WHEN COLLEGES LOBBY STATES

The Higher Education/State Government Connection

SOCIAL SCIENCE & HISTORY DIVISION
EDUCATION & PHILOSOPHY SECTION

Leonard E. Goodall

American Association of
State Colleges and Universities

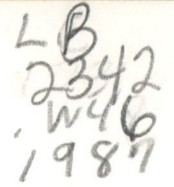

The following works appear herein by permission:

Dan Angel, "How to Play the State Capitol Game," *AGB Reports*, September/October 1980.

Patrick M. Callan and Richard W. Jonsen, "Trends in Statewide Planning and Coordination," *Educational Record*, Summer 1980.

M. M. Chambers, "Long-Term Expectations for Financing Higher Education," *Policy Studies Journal*, September 1981.

M. M. Chambers, "The Point of the Discourse," in *Higher Education in the Fifty States* (Danville: Interstate Printers, 1970).

Richard B. Crockett, "Constitutional Autonomy for Universities—The Current State of Judicial Opinion," *North Dakota Law Review*, 54:4.

Richard M. Cyert, "The Management of Universities of Constant or Decreasing Size," *Public Administration Review*, July/August 1978.

Heinz Eulau and Harold Quinley, "Legislators and Academicians," in *State Officials and Higher Education* (New York: McGraw-Hill, 1970), prepared for the Carnegie Commission on Higher Education.

Samuel K. Gove and Susan Welch, "The Influence of State Constitutional Conventions on the Future of Higher Education," *Educational Record*, Spring 1969.

John W. Hicks, "Lobbying for Limited Resources," in *The Future in The Making*, Ed. Dykeman W. Vermilye (San Francisco: Jossey-Bass, 1973).

E. Terrence Jones, "Public Universities and the New State Politics," *Educational Record*, Summer 1984.

Malcolm Moos, "The Future of the Land Grant University," *Change*, May/June 1982.

Malcolm Moos and Francis E. Rourke, "The State Story: Administrative Centralization," in *The Campus and the State* (Baltimore: The Johns Hopkins University Press, 1959).

Steven Muller, "Should States Support Private Colleges—Yes!" *AGB Reports*, September/October 1978.

Barry Munitz, "Memo to a Multicampus Trustee from a Flagship CEO," *AGB Reports*, September/October 1981.

James A. Norton, "Who's Afraid of the Statewide Board?" *AGB Reports*, September/October 1978.

Allen Rosenbaum, "University Reorganization in Wisconsin, *AAUP Bulletin*, Autumn 1973.

© 1987 by American Association of State Colleges and Universities
One Dupont Circle, Washington, D.C.

Library of Congress Cataloging-in-Publication Data

When colleges lobby states.
  Rev. ed. of: State politics and higher education, 1976.
  Bibliography: p.
  1. Higher education and state—United States.
  2. State aid to higher education—United States.
  3. Intergovernmental fiscal relations—United States.
  4. University autonomy—United States. I. Goodall, Leonard E.
  II. State politics and higher education.
  LC173.W46   1987   379.73   86-7946
  ISBN 0-88044-115-1

About the Author

Leonard E. Goodall has been engrossed in higher education and state politics all his adult life.

He was chancellor of the University of Michigan-Dearborn 1971-79 and president of the University of Nevada, Las Vegas (both of them state universities) 1979-85. Earlier in his career he served on the faculties of Arizona State University and the University of Illinois at Chicago Circle. He was associate dean of faculties and vice chancellor at the University of Illinois at Chicago Circle. He is currently professor of management and public administration at the University of Nevada, Las Vegas.

Goodall is a graduate of Central Missouri State University, with a master's degree in political science from the University of Missouri and a doctorate from the University of Illinois at Urbana-Champaign. His research has concerned urban politics and the politics of higher education. He has published The American Metropolis, Urban Politics in the Southwest, Gearing Arizona's Communities for Urban Growth, and an earlier companion to this volume entitled State Politics and Higher Education.

Contents

Acknowledgments   vii

Introduction   ix

State Constitutions and Higher Education

1. The Influence of State Constitutional Conventions on the Future of Higher Education   5
   Samuel K. Gove/Susan Welch
2. State Constitutions—An Update   17
   Leonard E. Goodall
3. Constitutional Autonomy for Universities: The Current State of Judicial Opinions   19
   Richard B. Crockett

Executive Leadership and the Universities

4. Governors and Higher Education   41
   Samuel K. Gove
5. University Reorganization in Wisconsin   54
   Allen Rosenbaum
6. The State Story: Administrative Centralization   72
   Malcolm Moos/Francis E. Rourke

Legislative Control of Higher Education

7. Legislators and Academicians   88
   Heinz Eulau/Harold Quinley
8. Lobbying for Limited Resources   100
   John W. Hicks
9. How to Play the State Capitol Game   104
   Dan Angel
10. Public Universities and the New State Politics   110
    E. Terrence Jones

Universities, Budgets, and Dollars

11. Long-Term Expectations for Financing Higher Education   123
    M. M. Chambers
12. State Tuition Policies and Public Higher Education   133
    Allan W. Ostar

13 The Management of Universities of Constant or Decreasing Size 150
   Richard M. Cyert
14 Should States Support Private Colleges—Yes! 162
   Steven Muller
15 Should States Support Private Colleges—No! 167
   Bill J. Priest
16 The Public-Private Debate 172
   Frank H. T. Rhodes

The Politics of University Planning and Coordination

17 Trends in Statewide Planning and Coordination 185
   Patrick M. Callan/Richard W. Jonsen
18 Ambiguities in the Administration of Public University Systems: An Organizing Perspective 194
   Lawrence K. Pettit
19 Who's Afraid of the Statewide Board? 210
   James A. Norton
20 The Point of the Discourse 218
   M. M. Chambers
21 Memo to a Multicampus Trustee from a Flagship CEO 225
   Barry Munitz
22 The Future of the Land-Grant University 232
   Malcolm Moos
23 State Colleges: An Unsettled Quality 243
   Robert Birnbaum

Acknowledgments

A predecessor to this volume, entitled *State Politics and Higher Education,* was published in 1976 under the auspices of the Rackham School of Graduate Studies of the University of Michigan and funded by a grant from the Lilly Endowment. I want to express appreciation here to the University of Michigan and to Lilly for having made the original project possible. Professor Sam Gove of the University of Illinois was chiefly responsible for developing my interest in the study of higher education politics. He is a contributor to both the first and second books.

Allan W. Ostar, president of the American Association of State Colleges and Universities, first suggested the possibility of a new version to address the current issues of higher education politics in the 1980s. AASCU's publications advisory board reviewed the proposal and provided valuable comments and recommendations. I want to thank Allan Ostar and AASCU for enabling publication of this volume.

I especially want to thank Joanne L. Erickson, AASCU's publications coordinator, who oversaw all details of production and publication. The skill of her and her staff made the project possible. I also want to thank Elizabeth Kielman, Joanne's predecessor, who provided valuable help during the early stages of planning.

I am grateful to the University of Nevada-Las Vegas for providing me with leave time, funds, and support services for work on the project, without which it would have been impossible for me to undertake preparation of this book.

Finally, I thank my wife, Lois, for her help in typing and organizing, as well as for her patience and encouragement, throughout my work on both books.

Introduction

One feature common to all fifty state governments is the support of one or more public universities and colleges, institutions important to the economic and political systems of their states. Citizens depend on them to educate their young (and their not-so-young). Business and industry look to them for employees and for research and consultative assistance. These universities and colleges spend large amounts of tax dollars, employ many people, and often have major construction programs that significantly affect the local economy. These institutions are key participants in the political process of their states.

This book provides an overview of the prime aspects of university participation in state politics. The chapters come from diverse sources—some from other publications, some from contributors writing especially for this book. Some are by research scholars, others by direct participants in the political process. In several instances, conflicting points of view have been presented to clarify the issues.

The emphasis herein is on the university as a participant in the state political system. It is not about the internal politics of universities: How does a dean get selected? How does the history department compete with the chemistry department for scarce budget dollars? These are interesting questions, but they are not addressed here. Rather, I examine how a university interacts with the governor's office, or how it competes with other universities or with the highway department for budget dollars.

I also emphasize the *process* of state politics rather than specific policy issues. I look at *how* decisions get made in the state political system, regardless of the particular issue.

Some readers may reject the idea of colleges and universities as "political" institutions or political participants. However, like it or not, they do have relationships with government. Some may be more effective in politics than others. Some may operate more ethically than others. But, for better or worse, these institutions (especially state-supported ones but, increasingly, all institutions) inevitably become involved in state politics.

The term *politics* herein refers to the process of resolving conflict over public policy. Political differences may occur along party lines. In California, for example, former governor Ronald Reagan and his administration were regarded by many as unsympathetic to higher education in general and to the University of California in particular. In Great Britain, the British Open University originated in a political issue supported by the British Labor Party.

So far as higher education is concerned, partisan politics is probably the exception to the rule in most states. It is more common for political division to occur among institutions, as when two or more universities compete for a law school. Sometimes the division occurs between types of institutions—for example, junior colleges against universities. Another common conflict occurs between higher education institutions and the legislature, as when institutions unite to oppose some particular legislative action.

Universities as Political Actors

The university occupies a unique position in state government. It must respond to public concerns but must also have sufficient independence to ensure academic freedom and freedom of inquiry in its research and scholarly activities. It acquires support from tax funds but also has other major income sources such as tuition and research funds. Universities are influenced by executive and legislative action but are governed primarily by their own boards. This complex position requires them to play various roles such as educator, fund raiser, protector of academic freedom, researcher—political agent.

Like other state institutions, public colleges and universities try to maximize their resources and minimize the external controls imposed on them. In this book, several chapters on legislative relations illustrate some of the techniques used by universities and colleges to gain increased legislative support. The reader will also find a recurring theme of autonomy because universities rely heavily on this concept in efforts to minimize involvement of legislators or other state agencies in their internal affairs.

Universities, like other political actors, attempt to develop strong clientele, such as alumni associations, to help mobilize political support. Institutions also try to build legislative support among legislators from their communities and regions.

The activity of garnering support from clientele illustrates the best and worst in universities as political actors. For example, institutions can cultivate alumni loyalty by improving their academic programs: a reputation as an outstanding university is probably the best political asset an institution can have. In sharp contrast, one will occasionally hear about a university that admits the legislator's son to medical school in return for his vote on a crucial issue. Fortunately, most universities having a reputation as effective political actors are seldom accused of using the latter political strategy.

The Uses of This Book

This book offers a general view of the interactions between higher education institutions and their political environment. It is intended to be useful to diverse audiences in various settings, such as students in higher education administration and policy, education, and political science (particularly state government or public policy).

Beyond its classroom applications, the book should prove useful to college presidents and other campus officials who interact with state officials and agencies. There may also be faculty members, university board members, state government officials, and informed citizens with an interest in this subject. To all such audiences, the editor extends his hope that *When Colleges Lobby States* will be useful and enlightening.

State Constitutions and Higher Education

This book begins with examination of the impact of state constitutions on higher education. Of course, any observer of state politics will readily note that a study of state constitutions can tell only part of the story of the political process. The informal relations, legislative traditions, lobbying activities, personalities of governors, and a host of other factors contribute significantly to the state political system. Likewise, the image and prestige of state universities, and their presidents and boards, will affect the relationship of higher education to the state.

A knowledge of state constitutions cannot reveal everything about state government and politics, but it does offer some enlightenment. Constitutions set the ground rules within which the debates, legislative process, and other aspects of state politics take place. The article by Gove and Welch provides a useful introduction to the subject. Although more than a decade old, it continues to provide a good summary of the more important constitutional issues facing universities and state government. It also describes the impact of state constitutions on many of the issues discussed in later chapters, including institutional autonomy, the role of state coordinating boards, and the budgetary and other authority of the executive and legislative branches of state government.

The update, prepared by the editor, indicates that constitutional changes since the writing of the Gove and Welch article have had relatively minimal impact on higher education. Other segments of the political process, such as legislation and administrative reorganization, have had a greater impact than have state constitutional changes on the governance of colleges and universities.

Crockett's review of judicial decisions concerning constitutional autonomy for state universities is a comprehensive view of recent court attitudes on the subject. As his review of the various states suggests, it is difficult to discern strong trends in this matter. Some state courts seem to lean one way, some another.

A careful reading of the Crockett chapter reveals that courts cannot have the last word on the issue of autonomy. As several of the opinions imply, regardless of the constitutional status of universities, state legislatures continue to have "the power of the purse" over universities. The *Kalamazoo Gazette,* in a May 21, 1973 editorial commenting on the Michigan case Crockett discusses, noted, "And if a college or university acts—or spends money—in a manner displeasing to the legislature, the legislature can take that into consideration when appropriations time comes around the next year."

This is a crucial point, and university officials recognize correctly, whatever their legally autonomous position, that they remain subject to gubernatorial and legislative influence and direction. These issues are discussed in subsequent chapters. It is appropriate, however, to begin with an analysis of the role of state constitutions.

1. The Influence of State Constitutional Conventions on the Future of Higher Education
Samuel K. Gove/Susan Welch

Two important but seemingly unrelated areas of interest to students of American government appear to be converging: concern for higher education in the state political environment and increased activity in state constitutional revision.

Public higher education has become an important and often controversial issue in state politics. All over the nation, state colleges and universities have undergone rapid and continued expansion, necessitating a substantial increase in state financial aid. This growth, together with the current campus unrest, has resulted in increased involvement in the state political environment for higher education.

Meanwhile, attempts at modernizing and simplifying state constitutions are taking place in the 1960s at a greater rate than in any decade of this century. Four states have adopted new or substantially revised constitutions; three others have defeated proposed documents. In each instance the vehicle for change—or proposed change—has been the constitutional convention.

Those involved in higher education have begun to recognize the importance of state constitutional provisions and to lobby in constitutional conventions. But those concerned with constitutional reform remain uncertain about including higher education in the state's basic document. The dilemma seems to focus on determination of which elements are so fundamental to the effective operation of state government that they should be included in the constitution, and which should be left to the discretion of state legislatures. The generally accepted assumption that conventions should frame a constitution of fundamentals implies that there is a dichotomy for all time between fundamental and legislative matters, and that a constitution of fundamentals is better than one of legislative matters.[1]

Constitutions often take into account the needs and conditions of the time and place of their adoption. Thus, a brief constitu-

---

Samuel K. Gove served for more than two decades as director of the Institute of Government and Public Affairs at the University of Illinois at Urbana-Champaign. He is now a professor in the institute and in the Department of Political Science. Susan K. Welch is a professor of political science at the University of Nebraska-Lincoln.

tion devoted to "fundamentals" is not always proposed in constitutional conventions. There are, however, certain costs in including a "nonfundamental" provision. The constitution is a more permanent and less flexible document than are legislative enactments; a constitution containing much detail is destined for obsolescence sooner, perhaps, than one treating governmental problems and institutions generally.

As Grad notes, the essential question is whether these adverse consequences are outweighed in importance by the intended provision, and whether the provision is so important as to justify the invalidation of all legislation and other governmental action which may come into conflict.[2]

The issue considered in this article is whether public higher education is indeed fundamental, and whether there should be higher educational provisions in a state's constitution. The reformers, represented by the National Municipal League, would say that higher education is not fundamental and, thus, should not be included. In that organization's *Model State Constitution* there is a passing reference to higher education, i.e., that the legislature may provide for such other public educational institutions of higher learning, as may be desirable.[3]

The authors of the model comment that the directive to establish higher education is not necessary but may advance the cause of higher education.[4] Many spokespersons for higher education would argue that a provision is not only necessary, but should be much more detailed than that provided in the model. They are far, however, from agreeing on specifics.

With the growth of public higher education, correspondingly more attention has been paid to higher education in state constitutions. Of the fifty states, however, nineteen have constitutions that are silent about higher education. These are Arkansas, Delaware, Illinois, Indiana, Kentucky, Maine, Maryland, Massachusetts, New Hampshire, New Jersey, New Mexico, Pennsylvania, Rhode Island, South Carolina, Tennessee, Vermont, Virginia, Washington, and West Virginia. The remaining thirty-one have constitutionally established higher education by various means: twenty-one states have constitutional provisions establishing a state university (Alabama, Alaska, Arizona, Georgia, Hawaii, Idaho, Iowa, Kansas, Louisiana, Michigan, Minnesota, Missouri, Montana, Nebraska, Nevada, New York, North Carolina, Texas, Utah, Wisconsin, and Wyoming); five states have constitutional provisions establishing a board of higher education (Colorado, Florida, Mississippi, North

Dakota and Oklahoma); one state constitution mandates the legislature to provide for a system of higher education (Connecticut); and three states indirectly mention higher education in constitutional provisions relating to trust funds (South Dakota), corporations and internal improvements (Oregon), public debt and public works (Ohio). California's document provides for a variety of higher educational systems, including a state university and its governing board, other institutions of higher education, and a state college system.[5]

Only one constitution now in use and drafted in this century (New Jersey) has no provision for higher education.

Major Convention Issues

In the last twenty years, the main discussions on higher education in state constitutional conventions have concerned university governance. The questions asked are: Should the constitution contain provisions on the method of selecting the governing board? If so, what kind? Should some degree of autonomy be granted to segments of the higher educational system? If so, how much, and to which institutions? Should the constitution provide for a statewide coordinating board? If so, how much power should it have?

Perhaps the issue causing most controversy is autonomy. Most educators, while realizing some outside checks are necessary and inevitable, prefer as much independence as possible. In general, existing legislative control over the university is regarded as excessive.

Providing a constitutional grant of independence makes it harder for various administrative agencies to exercise indirect controls over the university. Such a grant may also protect the university from direct interference by the legislature itself. For example, it may, in theory, serve as protection for a university administration that is attempting to negotiate a moderate path between the demands of student radicals and the threatened reprisals of irate state legislators.

Opposition to constitutional autonomy often arises from those who think that higher education should not be given preferential treatment over other state institutions, since the public colleges and universities are dependent upon money allocated by the legislature and provided by the taxpayer those who oppose constitutional autonomy think that the legislature should have final authority over how such public institutions are run. They fear that the colleges and universities will be "above" the elected officials of the states.

Some legislators wish to maintain final control over the university so they can deal more effectively with campus dissidents whom, they think, are not disciplined strictly enough by the university administration. If the university belongs to the public, this group would argue, then its internal processes should be supervised by the legislature, the voice of the public.

Still others oppose constitutional autonomy because they see it as an obstacle to effective coordination of the state's educational system.

Another problem concerns just which institutions should be given autonomy. In some states, the major university has constitutional autonomy, while the state colleges and smaller state universities do not. This situation existed in Michigan before the 1962 convention. Many think the "nonautonomous" institutions are placed at a disadvantage, while others believe state colleges are too small or too newly emerged from normal-school status to warrant autonomy.

A second and increasingly important issue is constitutional status for state boards of higher education. Proponents of a strong central body with constitutional powers to coordinate all higher education (or perhaps all education) within the state contend this would bring some order to the state educational system. Institutions no longer would compete in the state legislature for money, programs no longer would be unnecessarily and wastefully duplicated, gaps in the educational process would be filled, and long-range planning for the entire state higher educational system could be instituted.

On the other hand, those opposed to a strong state board often believe this would tend to homogenize the state's higher educational system, and that such a board would prove a detriment to the "better" institutions in the state. In addition, opponents of a strong governing body foresee only a locational shift in the competition for money—from the legislature to the state board.

A third issue is the composition of functions of the university governing board. Over half of the constitutions that include higher education provide for the method of selecting the governing boards, and these overwhelmingly favor appointment by the governor. In the remaining states, the legislature either is given a constitutionally enumerated power to determine how the board will be selected, or has assumed the power by virtue of constitutional silence.

Those favoring elective boards believe popular elections at established intervals would give the citizenry control over the public institutions. Those favoring appointive boards maintain that this method would keep "education out of politics," and that the average citizen, unfamiliar with the problems of higher education, is not equipped to engage in the policy-making process of public higher education.

Other problems relating to higher education—such as free tuition—surface in constitutional conventions, but these three issues—autonomy, state governing boards, and university governing boards—appear most frequently.[6]

Four Recent Conventions

To analyze more specifically the higher education issues that have appeared in recent constitutional conventions, we have looked at four conventions held in the last twenty years: Hawaii in 1950, Michigan in 1961-62, New York in 1967, and Maryland in 1967-68.[7] This analysis has been made from the pertinent documents and highlights the higher educational involvement in each convention.

In Hawaii, the major question concerned institutional autonomy. A provision mandating Hawaii to support the state university and other state educational institutions did not meet with much opposition in the constitutional convention; neither was there opposition to appointive regents, since this merely confirmed the existing practice. However, when the autonomy question was considered, there were sharp differences and lively discussion between those who wished the university to be tightly controlled by the legislature, and those who wanted it to have more freedom.

The Committee on Education at the convention reported favorably a provision that, in part, stated

The Board of Regents shall be empowered to establish policy and exercise full control over the university.

A supporter of this provision said:

There is no intention to put the university superior to other branches of government. The university of necessity will need to come to the legislature and get its appropriations as any other department of government. . . . It will, however, possess title to land.[8]

This position was supported by the president of the university, as indicated by another delegate:

I remember one time when the president of the university came to me and asked me whether you wanted to have a Uni-

> versity of Podunk or a University of Hawaii. . . . I think that we've got to be fair to the university, and I think they {the administrators} have . . . a better vision of what they are supposed to do at the state university than the average state legislator has.[9]

Those in opposition to such a broad grant of power complained that the university presently did not comply with the wishes of the state legislature in allocating its funds. This view was expressed by a delegate:

> I think we've got to give more power to the legislature to hold those fellows {regents} down out there.[10]

After considerable debate, a compromise was reached. The committee report was changed so the final version read:

> The Board of Regents shall have power in accordance with law, to establish policy.[11]

This apparently satisfied those in favor of limited power because the university was to act "in accordance with law." On the other hand, the university was given power to make policy and to control, as a corporate body, funds entrusted to it.

Academic Autonomy

The debate over autonomy was repeated in the Maryland convention of 1967. This convention was preceded by a study commission that made substantive recommendations and drafted a constitution with a proposal giving the University of Maryland exclusive general supervision of the institution and the control and direction of all expenditures from the institution's funds.[12] The state colleges also were to have academic autonomy and such other powers as given them by the legislature.[1pi163]

The president of the University of Maryland asked for autonomy for his institution in a letter to the commission and, in a personal appearance, testified that:

> Constitutional recognition will further enhance the reputation of the university and provide security for its future. In asking for this, the university does not seek independence from the legislature or executive branch of government, but it does plead for the power of internal management.[1pi164]

The board of trustees of the state colleges also wanted the commission to recommend autonomy for the governing boards of all institutions of higher education.[1pi165]

> The convention as a whole viewed both power requests as too broad. In convention, delegates granted the University of

> Maryland and the state colleges autonomy only in academic matters, leaving fiscal autonomy to legislative discretion. The governing boards of each level then were given power to formulate policies for their respective institutions. . . . The boards also would have general supervision over them in all academic matters.[16]

In the 1961 Michigan convention the issue of higher educational autonomy was present but was overshadowed by other issues. Since the University of Michigan, Michigan State University, and Wayne State University had been granted constitutional autonomy in the pre-1961 constitution, the autonomy issue concerned mainly the seven smaller state colleges and universities. Autonomy was granted to these institutions without much opposition. The provisions for separate elective boards for the University of Michigan, Michigan State, and Wayne were retained, but each of the other institutions was given its own appointive board. Previously each had been under the state board of education.

The major higher education issue in the Michigan constitutional convention was the composition and functions of the state board of education. Some wanted a "Super Board" that would exercise compulsory coordination over the entire state education system. Others opposed compulsory coordination as detrimental to individuality and excellence of various institutions of higher education.[17] The provision finally adopted included:

> Leadership and general supervision over all public education, including adult education and instructional programs in state institutions, except as to institutions granting baccalaureate degrees, is vested in a state board of education. It shall serve as the general planning and coordinating body for all public education, including higher education, and shall advise the legislature as to the financial requirements in connection therewith.
>
> The power of the boards of institutions of higher education provided in this constitution to supervise their respective institutions' funds shall not be limited by this action.[18]

Clarification of Power

Thus, the state board has supervisory powers over public education except in degree-granting institutions, but functions as a planning body for both higher and secondary educational institutions. Although it is stated specifically that the powers of the individual institutions are not diminished by the state board, it is difficult to see how effective overall planning by a strong state board would not diminish, at least to some degree, the powers of the individual institutions. The clarification of the state board's powers in higher education has not been completely resolved.

Institutional autonomy and free tuition were the major higher educational issues at the 1967 New York constitutional convention. However, the church-state dispute affecting all education was probably the major area of controversy in the convention.

The proposal that higher education be free received important political support, including that of the Democratic president of the convention and speaker of the state assembly. However, the trustees of the State University of New York issued a strong statement opposing the plan, expressing "grave concern" over the proposal's "serious repercussions" on the university's construction programs, which threaten the ability of the university to carry out its planned expansion.[19]

In addition, the proposal was opposed by most Republicans. Eventually a compromise was reached:

The legislature shall establish and define a system of higher education for all people of the state, encompassing both public and private institutions by programs which may include free tuition, grants, fellowships, and scholarships.[20]

Another issue of the New York convention—institutional autonomy—received far less publicity. There is no provision in the present constitution for higher education, except for reference to the Board of Regents of the University of New York, an overall coordinating and planning board for both public and private institutions. However, both the city university and the state university wanted constitutional autonomy.[21]

The chancellor of the state university urged constitutional autonomy for both the city and state universities as a protection against future political or administrative interference in the conduct of university affairs. He stated:

Vigorous development of institutions of higher education is best fostered in an atmosphere of independence and freedom.[22]

The mayor of New York City proposed that the city university be an autonomous unit of the state university, a proposal that received little support.[23]

In September the convention gave constitutional recognition and autonomy to the city and state universities, and continued the regents' powers of planning and coordination. The constitution as submitted provided:

> *The State University of New York and the City University of New York are continued and, consistent with other provisions of this article and with statute, each shall be responsible for the control and administration of the institutions and facilities therein.*[24]

It is clear that in all four states educators, in varying degrees, made known their views and sought to include their proposals in the constitution. All met with some success.

Higher Education in Conventions

Some general conclusions can be drawn from these four cases:

Higher education can be expected to play an important part in future constitutional conventions, but there is no consensus as to what higher educational provisions should be included in a constitution.

Many educators would like to see their university at least gain constitutional recognition with a directive that the legislature shall support the institution. This is true especially if the university is relatively new, or a subordinate unit of the state higher educational system.

For others, a grant of institutional autonomy is the highest goal obtainable in a constitutional convention. This is more apt to be granted to the major universities in the state, but in Michigan and Maryland, for example, all state institutions were treated equally. While a grant of institutional autonomy does not mean complete independence—the university will always be dependent on the legislature for funds—it may advance substantially the right of the university to administer its own affairs.

A "Super Board" with broad powers can be a threat to the individual university. Many public university officials have opposed granting such boards more than planning powers, and are particularly opposed to giving them a constitutional base. Although the Board of Education was given constitutional status in Michigan, proposals to further strengthen it met with strong opposition from university officials. In New York, the state board of regents was given no enlarged powers by the convention.

Free tuition has not been a major issue except at the New York convention. Only a handful of state constitutions have mentioned free tuition. there is some fear among university administrators that abolishing tuition without compensatory payments by the legislature would impair the university's financial position. Opposition to free tuition in state universities also comes from private universities.

Four "Oppositions"

In each of these four conventions opposition to the constitutional aims of the public universities can be subsumed into four types of opinion.

Proponents of a short, broadly phrased constitution are one source of opposition. These "good-government" advocates do not believe that higher education is a fundamental that should be found in a modern state constitution.

A second group favors strict control of public universities by the state legislature. These men believe the legislatures should be able to dictate policy to the university, if they wish, arguing that the universities are supported by tax money and, therefore, the representatives of taxpayers (the legislators) should have control. These persons view the university as another state agency, entitled to no special constitutional consideration.

Forming a third opposition are persons representing various parochial interests who wish to insert constitutional restraints on the university, such as geographical limitations or curricular restrictions.

Fourth, and finally, opposition to public universities sometimes arises from private higher educational institutions. However, private institutions often support public universities, perhaps in part because they believe state emphasis on education will be beneficial to them.

Higher education has played a significant role in recent state constitutional conventions, and there is no reason to believe this will change in future conventions. The examples given here do not cover all recent conventions and certainly are not an exhaustive list of areas of concern for higher education, or even of potential areas. They should strongly indicate, however, that higher education officials do have a stake in what goes on in constitutional conventions. A constitutional provision is much more lasting than a legislative act. A provision unfavorable to the growth of the university could have a permanent negative impact; likewise, a provision granting institutional autonomy could protect the university in future legislative conflicts.

Finally, it should be clear that the interests of the university cannot be separated from political struggles in constitutional conventions. Pressure groups similar to those appearing in the legislature most likely will be found in a constitutional convention.

Engaging in constitutional politics may reduce the need for other kinds of legislative "politics" later; that is, higher education, like other governmental functions, must protect its own interests. With constitutional protection, or at least recognition, a university and its officials may feel more secure and possess more defenses against attack from administrative officials, the state legislature, or an enraged citizenry. Constitutional silence may be misconstrued to mean that higher education is not fundamental.

Notes

[1] Frank P. Grad, *The Drafting of State Constitutions: Working Papers for a Manual* (New York: National Municipal League, 1967), fn. 2, supra, p. 4.

[2] Ibid., p. 22

[3] New York, 1963, p. 18.

[4] Ibid., p. 101.

[5] Millicent Y. H. Kim, "Article IX: Education [Higher Education]" *Hawaii Constitutional Convention Studies* (Honolulu: Legislative Reference Bureau, University of Hawaii, 1968). II, 6.

[6] Another problem that higher education shares with other educational levels is state aid to private schools, particularly religiously oriented private schools. In the New York convention of 1967, for instance, the controversy over the Blaine amendment, forbidding state funds to parochial and other religously supported schools, overshadowed all other issues pertaining to higher education, but seldom was discussed specifically in terms of higher education.

[7] The convention draft of Michigan was approved by the voters; the draft of New York rejected. Maryland voters rejected their convention proposal in May, 1968. The Hawaiian constitutional convention was a territorial one. The constitution drafted was approved, and when Hawaii became a state in 1959, the constitution, with only minor amendments unrelated to higher education, became the state constitution. There was another convention in Hawaii in 1968, but the revisions approved by the voters did not change the provisions relating to higher education.

[8] *Proceedings* (Honolulu: Constitutional Convention, 1950), II, 614.

[9] Ibid., p. 612.

[10] Ibid., p. 612.

[11] Hawaiian Constitution, Sec. 5.

[12] *Report of the Constitutional Convention Commission* (Annapolis: Office of the Secretary of State, August, 1967), p. 91. There was no mention of higher education in the Maryland constitution.

[13] Ibid.

[14] Ibid., p. 280.

[15] *Washington Post,* Nov. 19, 1967, p. D1.

[16] *Washington Post,* Dec. 20, 1967, p. B1.

[17]"Report of the Education Study Committee for the Constitutional Convention" (Unpublished MS, September 1961), pp. 50-54.

[18]Michigan Constitution, Art. VIII, Sec. 3.

[19]*New York Times,* Sept. 9, 1967.

[20]Ibid., Oct. 1, 1967

[21]Julius C. G. Edelstein, "Higher Education and the Constitutional Convention," *Modernizing State Government,* The New York Constitutional Convention of 1967, Proceedings of the Academy of Political Science, Ed. Sigmund Diamond (New York: The Academy, 1967), XXVIII, No. 3, 155-156.

[22]*New York Times,* June 16, 1967.

[23]Ibid.

[24]Proposed New York Constitution, Art. IX, Sec. 4.

2. State Constitutions: An Update

Leonard E. Goodall

The 1970s and 1980s have not been a period of major constitutional changes affecting higher education. Most of the discussion and activity concerning higher education organization and structure have taken place outside the arena of constitutional amendments. State study commissions have addressed questions of reorganization, and state legislatures have implemented changes of great significance but not written into constitutions. The far-reaching university reorganization in Wisconsin, for example, which resulted in the merger of two separate university systems, resulted from legislative rather than constitutional change.

Most of the constitutional amendments adopted in recent years have pertained chiefly to administrative, procedural and financial details. The State of Georgia, for example, adopted an amendment in 1976 giving the board of regents authority to grant senior citizens the right to take university courses tuition free on a space-available basis. In most states such action would not require constitutional or even legislative authority, but when state constitutions are lengthy, amendments must often be equally detailed.

Several states have had to enact constitutional changes to address the problem of student grants. Virginia (1974) and Nebraska (1976) both adopted amendments authorizing state grants to students attending nonpublic, postsecondary institutions.

In 1978 Hawaii enacted a general amendment intended to clarify that the board of regents has exclusive jurisdiction, subject to statewide laws, over the internal organization and management of the University of Hawaii. Although such amendments help reaffirm the public's intent to maintain an independent status for the university, they cannot ensure that specific issues will not remain for determination by the courts. Other articles in this part provide ample evidence of that fact.

The voters of various states have perhaps affected higher education over the past two decades as much by the constitutional amendments they have defeated as by those they have adopted.

Leonard E. Goodall is professor of management and public administration at the University of Nevada, Las Vegas. He formerly served as president of that institution and chancellor of the University of Michigan-Dearborn.

California voters in 1974 rejected an amendment to authorize the legislature, rather than the regents, to determine university tuition levels. Louisiana voters that same year rejected a far-reaching plan for governance of all of higher education by a single board and adopted instead a more moderate plan of coordination.

Nebraska voters in 1974 rejected a plan to enlarge the size of the university board by adding three nonvoting student members. In 1982 North Dakota rejected a proposal to replace the president of the North Dakota Educational Association with the Speaker of the House on the three-member panel that recommends candidates to the governor for possible appointment to the state board of higher education.

Higher education has felt the impact of some amendments that apply generally to all of state government. Open meeting requirements would be one example. Probably the best known would be various tax limitation provisions such as California's Proposition 13. Sometimes these amendments are written in general terms, but others are written in a manner applying directly to higher education. Arizona voters in 1980, for example, approved a limitation of annual increases in local property tax levies, including those of community colleges, to a maximum of 2 percent.

In spite of these changes, that the greatest impact on higher education in recent years has not come about through constitutional amendments. Legislative action and changes implemented by governing boards have been much more significant.

3. Constitutional Autonomy for Universities: The Current State of Judicial Opinion
Richard B. Crockett

Nebraska

In July 1977 the Supreme Court of Nebraska, in *Board of Regents of University of Nebraska* v. *Exon,* decided a declaratory judgment action that had been brought by the Regents against the Governor (Exon), the State Director of Administrative Services, and the State Director of Personnel. The purpose of the litigation was to determine the validity of several actions of the Nebraska legislature under Article VII, section 10 of the Nebraska constitution, which states as follows: "The general government of the University of Nebraska shall, under the direction of the legislature, be vested in ... the Board of Regents. ... Their duties and powers shall be prescribed by law."

Both the state district court which first heard the case and the state supreme court on appeal ruled that the phrase "under the direction of the legislature" did not give the legislature the power to direct the "government" of the university, but only the manner in which it shall "be vested" in the board of regents. The result, according to the Supreme Court, was that "it is the duty of the legislature to implement the constitutional provision by enacting legislation which vests the general government of the University in the Board of Regents." With regard to the constitutional language requiring that the regents' "duties and powers shall be prescribed by law," the court ruled that the legislature could set forth the powers and duties of the regents, but only in a manner consistent with the regents' control over the general government of the university. The court stated the following:

> *Although the legislature may add to or subtract from the powers and duties of the Regents, the general government of the University must remain vested in the Board of Regents and powers or duties that should remain in the Regents cannot be delegated to other officers or agencies....*
>
> *In prescribing the powers and duties of the Regents a legislative act must not be so detailed and specific in nature as to*

Richard B. Crockett is an attorney in North Dakota. He serves as legal advisor to North Dakota State University.

eliminate all discretion and authority on the part of the Regents as to how a duty shall be performed.

The court then applied these principles in determining the validity of each of the following challenged legislative actions:

First, provisions in the 1975 and 1976 appropriations bills adopted by the legislature directing the board of regents or employees of the university to take certain actions. The trial court had held that the legislature did not have the authority to do this, so that the statements would have to be construed as only advisory in nature. Although this question was not appealed, the Nebraska Supreme Court indicated that it agreed with the trial court, stating that "the legislature can not use an appropriation bill to usurp the powers or duties of the Board of Regents and to give directions to the employees of the University. The general government of the University must remain vested in the Board of Regents."

Second, a standing provision that money accruing to the university cash fund, which consists of money derived from the operation of the university (such as student fees, sales of commodities raised by the university, and medical center fees) shall become available "when appropriated by the legislature." In affirming the trial court's holding that an annual appropriation by the legislature was not required, the court cited a previous decision in which it had held that a legislative appropriation was not required in order for the board of regents to expend funds donated to the university by the federal government. The court reasoned that university funds which are not derived from state taxes have a different status than the general fund moneys, since such funds are equivalent to trust funds which can only be expended by the board of regents for the benefit of the university, rather than being available to the legislature for general governmental purposes. As an example of legislative recognition of the board of regents' control over such funds, the court cited a longstanding state law which declared that "all money accruing to the university funds is hereby appropriated to the use of the state university." It is significant that the court did not rely upon this statute as evidence that the institutional income had already been appropriated by the legislature, but instead used it to indicate the unique status of the university's nonappropriated funds.

Third, provisions in the 1975 appropriation bill adopted by the legislature requiring the approval of the governor (in the case of personal property) or the governor and the legislature (in the case of real property) before acceptance of any gift, bequest or devise of property in excess of $10,000 to the state, including the university. The court held that these provisions unlawfully delegated the constitutional authority vested in the board of regents.

Fourth, provisions fixing and determining the manner in which raises are to be given to employees of the board. The trial court had held that the legislature had the authority to determine such raises, but the Supreme Court overruled that finding and held that "the determination of salary schedules and the compensation to be paid to the employees of the Board of Regents is an integral part of the general government of the University." On a closely related issue, the Supreme Court held that the State Director of Personnel had no authority over university employees who had not been placed under the state personnel system by the board of regents.

Fifth, provisions prescribing certain requirements concerning planning, design, and construction of new facilities and the modification or repair of existing facilities. The Supreme Court held that these laws could not apply to the board of regents or the university because they would result in an unlawful delegation of the regents' constitutional authority.

Sixth, provisions making the university subject to a centralized purchasing and disposal program for property used by the state and its agencies. The Supreme Court held that these provisions would unlawfully delegate the board's authority if held applicable to the university.

Following the *Exon* decision, the board of regents at its September 1977 meeting adopted a general policy of continuing existing relationships with state agencies until recommendations for change were proposed to the board. Within a week of this action, the university administration established a task force composed of nine key administrators who were charged with "the responsibility of listing all of the issues and procedures which may cause some concern" in light of the court decision.

The task force issued its final report and recommendations in December, including an outline analysis of 199 areas of university policy or procedure that might be affected by the Exon decision.

In addition, the report identified nineteen critical areas of concern. Finally, the task force made the following recommendations:

- that a specific timetable for development of policies and procedures for an adequate personnel system be developed by the university's administrative staff as quickly as possible,

- that each of the nineteen critical areas of concern referred to above be assigned to a university office or staff team for design of timetables and approaches to be used in development of appropriate policies, procedures, and state agency interfaces and relationships, required to bring the university into compliance with the Exon ruling,
- that ongoing cooperation with other state agencies be maintained by the assignment of specific liaison responsibilities to university administrators,
- that administrative responsibility should also be assigned for improved development and management of administrative policies,
- that ongoing legislative support be achieved by assigning the responsibility for informing legislators of the impact of any bills introduced in response to the action of the Nebraska Supreme Court.

These activities and conclusions of the task force are important because they underscore the significance and impact of the Exon decision. Along with a guarantee of freedom from legislative interference in university governance, it implies a broad scope of responsibility that the board of regents must be willing to assume for managing the institution, not the least of which is the continued maintenance of a good relationship with various state agencies that used to be more involved in supervising university affairs and could still have a significant effect on its well-being. The task force emphasized the effect of the decision in both principle and practice by stating that it recognized the Exon ruling as not only a one-time incident of mere operational significance to the university, but also as a major guidepost of the State of Nebraska, reflecting its public policy for the relationship between state government and higher education through the twentieth century. As such, the task force offers the solemn admonition that the university and each of its employees build upon this increased clarity in public policy to improve cooperation between the university and other state agencies, and to improve the operational effectiveness of the university, in ways and amounts that may have been more difficult to establish before this clarification was available.

It is, of course, too early to tell whether or not the principle of autonomy will actually survive as Nebraska's "public policy for the relationship between state government and higher education through the twentieth century." Any thought that the board of regents would no longer have to worry about legislative involvement in educational policy making must have been dispelled by the action of the 1978 session of the Nebraska legislature in approving two comprehensive measures regarding postsecondary education, both over Governor Exon's veto. One of these acts provided for a "uniform information system for all public postsecondary education systems and institutions" in the state. Several broad purposes were stated in the act, including the provision of "timely and accurate information concerning the programs, personnel, students, finances, and facilities" of the educational systems and institutions, and the establishment of "an information base to support state level planning, budgeting, and performance evaluation activities for postsecondary education."

The legislature's intent to be involved in education policy making was even more directly stated in a second measure approved during the 1978 session. That act established "statements of role and mission" for the state's postsecondary education systems and institutions in order to provide for a "coordinated state system," and to "limit unnecessary program and facility duplication through coordinated planning." The act also established a legislative review process to ensure that the institutions complied with the role and mission statements and that the statements would be updated when necessary. Further enforcement was provided for in a section of the act that prohibits the expenditure of "funds generated or received from a general fund appropriation, state aid assistance program, or receipts from a mill levy authorized by statute . . . in support of programs or activities which are in conflict with the role and mission assignments."

In language that appears to be both self-contradictory and inconsistent with the Exon ruling, the act declares that "the legislature acknowledges the provisions of sections 10 and 13 of article VII of the Nebraska Constitution. The provisions of this act reflect the philosophy of the State of Nebraska and shall be acknowledged as such and implemented by the Board of Regents of the University of Nebraska." The board of regents is also directed to "adopt and promulgate policies and procedures necessary to assure compliance" with the act and the role and mission assignments for the University of Nebraska system and its campuses.

These directives are indeed very difficult to square with the principles of the regents' constitutional autonomy enunciated in Exon. Only time will tell whether the Nebraska Supreme Court's ruling will have any lasting effect or whether the fiscal power of the legislature will give it effective control of even those educational policy matters that have been determined to be legally within the scope of the regents' constitutional authority.

Minnesota

Within a month of the Nebraska decision, the Minnesota Supreme Court held in Regents of *University of Minnesota* v. *Lord* that an act of the state legislature requiring a state designer selection board to select designers for university buildings did not unduly infringe upon the authority over the "government" of the University of Minnesota that was vested in its board of regents by the state constitution. The case grew out of a controversy that began when the 1974 session of the Minnesota legislature enacted a state designer selection board act that was expressly made applicable to the University of Minnesota as well as to other state agencies and departments. The act established a citizen board appointed by the governor with the responsibility for selecting the primary designer for state building projects with estimated costs exceeding $250,000 or planning projects with estimated fees greater than $20,000.

During the same session of the Minnesota legislature, $30,000 was appropriated to the board of regents for planning the first phase of a learning resources center at the University's St. Paul campus. The university proceeded to select a primary designer for the project without going through the state designer selection board. When it requested payment from the state for the designer's planning services, the state Commissioners of Administration and Finance, under the direction of the State Treasurer, refused payment because of the university's failure to comply with the state designer selection board act.

The 1976 session of the Minnesota legislature added another dimension to the controversy by making its $4,897,489 appropriation to the university for completion of the learning resources center expressly conditional upon the university's compliance with the designer selection board act.

The board of regents then brought an action in state district court, seeking a declaration that the designer selection board act violated the regents' authority under the Minnesota constitution, and an injunction against the withholding of construction project appropriations from the university for its failure to comply with the act.

The basis for the regents' challenge was a section of the Minnesota constitution which states: "All the rights, immunities, franchises and endowments heretofore granted or conferred are hereby perpetuated unto the .. university. . . ." This language had earlier been held by the Minnesota Supreme Court in *State ex rel.*

University of Minnesota v. *Chase* to carry forward the authority of the board of regents for the "government" of the university under its original charter, with the power and duty "to enact laws for the government of the university."

The district court granted a summary judgment to the regents, holding that both the state designer selection board act and the condition requiring the university's compliance with it in the learning resources center appropriation measure were in violation of the autonomy granted the university under the constitutional provisions regarding the board of regents.

The state appealed the case to the Minnesota Supreme Court, which reversed the district court by a 5-4 vote, holding that the requirement that the state designer selection board select designers for university buildings is a valid exercise of legislative authority over appropriations made to the university, since the legislature has the power to impose reasonable conditions on the use of appropriated funds.

In its analysis of the "reasonableness" of the condition requiring compliance with the designer selection board act, the court began by quoting from the Chase opinion as follows: "at the one extreme, the legislature has no power to make effective, in the form of law, a mere direction of academic policy or administration. . . . At the other extreme it has the undoubted right within reason to condition appropriations as it sees fit."

While the Chase opinion contemplated the possibility of valid legislative conditions in appropriations to the university, the actual holding in that case invalidated a legislative act. The measure in question had authorized the State Auditor "to supervise and control" expenditures by all "departments, and agencies of the state government and of the institutions under their control." The act also required the approval by the State Commission of Administration and Finance of an "estimate" before any appropriation to a unit of the state could become "available for expenditure." When the commission disapproved an expense incurred by the regents for a preliminary survey of an employee group insurance plan, the regents brought a mandamus action, and the Minnesota Supreme Court affirmed the district court's judgment for the regents, holding that the act was an unconstitutional attempt by the legislature to interfere with the independent management authority of the board of regents.

This holding was distinguished by the court in Lord as involving a "direct attempt to control all university expenditures, rather than the limited conditions imposed by the designer selection board act." In stating the question to be resolved, the court also emphasized the need to examine the impact of the measure on the discretion and power of the Regents over the internal management of the university.

The court then discussed the purposes of the state designer selection board act. Its primary intent, according to the court, was "to avoid the conflicts of interest which arise when members of a state agency select a firm in which they have an interest, be it financial or otherwise." The university was perhaps uniquely affected by this objective because of the fact noted earlier in the court's opinion that the university had entered into several contracts with architectural firms which included faculty members in the university's school of architecture.

Second, the court indicated that the provisions in the act defining the membership of the designer selection board to include representatives of engineering, architecture, and the arts were designed to ensure competency in the selection process.

Third, the court noted the act's requirement that selection criteria be made public and that the selection process follow certain defined procedures.

The purpose of the act, according to the court, was "to promote the general welfare and to prevent conflicts of interest and fraudulent acts." Considering also the application of the act to all public agencies in the state, and not just the university, the court found the requirement to be a reasonable and limited condition for the legislature to impose.

The court noted, however, that the act would not apply to the university if it "were providing all funds for the construction of a building from its own revenues."

Moreover, the court held that the board of regents must be consulted during the negotiations between the designer selection board and the designer ultimately selected for a university project, and that the contract with the designer must be specifically approved for both form and content by the regents before it can be executed. Furthermore, the court ruled that the university "certainly has the right to direct his actions [the designer's] and to reject any design it finds unsuitable."

While the validity of legislative action was basically upheld by the court, it was actually subject ot the condition in the opinion that the final authority of the regents (and their exclusive authority, in the case of projects funded by the university's own revenues) be accommodated in a manner not specifically provided for in the act.

South Dakota

The most recent ruling of the South Dakota Supreme Court on the question of constitutional autonomy occurred in 1975 in *Board of Regents* v. *Carter*. That case was brought by the Board of Regents as a challenge to the authority of the State Commissioner of Labor and Management Relations (Carter) to rule on the definition of appropriate employee representation units and certify the designation or selection of representative units under the state's collective bargaining act for public employees.

The regents argued that such a legislative grant of authority was inconsistent with their charter in the state constitution, which specified that all state-supported educational institutions "shall be under the control of a board of five members appointed by the governor and confirmed by the senate under such rules and restrictions as the legislature may provide." According to the regents, the legislature's power under this section only extended to placing rules and restrictions on the appointment and confirmation process.

The court disagreed directly with this last contention, stating that it has consistently recognized the "rules and restrictions" phrase to also modify the word "control," so that it authorized some legislative restraint of the board's constitutional power of control over the institutions. The court indicated that such restraint was itself limited and that the legislature's "rules and restrictions" could not "erase" the Board's control or remove all of its power.

Proceeding, then, to an analysis of the public employee bargaining law, the court noted that it only required the board to negotiate in good faith with a representative employee unit. Since this obligation was defined in the law to mean providing a rationale for any position taken during negotiations, and not the making of a concession or necessarily agreeing to any proposal, the court interpreted this to mean that the regents' power "to unilaterally set salaries, discharge employees, or establish employment qualifications is left intact." The court concluded that the regents' "basic right of control" was therefore "left untouched," so it held that the act was "a permissible restriction on the exercise of that control."

Another question in Carter was raised by the state attorney general who intervened to protest the regents' action of hiring independent legal counsel in the case. While the court acknowledged the constitutional authority of the attorney general as the legal officer of the state, it pointed out that such authority had to be reconciled with the legislature's power to make rules regarding the form of the regents' control. Since one of those rules was a statute giving the board of regents the power to sue and be sued, the court held that such power necessarily includes the power to hire its own attorney, even without the consent of the attorney general.

This ruling of the South Dakota Supreme Court regarding the constitutional autonomy of the state's board of regents thus makes it clear that the board's authority is subject to legislative definition as well as limitation, although neither may be so expansive as to interfere with the basic right of the board to "control" the educational institutions under its jurisdiction.

In addition to the public employee negotiation process involved in *Carter,* a more recent lower court decision in South Dakota found another area of legislative authority to not be violative of the constitutional autonomy of the board of regents. In *Hines* v. *DeZonia,* a state circuit court held that the board (and hence the University of South Dakota School of Medicine under its jurisdiction) is a state "agency" subject to the state Administrative Procedures Act. The court accordingly enjoined the school from dismissing the medical student who brought the case until such time as the school promulgated rules for academic dismissals in accordance with the Act. The significance of this case may be somewhat diminished by the fact noted in the court's opinion that the board's own regulations on student discipline and academic standing required that any rules of implementation be promulgated in accordance with the provisions of the Administrative Procedures Act.

Another conflict in South Dakota surfaced at the August 1977 meeting of the board of regents. Inspired by the Exon decision in their neighboring state, and frustrated by the increasing involvement of South Dakota state agencies in campus affairs, the regents unanimously directed their attorney to draft a lawsuit resolution for their consideration. A specific point of contention at the time involved a decision by the state Personnel Bureau to reaudit the institutions of higher education in the fall, and the Commissioner of Higher Education was reported to have stated that the Personnel Bureau auditors would be escorted off the campuses if they tried to conduct another audit. Within a week of the board of regents' meeting, the state attorney general was quoted as saying that the regents were subject to the authority of executive agencies and that he didn't think "anybody will be escorting anybody any place." The regents subsequently decided to defer any further consideration of a lawsuit until an attempt had been made to resolve their differences with state agencies through legislation.

Montana

The legal status of the state governing board for higher education in Montana was changed significantly by the adoption of a new state constitution in 1972. Under the old constitution the "general control and supervision" of the state education institutions was vested in a state board of education "whose powers and duties shall be prescribed by law." The new constitution describes the responsibility of the board in much broader terms:

> *The government and control of the Montana university system is vested in a board of regents of higher education which shall have full power, responsibility, and authority to supervise, coordinate, manage and control the Montana university and shall supervise and coordinate other public educational institutions assigned by law.*

In contrast to the old constitution, the only reference in the new chapter to a legislative role in higher education is the following provision, which is quite limited: "The funds and appropriations under the control of the board of regents are subject to the same audit provisions as are all other state funds."

These provisions of the new constitution were considered by the Montana Supreme Court in *Board of Regents of Higher Education* v. *Judge,* an action brought by the board seeking a declaratory judgment regarding the constitutionality of several measures approved by the Montana legislature in 1975.

The measures in question required that the board secure the approval of the Legislative Finance Committee before expending in excess of amounts appropriated or making certain other budget amendments, and certify to the budget director compliance by the institutions with certain conditions related to the use of the appropriated funds.

In considering the budget amendment approval question, the court deemed it necessary to identify the funds subject to the appropriation power. The court thus considered provisions in the

1972 constitution that call for a governor's budget to be submitted to the legislature "setting forth in detail for all operating funds the proposed expenditures and estimated revenue of the state" and that require the legislature to "insure strict accountability of all revenue received and money spent by the state." The result, according to the court, is that the legislature's appropriation power "extends beyond the general fund and encompasses all those public operating funds of state government" except for "private funds received by state government which are restricted by law, trust agreement or contract."

Having thus clarified one limitation of the appropriation power, the court created another by holding that the budget amendment approval process approved by the legislature was an unconstitutional delegation of its power to the finance committee.

The court related the certification question to the power of the legislature to make line item appropriations, since the certification requirement at issue was preceded by a statement of legislative purpose "to restrict and limit . . . the amount and conditions under which the appropriations can be expended." Although the board of regents had argued that its constitutional autonomy precluded appropriations from being restricted on a line item basis, the court held otherwise, stating that the legislative exercise of control over expenditures goes "hand in hand" with the appropriation power. The court acknowledged, however, that line item appropriations would be impermissible if they involved such a degree of legislative control over expenditures as to infringe upon the regents' authority to "supervise, coordinate, manage and control" institutions under its jurisdiction.

Following the same line of reasoning, the court also held that the legislature had the authority to impose certain conditions on its appropriations and to require certification of compliance with those conditions, so long as the conditions "do not infringe on the constitutional powers granted the Regents." The court then scrutinized each of the conditions imposed by the 1975 legislature and held the following to be unconstitutional: first, a requirement that "all moneys collected or received by university system units subject to this act from any source whatsoever, including federal grants for research and operations, and any moneys received from a foundation shall be deposited in the state treasury. . . ." This provision was in conflict with the general principle discussed earlier that private moneys restricted by law, trust agreement or contract are not subject to appropriation.

Second, a prohibition of more than a 5-percent salary increase for university presidents and the commissioner of higher education during each year of the biennium. The court reasoned that control of such salaries was not a "minor" matter, but rather an effort to dictate personnel policy in violation of the board's authority.

Third, a requirement that "the Regents shall grant classified university employees salaries in accord with House Joint Resolution 37. . . ." An inherent responsibility of the board under its constitutional powers is the determination of priorities in higher education, according to the court, and this attempted legislative condition impaired the regent's power to function effectively by establishing policies and determining priorities related to the hiring and retention of competent personnel.

The holdings in *Judge* affirming the legislative power to make line item appropriations and conditional appropriations mean that the Montana legislature can be expected to exercise a great deal of influence on the university system in the state. The case reveals a considerable amount of judicial respect for the broad scope of control and authority granted to the board of regents under the 1972 constitution, however, and the appropriation power will accordingly have to be exercised with some restraint in order to avoid any further challenge.

Michigan

In October 1975, the Supreme Court of Michigan added another significant decision to a long line of opinions regarding the constitutional autonomy of higher education institutions in that state. *University of Michigan* v. *State* was a declaratory action brought by the constitutionally established universities to determine the validity of several provisions of the State Higher Education Appropriation Act of 1971, and the Michigan State Board of Education intervened as a defendant to raise the question of its constitutional authority with respect to the universities. The constitutional language relied upon by the universities stated that each of their governing boards "shall have general supervision of its institution and the control and direction of all expenditures from the institution's funds."

Several of the appropriation act provisions challenged by the universities made it an express "condition" of the appropriation that the number of out-of-state students be limited in certain respects, that none of the appropriated funds be used to construct buildings not authorized by the legislature, and that the general fund subsidy appropriated for an institution be automatically reduced by the amount of any tuition or student fee revenue not reported for budget purposes.

Both the trial and appellate courts had found these conditions to be an unconstitutional infringement of the universities' autonomy, but the Michigan Supreme Court noted that the statement of express "conditions" in the 1971 act had been changed in subsequent appropriations acts to declarations of "legislative intent." Since the legislature clearly has the right to merely state its intent or wishes, according to the court, no constitutional conflict existed at the time of the decision, and the court declined to rule on the questions raised by the universities regarding the "conditions."

Another appropriation act provision challenged by the universities prohibited their letting of any construction contract for a self-liquidating project unless they had first submitted "schedules for the liquidation of the debt for the construction and operation of such project" to the appropriate legislative committees. The court described this as a "mere reporting measure" and noted that there was no requirement of legislative supervision or control. Given also the legitimacy of the legislature's interest in the information, the provision was held by the court to be constitutional.

The final appropriation act question considered by the court was a prohibition of the use of the appropriated funds to "pay for the construction, maintenance or operation of any self-liquidating projects." The court refused to rule on that question, due to the lack of any specific facts or impasse that would provide a contest for its decision. In very strong language, however, the court indicated that the universities "would be wise to comply" with the "perfectly proper" expression of the legislature's desire to separate the funding of self-liquidating and state-funded projects. Because of the power of the purse held by the legislature, the court warned the universities of the "understandable legislative reaction" that would result from their disregard of the provision. Rather than a legal question that could be judicially resolved, therefore, the court described the matter as "one of power and politics" from which it should abstain.

The question raised by the state board of education required a reconciliation of the constitutional grant of autonomy to the universities with the following grant of constitutional authority to

the board:
> *Leadership and general supervision over all public education, including adult education and instructional programs in state institutions, except as to institutions of higher education granting baccalaureate degrees, is vested in a state board of education. It shall serve as the general planning and coordinating body for all public education, including higher education, and shall advise the legislature as to the financial requirements in connection therewith. . . . The power of the boards of institutions of higher education provided in this constitution to supervise their respective institutions and control and direct the expenditure of the institutions' funds shall not be limited by this section.*

Since the universities were excepted from the board's "general supervision" by the express terms of this provision, the court analyzed the impact of the other designated responsibilities of "leadership," "general planning and coordination," and advising the legislature. In light of the specific language negating any limitation of the university boards' powers of supervision and control, the court held that the state board of education could act as an advisory body to the universities, but without any power to veto their programs. In order for the board to properly fulfill its constitutional mandate of advising the legislature, the court noted that the universities must inform the board of any proposed programs and their financial requirements.

A very important element of this decision by the Michigan Supreme Court is its recognition of the significance of the political factors involved. In addition to its acknowledgment of the legislative power of the purse, the court indicated in the following paragraph the necessity for mutual respect between the legislature and the university governing boards in their exercise of overlapping responsibilities:

> *This case arises because two important elements of our government, the legislature and the universities, are zealous to perform well their constitutional missions in the service of the people. The legislature has taken certain action pursuant to its responsibilities to supervise properly the spending of the people's money. The universities seek to maintain their constitutional integrity to manage funds given into their charge in order best to perform their educational mission. It is obvious that these two functions can touch or overlap each other. Therefore*

understanding and good will is necessary that the people whom both elements represent be served.

Following the state Supreme Court decision in *Regents,* the Michigan Court of Appeals was asked to resolve a question regarding the constitutional autonomy of public community and junior college boards in that state. *Kowalski* v. *Board of Trustees of Macomb County Community College* held that the constitutional language indicating that such colleges "shall be supervised and controlled by locally elected boards" meant that the boards had the authority to set tuition rates in excess of a legislatively prescribed schedule. The court reasoned that this language was "almost identical" with the constitutional language considered in *Regents* and that, although the supreme court's opinion did not address the issue, the court of appeals decision in that case had held that the board of regents had the authority to establish tuition rates.

Executive Leadership and the Universities

Although the governor is commonly regarded as the chief executive of state government, governors often find they have executive authority over only a portion of the state's activities. The direct election of other state officials; independent boards and commissions with lengthy, overlapping terms; "federalized" functions, such as welfare, that are subject to national as well as state regulations; and limitations imposed by state constitutions all impinge on the executive authority of state governors.

In most states, higher education institutions are prime examples of institutions expending large amounts of state funds but operating independently of the governor. The independence comes from constitutional provisions in some states, as pointed out in the preceding chapter, but also arises from the administrative and political structure of the universities. For example, university boards are sometimes elected directly by the people and thus have clear structural independence from the governor.

Even when appointed by the governor, board members may come to play a role more as university advocate than as gubernatorial spokesperson. The Rosenbaum article on Wisconsin illustrates the sensitive nature of the attempts to balance autonomy and accountability in defining the relationship between state universities and the governor.

The governor is by no means powerless, of course, to influence the policies of the state's colleges and universities. His or her clout probably results largely from budgetary authority. Although governors do not have final authority over the budget in most cases, their recommendations to the legislature in the executive budget usually establish the general level of expenditure around which legislative debates will center. Legislative action may raise or lower governors' recommendations somewhat, but their figures tend to set the "arena of debate" for the legislature.

The Gove article provides a general summary of the governor's role in influencing higher education policy and points out both the formal and informal means available to governors to achieve this task. (The first version of this book contained a different article on the Reagan years as governor; it is interesting to note that Martin's article, written much later, presents a somewhat more sympathetic view of his gubernatorial years.) The article by Moos and Rourke, which appeared in the first book, is also included here because it presents almost a classic analysis of the conflicting values of university autonomy on the one hand and centralized coordination and authority on the other. They draw attention to the dangers to institutional autonomy that may result, even unintentionally, when state governments attempt to apply "good" administrative principles to a university setting.

4. Governors and Higher Education
Samuel K. Gove

Higher education systems (both private and public) have long had a special relationship with their states and governors. In some states higher education has been put on a pedestal and granted constitutional or statutory autonomy. At the same time, most governors actively participate in some aspect of higher education governance. And everywhere there is that elusive something called "academic freedom," a concept unique to higher education and difficult to describe to those outside the academy.

The relationship of the governor to higher education varies from one state to another; it has also varied over time and within a state from one governor to another. At times there has been a concerted effort to keep higher education out of "politics." Education leaders liked to think of themselves as part of state government's fourth branch. Governors were not to have direct involvement with the universities, which were regarded as autonomous and independent.

According to John D. Millett,
> *It is my observation that the key person in the development of higher education policy in a state is the governor of the state. If a state has a governor who by reason of experience, conviction, or predisposition is inclined to make higher education a major interest, then legislation and appropriations for the development of higher education are likely to be enacted. The momentum of such action under one or more governors is likely to be maintained under succeeding governors who may be less included to favor higher education expansion or affluence.[1]*

The past is replete with well-documented examples of governors who have become ultimately involved in the internal affairs of universities. Stories from several southern states come to mind: *Our Invaded Universities* by Ronnie Dugger (Texas), *The Tower and the Dome* by Homer Rainey (also Texas), *The Wild Man from Sugar Creek* by William Anderson (Georgia), and *Huey Long* by T. Harry

---

Samuel K. Gove is a professor in the Department of Political Science and the Institute of Government and Public Affairs at the University of Illinois at Urbana-Champaign. He spent over two decades as director of the institute.

Williams (Louisiana).[2] Other examples of governors' attempts to get rid of governing boards or university presidents can be found in Arkansas, Georgia, and Oklahoma. Brazen involvement seems to be a thing of the past, although an occasional story in *The Chronicle of Higher Education* suggests that the relationship in some states is not ideal, at least from the university's perspective. For example, the Maryland governor's involvement in a fairly recent academic freedom case at the University of Maryland has been quite well documented. More recent, positive involvement is Governor Rockefeller's role in the expansion of the SUNY system.[3]

In most states the governor appoints the members of the governing and coordinating boards and is usually the key actor in determining how much state money will be given the public and private universities. At the same time, most state governors look to the higher education establishment for help in determining economic policy.

Despite long-standing interest how governors interact with higher education, several studies on specific examples, and general information available, the gubernatorial role in higher education policy is largely unexplored.[4] Given the many serious problems facing higher education today, the time has come for attention to this issue.

Many states face declining enrollments and the possibility of campus closings. Fewer dollars from federal agencies require a search for new funding sources. Some states are concerned about higher education's governing structure, and proposals for reorganizations or reorganization studies have been made. What should the governor's role be in these situations? And is the issue public or academic policy? At present, there are no clear answers, but a look at some of the issues may help.

The "Ideal" Relationship

Many scholars have written about the ideal relationship between universities (primarily public) and state government. In *The Efficiency of Freedom,* the Committee on Government and Higher Education wrote,

> *Most governors are scrupulous in keeping higher education out of politics. Indeed, in a great majority of states, the governor is a source of understanding and support for the state universities and colleges. The importance of the governor's office for higher education is marked in several ways: a high degree of authority is concentrated in the governor's hands; his personal staff is influential in state affairs; in most*

states he has authority to appoint board members and many state officials whose work is related to the state colleges and universities; he serves as ex-officio member on academic governing boards in several states, a role which often places him in close personal contact with higher educaton. This can be of benefit, but in some cases his membership has resulted in unfortunate political involvements or has drawn the governor into the position of having to arbitrate petty differences. But even in states where he does not sit on the board of trustees, the governor, more than any other state official, is in a position to improve the relationship between the state government and higher education. His influence within the executive arm of the state government is strong, and state officers, taking their cue from the attitude of the governor, can be encouraged to deal cooperatively with educators.[5]

The committee made many recommendations for improving the relationship between state government and higher education. Three involved the governor's office:

1. The committee calls attention to the fact that a large measure of the success of higher education will depend on the caliber of members serving on governing boards.

2. Governors are encouraged to survey the administrative controls over higher education and to issue administrative orders (where statutory changes are not required) to eliminate those that are unnecessary or harmful.

3. Governors are encouraged to exercise their influence to keep higher education out of any partisan conflict.[6]

The committee also made a number of recommendations to state legislatures. One deserves special mention here: "Legal autonomy should be given to every institution of higher education that carries on a substantial program of teaching and research."[7] The committee continued with related recommendations on budgeting, purchasing, auditing, personnel, and building.

One aspect of these recommendations should be especially noted. Both the governor and the legislature were admonished to preserve and encourage the independence of higher education. Other studies since then have made similar observations and recommendations.[8]

This concern with autonomy continues today. At last count, six states have given unlimited constitutional autonomy to their institutions of higher education: California, Georgia, Idaho, Michigan, Minnesota, and Oklahoma. Three other states have granted limited constitutional autonomy. There have been no recent attempts to increase such autonomy. Many states have constitutional provisions describing only some aspect of higher education, such as the organizational structure, and some fifteen state constitutions make no mention of higher education. State constitutions should contain fundamentals. Neglecting to mention higher education sugggests that the enterprise is not necessary, especially if the same constitution mentions K-12 education.

The 1959 report also urged universities to stay out of "politics." At that time most higher education leaders would have argued vociferously that no politics existed in higher education. They would have said higher education's cause was "right" and, hence, not debatable. Today higher education's cause has become political, if politics is defined as a method for securing needed financial support. As John Millett has written, "It is illusory to believe that any separation of higher education from politics is possible or desirable in our liberal democracy."[9] Nonetheless, most academics, though not all, would agree that higher education should avoid partisan politics, particularly in elections.[10]

Governors and Academic Issues

Throughout the years, governors have been involved in broad academic issues with statewide implications. For example, governors have involved themselves in student tuition issues because of the impact on state finances. While governor of California, Ronald Reagan took a strong stand to end the state's no-tuition policy. In 1984 Governors Cuomo (New York) and Deukmejian (California) called for increased tuitions in their state-of-the-state speeches; in Michigan, Governor Blanchard took a strong stand against tuition increases.

Another issue is state aid for private higher education institutions. In some states such aid is prohibited constitutionally. But most states have established elaborate student aid programs. Every year the Education Commission of the States catalogs these programs. They are impressive. Because of the broad implications, governors frequently take the leadership in starting and expanding them. Sometimes the impetus comes from a study commission appointed by the governor. An early and visible commission was the McGeorge Bundy Commission in New York, which recommended a greatly expanded aid program. Similar commissions were established in other states, and in each case the governor took the initiative.

The structure of the public university system in a state is another area of concern in higher education policy making. In times of expansion, governors feel there may be program duplication or a lack of communication among institutions. Sometimes governors appoint commissions to make recommendations about these matters. Sometimes the governor leads the reorganization battle. The most recent example occurred when Governor Lucey united all the Wisconsin state institutions in one statewide University of Wisconsin system.[11]

Although not new, another issue is the governor's role in permitting or discouraging controversial speakers on campus. In the 1960s governors differed on whether to permit communist speakers on campus: thus the governor of Oregon permitted a communist to speak, while the governor of neighboring Washington discouraged the same speaker. North Carolina, during the same period, banned controversial speakers. At the moment this is not a volatile issue on American campuses, although there is concern about speakers being shouted down: still, the notion of academic freedom seems to prevail.

A recent issue that frequently involves governors is collective bargaining at public universities. The governor can and frequently does take a role in developing state policy on this matter. Moreover, when the legislature becomes involved, the governor can help shape legislation and work for its passage. He or she can help determine the type of bargaining unit and, more important, whether it will bargain with the state (possibly the governor's office) or with the governing board. In New York State, after the Taylor Law on public employee collective bargaining was enacted, Governor Nelson Rockefeller determined that all bargaining units of state employees would negotiate with the governor; he even appointed a special counsel for this purpose. Pennsylvania adopted the same arrangement.

Governors sometimes involve themselves in another aspect of higher education, namely, athletic programs. Louisiana seems to be a prime example, as evidenced in this quotation from a 1976 Carnegie Commission study:

> *To a large degree, however, this interest in higher education is not focused on academic matters. Scandals and sports are perhaps equal sources of interest. A winning football team at Louisiana State is seen as worth 100,000 votes. The Governor appears on television when a new coach is being signed, not infrequently has breakfast with high school students who are being recruited to a state college football team, and in*

general indicates his interest in the LSU athletic program.[12]

Gubernatorial Involvement in Campus Affairs

How often and when do governors get involved in campus affairs? As with most such relationships, they vary from state to state. There has been no national survey on this. Many surveys have been conducted on the executive branch of state government but none, to my knowledge, on gubernatorial involvement in higher education policy.

Another reason for this lack of information is that governors, unlike state legislatures, do not operate in the open. It is not known how often (if ever) the governor and the president of the leading public university communicate. Such contacts are privileged, and properly so. What the governor recommends for higher education in the budget, and what he or she approves after the legislature has acted, is public knowledge, as is what the governor says about higher education (if anything) in a state-of-the-state address. However, it cannot be known how involved a governor gets behind the scenes. Clearly, there is a good deal of involvement. In four states the secretary of education is a member of the governor's cabinet. But the usual form of governance is by means of a governing board. In fact, according to Millett, "The idea of a board of education or a board of trustees is so deeply imprinted in the governmental thinking of this country that any other arrangement is usually dismissed out of hand."[13]

In most states the governor appoints the governing board; in about a half dozen, members are elected. In a few states the governor is even a board member. The extent of gubernatorial involvement in the boards also varies from state to state. At the beginning of his administration Governor Jerry Brown was an active member of the University of California board. In Illinois the governor sits on the University of Illinois board by statute but customarily does not attend meetings. Not everyone is happy, however, with the structure of these governing boards. According to a 1976 Carnegie Foundation report,

> *The governor, in many states, is now the one dominant figure in higher education. We consider this to be an unwise long-term development. We suggest, as a check and balance, that governing boards be structured so that, first of all, governors not be members of them, and second, that appointments to these boards be recommended through appropriate screening mechanisms and be subject to some form of legislative approval. The governor, with his control over budget*

and his power of final appointment, will still be a forceful figure but less dominant.[14]

In addition to higher education boards or trustee boards, most states now have statewide coordinating boards. In fact, in the 1970s the small number of states that did not already have them were strongly encouraged to create them with the passage of Section 1202 of the federal Higher Education Act. Michigan is one of only a few remaining states without such a statewide body: currently, there is no long-range planning system for higher education, and the state constitution guarantees autonomy for the colleges. They can freely expand or reduce programs (depending on available funds), set tuition, and open branch campuses.

Except in Virginia, where the board is a legislative agent, members of these coordinating boards are appointed by the governor, and the boards have become a buffer between institutions and governors. As a result, they have a difficult balancing role to play. They must decide whether to be spokespersons for higher education or advocates of state government and state agencies. This does not usually present any great difficulties—except when financial questions arise.

Some people in higher education consider gubernatorial involvement beneficial. A 1970 Carnegie Foundation report said of the Kentucky governor,

A relatively poor state has invested very heavily in higher education—largely because of the initiative of governors. Higher education has strong support in the state and in the Legislature, but the advances that have been made result in part from the Legislature's habit of approving budgets with little or no change.[15]

According to the same study, the same was true in Texas:
It may seem odd to attribute so much power to a governor whose formal powers are relatively limited. Nonetheless, the progress of higher education in the past decade, or half-decade, has depended to a large degree on the incumbent governor. Perhaps in California there are enough other liberalizing influences to enable higher education to weather the storm of an arch-conservative, but this is not the case in Texas, where a governor who is not oriented to higher education and its problems could bring progress to a screeching halt.[16]

In recent years few governors have tried to articulate their own role in higher education matters. One exception is former Governor Terry Sanford of North Carolina:

> Terry Sanford carried the strong governor theory a step farther: The governor's role with the independent board should be a powerful one not only so that he can govern in general more coherently but also because his influence is necessary to protect the public interest in particular fields. Sanford criticizes the "self-serving" behavior of some professional leaders in fields like health and education; he is skeptical about the ability of so-called independent boards to resist being captured: "Too often they become 'dependent,' harking to the direction of the professionals." Sanford's thesis is that, the governor, having played a strong role in setting goals for higher education and thus being assured that they are, in fact, in the public interest, will throw his full weight behind efforts to find adequate support for those goals. Previous efforts to hold the governor at arm's length from higher education policy have probably harmed the cause more than they have helped it: "More universities have suffered from political indifference than have ever been upset by political interference."[17]

Former Governor Albert Quie of Minnesota has also made his views known. Speaking of higher and secondary education together, he listed ten functions for the governor:

- the state's foremost public educator
- a powerful advocate for the public interest
- a priority setter (through the budget)
- an appointer of leaders who influence education policy
- the state's most influential convenor
- a legislation proposer and initiater through executive action
- an influential linker, broker, and mediator
- an agent for making quality education a priority of his or her political party
- the state's senior representative in national affairs
- a visionary in the pursuit of quality education.[18]

Higher Education as a Gubernatorial Priority

Those associated with higher education want it given the highest priority by the governor. But this does not always occur: higher education priority varies from year to year, state to state, and governor to governor.

In interviews with former governors by the National Governors' Association, almost no mention was made of higher education. Perhaps governors do not worry much about it, or they assume their universities are in good hands. One exception was former Governor Walker of Illinois. Unlike the other governors, he was specifically asked, "Do you think more agencies dealing with education and higher education should report to the governor? Did you feel that you were blamed for things they did independently?" The governor responded,

> *Higher education—no question about it. Higher education needs a bridle and more responsiveness to the executive branch of government. The splintering of responsibility through boards makes it possible for the vice president of the university to have a limousine when he shouldn't have a limousine, just to give you a very small example.*[17]

A more recent study of gubernatorial styles and management skills, entitled *Being Governor*,[18] also pays no attention to the governor's role in higher education. Perhaps this is not surprising when one considers that the field is contracting rather than expanding. How much contraction will actually take place remains to be seen. Declining enrollments have been well documented, cutbacks in federal programs have been given considerable attention, and many institutions are threatened with total extinction.

Higher Education, High Technology, and the Governor

A growing number of governors see the marriage of high technology and higher education as one made in heaven that could save their state's economy.

Even this blessing poses problems, however. Despite the hope that high technology will help bring recovery and prevent future economic problems, most state budgets are still hurting from the recession, and there is not enough extra cash in the till to give higher education the funds needed for high-technology development. And so the dilemma: should a state keep a lean budget for these tough times, or should it increase aid to those higher education programs involved with high technology? If the latter is chosen, increasing emphasis on high technology could involve governors more closely with higher education than in the past.

High technology involves risk, but many governors are willing to take it. According to former Democratic Governor James B. Hunt, Jr., of North Carolina, "States should be strengthening their colleges and universities for the challenges and needs of a new technological age."[19] Hunt was Chairman of the National Governors' Association Committee on Technological Innovation. The committee saw disturbing state trends that would need to be reversed before the high technology-higher education marriage could be consummated. These included faculty losses in engineering and computer science programs, reductions in engineering research, and deteriorating laboratory equipment.

Successful high-technology ventures require four basic prerequisites, according to the committee's report:
- A sufficient research base generating scientific and technical advances
- A managerial structure with sufficient vision, experience, and know-how to transform good ideas into marketable products and services
- A well-trained labor pool of scientists, engineers, technicians, and skilled workers
- Investment capital, available long term and at reasonable rates.[20]

Practicing what he preached, Hunt asked the North Carolina legislature for $7.25 million in fiscal 1984 and $10 million in fiscal 1985 to operate the Microelectronics Center of North Carolina, now under construction. The center will conduct research and training in microelectronics.[21]

Hunt's committee surveyed the states on high technology commitment and found that Hunt is far from alone in his beliefs. Governors in nine of the thirty-two states that responded have appointed special boards to coordinate state action related to technological innovation. The boards include representatives of higher education, government, and industry. They not only advise the governors but also foster cooperation between industry and universities.[22] One result is deeper gubernatorial involvement in higher education.

Pennsylvania's Ben Franklin Partnership is a good example of how a board and a governor can work together on high technology. The partnership helps establish advanced technology centers, operated by universities, business, labor, and financial institutions. Governor Richard Thornburgh (also vice chairman of Hunt's committee) requested a 1,000-percent increase in state matching funds for the program last year, which would have increased the program's budget from $1 million to $10 million.

Colorado Governor Richard D. Lamm showed a similar commitment to bringing high technology and higher education closer. To the legislature he said, "There is a raw material in the new industrial order that is taking precedence. That raw material is education. In a real sense, the education of today is the economy of tomorrow."[23] Lamm also echoed Hunt's warnings about state readiness for high technology. He said that in 1982 Colorado's universities granted only twenty-nine advanced degrees in microelectronics and fewer than one hundred graduate degrees in biotechnology. However, state jobs in electronics increased 116 percent year year from 1975 to 1980; manufacturing jobs increased less than 5 percent each year.

Governors in Hawaii, Kansas, Maryland, Massachusetts, South Carolina, New Jersey, and New Mexico have also stressed the importance of uniting high technology and higher education. Proposals have ranged from monetary commitments to promises for studies. But not all governors can afford such commitments, even though high technology might help cure the problems that cause the restrictions. California pursues high technology with its Investment in People program, which supports community college training programs in new technologies and improvements in university engineering programs.

Despite poor finances in so many states, the allure of high technology should continue to attract the attention of governors and universities alike.

Outlook

This discussion has pointed out the myriad ways governors are involved in higher education. There is no model for that relationship; it is still evolving. Clearly, however, governors are becoming the dominant figure in higher education policy making, especially when the budget is at issue. At present there does not seem to be any widespread or serious violation of academic freedom. Institutions are generally free to make academic decisions. But when finances are at stake (for instance, when tuition levels are set), governors frequently get involved. Similarly, when decisions concern aid to private institutions, governor step in.

Higher education leaders want their institutions given the highest priority. So do people representing other functional areas. This contest will thrust higher education into the political arena, whether higher education leaders are prepared or even willing. Higher education will have to lobby for its interests and keep its political fences in order. Most important, higher education will have to develop good relations with state governors.

Notes

[1] John D. Millett, "State Administration of Higher Education," *Public Administration Review,* March/April 1970, p. 105.

[2] Ronnie Dugger, *Our Invaded Universities: Form, Reform, and New Starts* (New York: W. W. Norton, 1974); Homer P. Rainey,

The Tower and the Dome (Boulder: Pruett, 1971); William Anderson, *The Wild Man from Sugar Creek* (Baton Rouge: Louisiana State University Press, 1975); and T. Harry Williams, *Huey Long* (New York: Alfred A. Knopf, 1969).

[3]Robert H. Connery and Gerald Benjamin, *Rockefeller of New York* (Ithaca, N.Y.: Cornell University Press, 1979), p. 313.

[4]*The Efficiency of Freedom: Report of the Committee on Government and Higher Education,* Washington, DC: American Association of State Colleges and Universities, 1985, p. 32.

[5]Ibid., pp. 33, 34.

[6]Ibid., p. 30.

[7]*See for instance* Lyman A. Glenny and Thomas K. Dalglish, *Public Universities, State Agencies, and the Law: Constitutional Autonomy in Decline* (Berkeley: Center for Research and Development in Higher Education, University of California, 1973).

[8]John D. Millett, *Politics and Higher Education* (University, Ala.: University of Alabama, 1974), p. 59.

[9]Allan Rosenbaum, "University Reorganization in Wisconsin," *State Politics and Higher Education,* Ed. Leonard E. Goodall, pp. 62-84.

[10]Heinz Eulau and Harold Quinley, *State Officials and Higher Education* (New York: McGraw-Hill, 1970), p. 16.

[11]Millett, p. 59.

[12]Carnegie Foundation for the Advancement of Teaching, *The States and Higher Education* (San Francisco: Jossey-Bass, 1976), p. 19.

[13]Eulau and Quinley, p. 15.

[14]Ibid., p. 29.

[15]Robert O. Berdahl, *Statewide Coordination of Higher Education* (Washington, D.C.: American Council on Education, 1971), p. 265.

[16]Albert Quie, "Quality Education: A Personal Perspective on Ten Roles for Governors," from a 1979 speech reprinted by Education Commission of the States.

[17]National Governors' Association, *Reflections on Being Governor* (Durham, N.C.: Duke University, 1983).

[18]Thad L. Beyle and Lynn R. Muchmore, eds., *Being Governor* (Durham, N.C.: Duke University, 1983).

[19]*Chronicle of Higher Education,* 9 March 1983, p. 1.

[20] Ibid., p. 8.
[21] *Chronicle,* 2 February 1983, p. 12.
[22] *Chronicle,* 9 March 1983, p. 8.
[23] *Chronicle,* 23 February 1983, p. 1.

5. University Reorganization in Wisconsin
Allen Rosenbaum

The game of higher education politics in Wisconsin is called "merger." Just what kind of game it is, however, or indeed what it is likely to become in time, is something about which even those most directly involved are still not certain. Thus any attempt to analyze the politics of public higher education in Wisconsin must begin by noting that the present situation is seemingly one of transition and consequently also one of uncertainty. The organization and structure of public higher education in Wisconsin is notably different today from what it was two years ago and it is not at all inconceivable that there may be more changes. Furthermore, while it is less likely it is nevertheless possible that future changes could go beyond simple organization and structure to affect significantly the basic character and quality of public higher education in Wisconsin. Whether such changes, were they to come about, would amount to taking a step forward or backward, or simply marching in place but to a different tune, is a matter on which there is still little agreement.

Obviously, uncertainty about what the future holds is not a condition that is unique to public higher education in Wisconsin. Indeed the combination of heightened political skepticism about the manner in which public higher education has been governed (a legacy of the tumultuous student demonstrations of the last several years), the recent leveling-off if not actual drop-off in enrollments, and a much more tight-fisted attitude toward funding on the part not only of the states, but of the federal government and major foundations as well, has served to add much uncertainty to the future of public higher education almost everywhere. The Wisconsin situation is, however, even more complicated as a consequence of action taken by the state legislature in the fall of 1971. At that time the legislature, after a spring and summer of heated controversy, approved a bill that resulted in merging the state's two previously independent university systems—the University of Wisconsin (U of W) system and the Wisconsin State Universities (WSU) sys-

---

Allen Rosenbaum had a close-up view of the reorganization debates in Wisconsin. He was a member of the political science department at the University of Wisconsin-Madison during the restructuring of the university.

tem—into a single system of 130,000 students. In signing that bill, the governor set in motion what in all probability is the single most dramatic change in the organizational structure of public higher education in the state's history. Moreover, in so doing, he had, with the proverbial stroke of the pen, created what is today the nation's fourth largest university system.

Not only are the ultimate consequences of this action still uncertain, but they are indeed still the subject of much controversy, at least among the state's higher education community. The merger of the two systems, which was initiated and in the main brought about through the determined efforts of the state's Democratic governor, Patrick Lucey, left many of the major issues involved in any real merger unresolved. Other than creating a single board of regents governing all of the state's public institutions of higher education and a single system president, the legislation effecting the merger did not in itself bring about any substantive changes. This was not by choice; rather, it was the political price that the governor had to pay for achieving legislative approval of the merger. As the proposal had become increasingly controversial, at least to those affected by it, Lucey was forced to limit its scope.

The merger legislation did, however, create a committee made up of representatives of most of the major interests that were directly involved; and this group has made a set of recommendations to the 1973 session of the legislature regarding the statutory enactments needed to implement the merger. The extent of this committee's ultimate impact is, however, despite steady meetings throughout 1972, by no means clear. Changes in legislative personnel, the sometime estrangement between the governor and the university administration, and the emergence of faculty unionism as a complicating factor, may all have resulted in the erosion of much support for several of the committee's proposals. The committee has, however, avoided one potential source of much political controversy by ignoring the legislative mandate that it evaluate the initial success of merger and instead recommended that the 1977 legislature undertake such a task.

There is no question that the resolution of the multitude of issues involved in any effort to achieve merger in more than name will continue to be the subject of much debate and political maneuver during the course of the next few years. The new board of regents, two-thirds of whose present membership was carried over from the old U of W and WSU boards and thus had been appointed by the present governor's Republican predecessor, certainly has given numerous signs that it plans to be an active rather than passive participant. Likewise the governor—who now has an obvious political stake in merger—and the legislature, where several Republicans occasionally threatened to try to repeal the merger legislation (a very unlikely possibility), will be actively concerned about the shape of future events. Needless to say, the university's president—who has from time to time been under attack from the governor for failing to be fully committed to the "spirit" of merger while still seeking to gain control of the administrative behemoth astride which he now finds himself—will be deeply involved in future developments. And of course the faculties and administrations of each of the now thirteen four-year-plus campuses of the University of Wisconsin (who are likely to be the most affected by these events) will be deeply involved in them. Perhaps not surprisingly the groups which on the whole seem most notably uninterested in merger are the students (who, as the governor's aides are quick to point out, now represent a very much bigger bloc of voters than the faculty and staff of the institutions) and the state's citizenry.

The consequence of all this is that, depending on with whom one talks, the future of public higher education in Wisconsin may be viewed as portending either the best or the worst of all times. The one thing that can be said with absolute certainty in the midst of this uncertainty is that the occurrence of merger guarantees that future state-university political relationships, however they develop, will not be what they once were, or at least once seemed to be. In the past it has always been assumed by all involved in or concerned with such matters that the Madison campus of the University of Wisconsin was far and away the most dominant, indeed the unchallengeable force in any political equation that would result in the establishment of state policy for public higher education. But at least the initial outcome of the several-month controversy over merger suggests that the Madison campus will never again appear as all-powerful and totally dominant as it did prior to the events of 1971. In at least that sense, then, the politics of higher education in Wisconsin will not again be quite the same. By no means, however, does this necessarily mean that the future of the Madison campus, as well as the state's other university campuses, is any less bright than it was a few years ago. That remains yet to be determined and is likely to be affected by social forces far more significant than institutional organization structures. Having said all this by way of introduction, let me now turn to look at some of the factors that led up to merger and then examine some of the issues that ultimately have been at stake.

A Brief History of Institutional Development

The thirteen four-year-plus campuses and eleven two-year centers that now make up the University of Wisconsin system are the product of two very different patterns of institutional development. These were the patterns followed by the pre-merger University of Wisconsin, the development of which will be briefly examined first, and the Wisconsin State Universities system to which we shall subsequently turn our attention: What was to be the University of Wisconsin system began with the founding in 1849 of the Madison campus.

In the final decades of the nineteenth century, the Madison institution grew to be a state university of some national renown. During this period, and during the period 1900-1920, certain patterns of development and institutional characteristics emerged which would have a profound impact upon the relationship of the school to both the state's political leaders and the mass of its citizenry. The most notable of these were the institution's early commitment to applied scholarly research and service to the state of which it was a part. Both of these developments were embodied in the emergence of what has popularly come to be known as "the Wisconsin idea," which we will examine more closely in our subsequent discussion of the political resources of the university.

The university's pioneering activities in the establishment of a statewide extension program also served as the initial impetus for the establishment of branch campuses outside of Madison. During the Twenties and Thirties, a number of educational extension centers were organized in communities around the state. A second major step toward institutional expansion occurred in the aftermath of World War II. Responding to returning war veterans' demands for higher education, the university increased its enrollment from 9,802 in 1946 to 23,892 the following year. In part this was accomplished through the establishment of over a dozen more two-year centers around the state. In subsequent years, as university enrollments declined, many of these centers were closed. However, nine of them, including one in Milwaukee whose history as an extension center well predated the war, continued in operation.

In 1956, as a consequence of the first major political controversy ("first" in the sense that both systems actively battled) between the University and then Wisconsin State College (WSU) system, a permanent four-year campus of the University of Wisconsin was established in Milwaukee. This was done by combining the university's Milwaukee extension center with the then Wisconsin

State College of Milwaukee into a four-year branch of the university. As a part of an informal compromise worked out in the aftermath of this controversy, two four-year technological institutes at Stout and Platteville, which up to this time had been governed by their own boards of trustees, were assigned to the state college system and its board. In addition, the victorious university, in order to pacify further the anger of the state college supporters (who had lost their bid to have the new Milwaukee institution established as part of that system) agreed to the creation of a statewide coordinating body for public higher education. What emerged from this was the ill-fated Wisconsin Coordinating Committee for Higher Education (CCHE). In response to the demands of the university's supporters, this body was composed almost entirely of regents from the two system boards and its staff was, until 1965, when the structure of CCHE was changes, drawn from U of W and WSC personnel.

It was during the course of the rapid expansion of student enrollments that took place in the 1960s that the University of Wisconsin was fully converted into a multicampus state university system. In 1964, the several two-year extension centers, which had continued to operate in the aftermath of the decline in student enrollment in the university in the early Fifties, were reestablished as two-year university academic centers independent of the extension program. Between 1964 and 1968, four more two-year centers were established. In 1968, four of the university centers in the Green Bay area and two in the Kenosha-Racine area were combined and reestablished as four-year campuses of the university. As organized by the university, these two new campuses, the UW-Green Bay and the UW-Parkside, would not only be four-year degree-granting institutions, but would in addition offer certain specific programs of graduate education that would ultimately lead to the M.A. and Ph.D. degrees.

The establishment of the two new university campuses at Green Bay and Parkside were certainly in part the consequence of growing aggregate demands for public higher education. At the time that planning was beginning on these campuses in the mid-sixties, it was optimistically expected that in all probability the demand for public higher education was likely to continue in a steady upward climb throughout the next several decades. There were, however, other factors that appear to have played a part in the decision of the university to commit itself to the establishment of these new campuses. Among the most important of these was the growing rivalry between it and the by-then rapidly expanding Wisconsin State University system. The two areas involved were, after Madison and Milwaukee, the state's two largest population centers. Moreover, they were also unserved by any four-year public institution of higher education. Establishing U of W campuses there would serve to keep the expanding WSU system out of these areas, as well as to add substantially to the population base that was directly served by the U of W campuses. As will later be seen, however, these two campuses may well have had consequences for the U of W system which were quite unpredicted by those then engaged in their establishment.

What was prior to merger the Wisconsin State University system had its beginning at Platteville in 1866 with the founding of a state normal school to provide two years of training beyond high school for future elementary school teachers. In the course of the next fifty years, eight more such institutions were opened, all of which were governed by a Board of Regents of Normal Schools. In 1927, the normal schools were by legislative action changed into four-year state teacher colleges offering a bachelor of education degree. This was a change which had been actively opposed by the various presidents of the University of Wisconsin during the first two decades of the twentieth century.

In 1951, the "teacher's" designation was dropped from the names of the institutions and they were given authority by the legislature to offer a liberal arts program. In 1964, the board of regents which governed the institutions (and which traditionally was composed of one regent from each community in which an institution existed, plus the Superintendent of Public Instruction), changed the names of the institutions from state colleges to state universities. Subsequently the legislature in turn changed the name of the governing board itself in order that it would conform with the institutions.

The growth of the state universities system, particularly during the course of the 1960s, was quite rapid. Indeed, where it began the decade of the sixties with a combined student body that was equal to only about half that of the U of W system, by the end of the decade the WSU system was almost equal in number of students to the U of W system. Equally as important, while in its entirety the WSU system was slightly smaller than the U of W system, it had by the beginning of the 1970s actually surpassed the U of W system in terms of the number of Wisconsin undergraduates being educated.

The Politics of Institutional Coordination

The question of establishing some form of coordination of public higher education in Wisconsin was one of those perennial issues that regularly concerned the state's public policy makers. Throughout the nineteenth century, proposals were put forward which would have brought the U of W, the normal schools, and publicly supported elementary and secondary education under the control of a single board of education. Moreover, in several instances during the first half of the twentieth century, legislation was proposed that would have resulted in the merging of the university and board of regents of the normal schools.

In 1953 and again in 1955, Governor Walter J. Kohler made concerted efforts to achieve the merger of all public higher education into one system. In 1955, he made this issue a high priority item in his legislative program. As a consequence, the Kohler proposal, which was supported by the then State College Board, and opposed by the university's board, was a matter of some controversy in Wisconsin during much of 1955. The university was, through its support of a compromise proposal, ultimately able to defeat this proposal in the state legislature by undermining the governor's support in his own part. (Kohler was then in his last term and had in the preceding election won by only a small margin.) This was the compromise that, as was noted earlier, resulted in the merger of the state college and the university extension program in Milwaukee under the U of W's control, while providing for the establishment of a statewide coordinating committee for public higher education (CCHE).

The coordinating committee as originally organized included as members five university regents and five state college regents, four public members appointed by the governor, and the state Superintendent of Public Instruction. The character of the agency—its lack of independent staff and domination by individuals representing the established institutions—combined no doubt with the fact that it was presiding over a period of very rapid expansion of public higher education, served to limit effectively its potential for success. Quickly the coordinating committee found itself in a virtually untenable position, at least in seeking to exercise some control over the future expansion of public higher education. Competition between the U of W system and the State Universities system over new programs and new campuses was throughout this period rapidly intensifying. The coordinating body responded to this situation by avoiding major controversy and granting to the two systems most of the programs and new campuses sought by each. That this body should be sympathetic to the desires of each of these university systems is hardly surprising when one considers the character of its make-up.

As a consequence of this situation, in 1965 the then newly elected Governor Warren Knowles requested and received legislative authorization to reorganize the coordinating council. The newly reorganized board was provided with funds for the appointment of independent professional staff, as well as reconstituted in such a fashion as to provide that a significant majority on the board would be citizen members appointed by the governor. By this time, however, it was probably too late to achieve the kind of coordinating body that would do the job the governor and the state legislature sought. Due to its lack of a significant political base, as well as the aggressive institutional rivalry that had developed by this time, and perhaps in part because of the turmoil and uncertainty that characterized the latter years of the sixties, the board simply was not able to emerge as a major restraining force on the rapidly expanding public universities.

The consequence of this situation was the 1971 proposal by the then newly elected governor to merge the state's two public university systems. Indeed, one of the reasons most widely circulated in attempting to explain the adamant position assumed by the governor on the issue of university merger was that he was determined to bring about the elimination of the by then widely condemned coordinating council. While this is no doubt a less than totally sufficient explanation of the governor's motives in supporting merger, it is nevertheless an accurate reflection of the high degree of disregard in which this agency had come to be held by this time. It is in fact usually figured as one of the major scapegoats in any attempts to explain what was wrong in public higher education in Wisconsin.

An attempt to provide here the final definitive analysis of either the real causes or ultimate consequences of university merger in Wisconsin would be premature. There is still speculation by even those most intimately involved in this affair as to the meaning and significance of some of the events that transpired either during the course of the heated controversy that occupied much of 1971 or in the year and a half that has elapsed since then. There are, however, several things that can be said about the process by which merger was accomplished. In the first place, merger was from the outset and still is a reality only as a consequence of the governor's efforts. In that sense the merger controversy serves to illustrate both the extent and the limits of a governor's power over the state's university system. Quite clearly, if a governor chooses to do so he can exercise a good deal of authority over the development of state-supported higher education. There are, of course, certain conditions that must be met to do so, including being able to exercise strong influence, if not actual control, over the legislature. But, as we will shortly note, if a governor is willing to make higher education one of his top priority issues, there are ways that this can be done even if he has only partial control over the legislature.

To many of those immediately involved, the most perplexing aspect of the whole process is why the governor initiated the merger in the first place. The governor himself has stated publicly on numerous occasions that his main purpose in bringing forth the proposal was to achieve greater administrative and fiscal efficiency through ending the unchecked competition of the two state university systems and eliminating the CCHE. There are in addition a host of other possible reasons, some of which are frequently cited by those who either supported or opposed the merger effort. These include but are by no means limited to the following:

1. The governor desired to get rid of the regents appointed by his predecessor (subsequently, however, he was to agree to carry over to the new board of regents many of the individuals who had been appointed by his predecessor).

2. Certain key advisors to the governor had convinced him that by shaking up the established system the quality of higher education and in particular undergraduate education could be vastly improved on both the U of W and WSU campuses.

3. The governor was attempting to build a record for the next election, and this was an area in which there had been such turmoil that there was a unique opportunity to make a record as a vigorous leader. Moreover, in so doing he eliminated the possibility that if the turmoil had continued he could have subsequently been charged by the Republicans with having been "soft" on the university.

4. The governor felt that a significant portion of the states' citizenry wanted "something done about the troubles at the University." While in fact not related, merger might be vaguely perceived as representing a response to this problem, particularly three years after the event when at the next election it could be pointed out that the "troubles" subsided at about the same time the governor was taking action.

5. The governor and his aides were seeking a means by which they personally could get a much firmer grip upon the financial affairs of public higher education, which by this time had become one of the largest items in the state budget.

6. The governor was seeking to gain the favor of the WSU students (now voters) and faculty by making them a part of the more prestigious University of Wisconsin.

7. The governor was seeking to build a permanent monument to the fact that he had been in office and the merged university served this purpose.

8. The governor was engaged in an attack upon (or, depending upon one's perspective, legitimately seeking to influence) the Madison faculty because it was overly concerned with research at the cost of undergraduate teaching.

9. The governor didn't really care about merging the universities until late in the controversy when his prestige had been put on the line over the issue. Rather, he had originally intended to sacrifice the issue willingly to Republican opposition in order to obtain passage of a proposal for tax reform that would appeal to urban constituencies throughout the state.

10. The governor simply didn't know what he was doing.

Although in some states and with some governors, it would not always be so, one can in this particular instance be reasonably certain that the last of these proposed explanations is probably of little use in understanding the why of merger. Nor for that matter is it likely that the next to the last of these explanations is of much use, although in both cases some knowledgeable observers have seriously put both explanations forward. Beyond these last two, however, it is not unlikely that each of the other explanations suggested have in varying degrees some measure of validity in helping to explain why there has been a merger. The key point in all of this is simply that irrespective of whether merger resulted in any fiscal saving or not (for the record, money was saved at least by eliminating the CCHE staff), there were, as seen from the vantage point of those around the governor, a number of political and policy benefits that might result from merger. At this same time, other than a few votes from the faculty at the Madison campus, there was, if the governor did not stumble in the legislative struggle, little that he could lose.

While the governor's reasons for proposing the merger may be less than fully clear, the political strategies which he utilized in seeking this goal are a good deal more evident. At the outset he sought to avoid potential opposition from the University of Wisconsin by providing that the new board would be dominated by regents from that system. This, however, was greeted by ambivalence at the U of W while providing vigorous opposition from individuals associated with the WSU system. Thus the governor modified his original proposal so that it would provide for equal representation of both systems on the merged board. This was an important element in his ability to achieve merger in that it not only removed most of the concerted WSU opposition, but resulted in producing significant informal support for his proposal from these same sources.

Another important factor in Lucey's ability to gain approval of the merger proposal was the manner in which he was able to neutralize potential opposition from the U of W president early in the developing controversy by appointing the then still new president as his choice to head the merged system. In such a situation, the U of W president, who was still something of a novice in both his job and the state's political environment, found himself in the position in which he either felt unable, or simply chose not, consistently to lead university opposition to the proposal. In part as a consequence of this situation, one of the university regents, who had been very active in Republican party politics, undertook to mobilize opposition in the Republican-controlled state senate to the governor's proposal. Ultimately, however, he failed in this effort. By having made the dispute a party issue in the lower house, the governor was able to hold his own party members (who held a large majority there) in support of the proposal. At the same time, by striking bargains with various key Republicans in the state senate and skillfully downplaying partisanship there by using a Republican who had been a long-time proponent of the concept of merger to sponsor the bill, Lucey obtained senate passage. To do so, however, the governor ultimately had to pacify the U of W Board of Regents by eliminating most of the substance of the original bill; and in this sense, then, the Republican regent-led efforts were by no means without some success.

Certainly when all is said and done, an important part of the governor's ability to obtain legislative merger was to be found in the ambivalence and the notably weakened political situation of the University of Wisconsin. In this respect, the years of campus turmoil in Madison had taken their toll upon the institution in terms of both public and interest-group support. The latter was illustrated by the fact that opponents of merger within the U of W, primarily senior faculty from Madison, wound up fighting the battle, virtually without any allies. In fact most of the state's major interest groups, many of which as noted earlier had previously been staunch supporters of the U of W position in prior legislative controversies, simply sat the issue out or at most registered a token indication of preference one way or the other.

Some indication of the loss of public support suffered by the institution during the years of turmoil is found in a study of citizen attitudes toward the U of W done by Leon Epstein. Using statewide survey data, Epstein found that public support for increased expenditures of state money or behalf of the Madison campus of the university had fallen from 72 percent positive responses in 1966 to 48 percent in 1970. The permanence of this decline in support is obviously another question, but certainly in terms of the merger controversy it seems to have placed the institution in a significantly weakened position. No matter how closely one might have been listening, there simply wasn't any public response to the contention of many at Madison that the governor was playing politics with the university. Indeed a couple of public opinion polls taken during the summer of 1971, when the controversy over the governor's proposal was at a peak, indicated that the large majority of the state's citizenry either didn't know or didn't care about the merging of the state universities.

Finally, in seeking to understand how the governor was able to achieve passage of his merger proposal, one must also take into account the extent to which the U of W's ambitious educational and political maneuvering during the course of the preceding decade seems to have worked against it in 1971. To a degree that would appear, at least impressionistically, to be unmatched in most other states, the U of W has been dependent upon its image locally as a "great" and "unusual" kind of public institution to aid it in its efforts to protect its interest. The Madison campus has, as we have already noted, been viewed as a rather special university by, at least, the state's political and economic elite. The fact is, however, that such an image and its consequent political benefits in terms of legislative support were much more easily maintained when the university was just the Madison campus and consequently did seem to be a rather unique institution in not only state but national higher education as well.

While the establishment of the Milwaukee campus may not have done irreparable harm to such an image, it probably didn't help it. The establishment of the Green Bay and Parksides campuses, however, at least for many in the state legislature, seems to have destroyed this image. Thus when the Madisonians who opposed merger sought to gain legislative support by arguing that the governor's proposal would destroy the unique character of the U of W, their pleas for the most part fell upon deaf ears. The typical legislative reaction, whether right or wrong, was that the Green Bay and Parkside campuses were little different from the state colleges; thus it seemed at least to legislators that the U of W could no longer legitimately claim to be either unique or special. Consequently there was no longer any reason to argue that the proposed merger would jeopardize the unique character of the institution.

State Higher Education Policy and Merger

Ultimately, whether merger is simply shadow or really substance may very well have, despite the fear of some of those affected, only the most limited impact upon the future of higher education in the state of Wisconsin. A far more significant determinant of the future is likely to be the extent of political support for higher education, particularly as manifested in both the absence of oppressive measures directed against the universities and the willingness of Wisconsin public officials to continue to provide adequate financing. At this point, it seems that legislative ire toward higher education, which only a few years ago was a matter of grave concern to many connected with the old U of W, is now, with the ebbing of student activism, also beginning to recede. This in part would seem to help explain why there has been comparatively little legislative enthusiasm for the anti-tenure effort. The question of state financial support for public higher education, is, however, a rather different matter. Not only is there the issue of how much state money will be forthcoming in the future, but there is the equally interesting and uncertain matter of for what purposes (and consequently at what campuses) that which is available will be spent.

As is not infrequently the case in governmental reorganization efforts, those events which seem to attract the least attention may have in the long run the most profound impact on the institutions involved. In this case, the whole question of the central administration—local campus relationships—which, unlike the tenure and budget issue, have attracted little or no attention in the Wisconsin press, or for that matter in most of the university community as well, may hold the key to the future of the institutions involved. The present or future character of the relationship between the university's central administration and its individual campuses (and consequently between individual campuses and state public officials as well) is by no means settled. While it seems to appear that the state Department of Administration (the governor's equivalent to the Office of Management and Budget at the federal level) is itself committed to the idea of working through a strong central university administration, it is not at all clear that the relationships between the chancellors of the individual campuses and the state's politicians in particular its legislators, have been severed once and for all. Indeed it is not inconceivable that future budgetary proceedings will witness increasing wheeling and dealing between individual campuses and state legislators.

If this were to be the case then in the end merger might result not in the savings that the governor sought but rather in a substantial increase in higher education spending as the individual campuses united with each other, and their local legislative representatives in a sort of one-for-all and all-for-one grand alliance. With a leveling off in enrollments combined with the fact that higher education spending has in the last two decades become a large and important part of the state's budget, this is probably a less likely possibility than it might have been a few years ago. Rather, it is likely that there will be a belt-tightening of some sort, which in turn raises the question of whose belt will be tightened the most. Here once again the issue of local campus-central administration-state political arena relationships could be the crucial one. Will there be a free-for-all among the various state campuses to get the most of what there is to be gotten, or will some more rational approach prevail? And if there were to be a political free-for-all, would the various institutions form coalitions, perhaps along the old U of W-WSU divisions, in such a fight? All of this is obviously still a matter of speculation, although the likelihood of open institutional warfare seems very slight at present.

An indication of what the future could hold in this regard came in the December 1972 speech by the governor to the Madison faculty. At that time Lucey mentioned in passing that he was planning to organize the University budget into two categories. There would be one for the graduate institutions (Madison and Milwaukee) and one for the rest of the campuses in the state. Such an arrangement has a number of serious implications built into it. It would significantly cut down the flexibility of the universities' central administration by greatly limiting their capacity to transfer funds between these two campus groupings. It would also mean increased limitations on the possibility of the old WSU campuses' expanding most of their recently begun graduate programs in various fields (which in all probability will occur in one way or another). For the Madison and Milwaukee campuses of the old U of W system, such an arrangement could prove to be of great benefit or a mild disaster, depending upon what effect it has upon the formulas for funding graduate and undergraduate teaching on these campuses. In all probability, the greatest losers under such a situation may be the Parkside and Green Bay campuses of the old U of W system. Planned a decade ago to be campuses with unique institutional missions which would distinguish them from the typical state college, these institutions may in the future be just simply two more small state university campuses.

It is in this particular context that one finally confronts the issue which, from the day that the governor proposed merger and right up to the present, has continued to agitate many of the old U of W campuses and still motivates those who vigorously oppose the idea. This is the question of whether, in the face of merger, the old U of W campuses will be able to continue to sustain their national position as seemingly rather more elite institutions than the old WSU schools. Viewed from the not-so-placid shores of Lake Mendota as well as the almost as turbulent environs of Green Bay and Parkside, merger obviously meant first that all state-supported campuses would share the presumably much more lofty U of W name. Might it then not also mean that at some future time all campuses would share the same faculty salary levels and teaching loads and finally in the end the same institutional character and status? And since Wisconsin is not a large and wealthy state, was it not equally logical to assume that the changes brought about by such a process would be in the direction of making the old U of W campuses more nearly like the old WSU campuses rather than the reverse?

Ultimately these were and still are the issues that provoke the greatest concern about merger at Madison. There, where the collective faculty self-perception has (whether accurate or not) long been one of established excellence, merger to many portended the beginning of the end of such a status. No less concerned than those at the Madison campus are many at the Green Bay and Parkside campuses. Not only has merger threatened the aspirations of these two campuses to become institutions rather like a public Oberlin or a Santa Cruz of the Mideast, but it also has opened up the very real possibility that whatever unique or special identity they now possess might be quickly lost in the shuffle of merger.

On the other hand, the matter of merger was and is a much less compelling issue on the Milwaukee campus of the old U of W system. Having been well established as the state's second large public multiuniversity campus when the merger occurred, its position in the state system of higher education never really seemed to be in any jeopardy. Located in Wisconsin's largest population center, it, like Madison but unlike all other campuses, had little to fear about the possibility of any serious cutback in its wide range of academic offerings at the undergraduate and graduate levels. Moreover it is not unlikely that the chances of the campus for achieving a measure of the national eminence that many connected with it obviously desire may indeed have been significantly enhanced as a result of merger. Conceivably, a far greater impediment than merger to the chances of the Milwaukee campus to move in such a direction might have been the likelihood that the old U of W administration during the 1970s would have concentrated much of its energy and extra funds on the task of building up Parkside and Green Bay. With that prospect considerably less likely now, the outlook of the Milwaukee campus for future development is probably brighter than it might otherwise have been. No doubt it was as a consequence of such a combination of circumstances that the Milwaukee faculty position on merger was in fact noticeably more ambivalent and muted than that of the other campuses of the old U of W system.

Whereas the main concern of the old U of W campuses in the post-merger period has been to preserve the more exalted status of their past position in state higher education, the concern of the old WSU campuses has been the opposite—to enhance their standing relative to the old U of W campuses. On issues like campus governance, academic prestige, and faculty working conditions, many of those connected with the former WSU institutions have long felt themselves to be more or less like second-class citizens within the state's higher education system. Merger and the acquisition of both a new name as well as a new set of institutional relations has been viewed by many both on and off the campuses as a means to make them more like the old U of W campuses with regard to such matters.

Needless to say, merger has had only the most minimal impact as of yet upon any of these campuses. Moreover, any speculation upon the likelihood of the fears or hopes of the various U of W campuses actually becoming a reality would be no more than that—simply speculation. What is clear, however, is that involved in all of this have been some serious and fundamental questions about both the form and function of higher education in Wisconsin. Equally as clearly, these matters need to be considered and debated by educators, policy makers, and the citizenry of the state. In fact, those involved have often seemed to be preoccupied with matters of form while the essence of the situation becomes increasingly obscure.

Conclusion

The events of merger may or may not be of very much importance to the shaping of the future of public higher education in Wisconsin. For that matter, in and of themselves they may have only the most limited consequence for the bringing of greater fiscal economy to higher education in Wisconsin. The fact of the matter is that if the governor really desires it, there will no doubt be a savings in state money spent for public higher education within the merged system—just as there would have been if there had not been merger. The point here is simply that savings in state expenditures for any agency are not the product of some kind of magical formula or a particular sort of administrative reorganization.

Economy in government begins with a governor who takes a tough line (to whatever agency might be involved) and simply says, "You cannot have this or that program or more than a certain amount of dollars." This is a reality which post-merger politics suggests that the governor either knew all along or else learned about very quickly. The problem with such an approach, however, and consequently the reason that this governor (as well as any other) would just as soon not act in such a manner, is that there will always be certain political costs involved. Agencies, be they universities or otherwise, have, as we have seen, their own political resources. And when they can, they most certainly will act to protect their own institutional interests. Consequently, most governors are often reluctant to fight the battle needed in order to impose much in the way of economies. If in a particular case a governor decides that it is a good policy or politics or both to hold the line tightly on higher education budgets, merger or any other administrative shuffling will in all probability make little or no difference regarding his or her ability to do so.

In the long run, the events of merger in Wisconsin are probably most important not so much for what has actually taken place but rather for what they have symbolized. During much of the Fifties and Sixties not only did many individuals in state universities across the nation forget that it was state governments that ultimately had final authority over their fate, but indeed it became sort of fashionable almost to ignore that fact. In a very real sense, merger in Wisconsin has been the vehicle by which state policy makers—in both the executive branch and the legislature, and Democrats and Republicans alike—have sought to remind all concerned that they are still the boss. This no doubt is both a good and an overdue occurrence. If there is a problem implicit in all of this it is that it is not unlikely that this sudden flexing of muscle at the state capital may have occurred for some of the wrong reasons and may be of too little duration. Indeed, some signs are already evident that, having done their thing in 1971, most state policy makers, and in particular those in the legislature, would just as soon avoid participating in the difficult and time-consuming process of formulating the goals and priorities for the future of public higher education in Wisconsin. Even the governor at times seems to be suggesting that if only the U of W administration would do things in such a way as to make merger appear to be an obvious success (however that is defined), he would happily get out of the higher education game. Unfortunately no one seems to recognize that just as war is too important to be left to generals alone, so education is too important to be left to educators alone.

6. The State Story: Administrative Centralization
Malcolm Moos/Francis E. Rourke

Finding the proper position for public institutions of higher education within the overall scheme of state government is an old problem. Certainly, the difficulty has not, as some modern observers have often believed, been born entirely of recent attempts to reshape the architecture of state government. The legitimacy of certain controls the state established over the campus first became an issue well back in the nineteenth century. Early litigation before Michigan courts involved such pointedly contemporary issues as how far a legislature may legally attach conditions to funds appropriated for support of a state university. The same cases also discussed the propriety of attempts by a state fiscal officer to control college expenditures from appropriations duly authorized by the legislature.

But the concern of college administrators with drawing a line between proper and improper controls by the state has become particularly acute in recent decades. Everywhere in state government there has been a gradual movement toward administrative centralization, and this move, coupled with the growth of state appropriations, has brought a burgeoning variety of controls over state colleges and universities. In some states it has opened up entirely novel avenues of supervision with the establishment of building authorities and central purchasing offices. In other instances it has meant the revival of previously dormant power in a comptroller's office to exercise a close preaudit check upon the legality and economy of all state expenditures. Inspired as it is by the entirely praiseworthy goals of economy and efficiency, the new centralization has nevertheless seemed to many educators to pose a grave threat to the traditional freedom of state colleges and universities and to open up avenues of political pressure on the campus.

Administrative Reorganization: The Wellspring of Control

Malcolm Moos was a member of the Department of Political Science at Johns Jopkins University at the time this article was written. He subsequently served as assistant to President Eisenhower and as president of the University of Minnesota. Francis E. Rourke was also a member of the Johns Hopkins political science faculty and continues with that university today.

College officials have been increasingly worried over the steady infiltration of state administrative power into the internal affairs of public institutions of higher education for almost forty years. At the same time, these have also been years in which there has been a growing effort in most of the states to redesign the administrative architecture of state government. Nor have these simultaneous developments been unrelated. For the trend toward administrative reorganization is widely believed to lie at the root of most of the controls attacked by college officials.

Historically, the movement to revamp state government had its origins in 1909, when the People's Power League of Oregon came up with proposals for centering executive power in the governor. It gathered much of its modern momentum in 1917, when Governor Frank Lowden won approval for a comprehensive plan of administrative reorganization in Illinois. Since that time the Illinois experiment has served as something of a precedent as state after state has moved to streamline its executive machinery. As one author states it:

> *The Progressive era was the period in which the doctrines of centralization began to be accepted as axiomatic, the period in which the formulae for reconciling "true democracy" and "true efficiency" became completely crystallized. Generally the case was accepted as proved in the following years, and the tenets of centralization were used as guiding principles in local, state, and national reorganization schemes.*[1]

The zeal to reorganize has been particularly strong during the past decade, when "little Hoover commissions" have been sprouting all over the landscape of state politics. No fewer than thirty-three states set up such agencies during the legislative biennium of 1950-51.

The recommendations of reorganization groups are virtually uniform in all the states and parallel very closely the proposals usually set forth in the leading studies of national administration. Recent state reports have in fact been largely inspired by and modeled after the Hoover Commission studies of the organization of the Executive Branch of the government. Underlying all these surveys is the belief that administrative reorganization cheapens costs while improving the services offered by state government. The slogan of "economy and efficiency" with which it is associated has done more than anything else to promote the cause of reorganization with the general public.

Integrating State Administration

The most familiar aspect of the reorganization movement is the effort it has made to shift agencies around until they are located in a few recognizable departments and agencies within the executive branch of government. Traditionally every state activity has tended to move within its own private orbit. And this isolation has meant that policies followed in one area often duplicate or conflict with those pursued in closely related areas of administration. The consolidation of related activities in fields such as transportation, highways, and health, has been widely regarded as promising some savings as well as heightening the efficiency of executive operations.

Yet studies calling for administrative consolidation ordinarily meet with stiff opposition in the rough and tumble of state politics. For any such proposal, however innocent on the surface, threatens some disturbance of vested interests within the state. Legislators and legislative committees have working arrangments with administrative agencies which a shift in the location may easily upset. The same fear of change grips interest groups that regard a more tightly knit administrative system as less accessible to their own influence. And as the third dimension of organized resistance to administrative integration, executive agencies themselves are less than enthusiastic about consolidation proposals that threaten to reduce their status or restrict their traditional freedom of operating.

In the face of stubborn opposition that proposals for administrative integration ordinarily generate, it is not surprising that a great many plans for consolidation in state governement never get off the ground. As one study reveals: "With very few exceptions, the numerous postwar movements for state reorganization appear to have resulted in only moderate or negligible legislative acceptance of the reorganization proposals."[2] In some instances, of course, the establishment of groups to suggest changes in executive organization represented merely an effort by a skillful governor to dramatize his own zeal for economy and efficiency. Once their reports are turned in, the political utility of a reorganization commission and the impulse to reform may both be exhausted.

The effort to weld state administration into a coherent unity through the reshuffling of agencies and functions has not in itself resulted in any substantial transfer of power from colleges and universities to other state agencies. No state has proposed that governing boards be abolished and the colleges be absorbed by an ordinary state agency. In some states the lack of political vitality in consolidation plans serves to immunize institutions of higher education from the effects of these proposals, while in other areas the legal independence of the schools bars any drastic change in their status. What has actually happened is that in every state the system of higher education has been under growing pressure to "set its own house in order." Every year special state educational commissions are established to look into the way in which schools of higher learning are equipped to meet the challenge of present and future enrollment trends. And high on the agenda of these groups is the objective of developing some rational scheme for avoiding needless duplication of facilities—the same goal that animates little Hoover Commissions in recommending administrative consolidation in state government.

Centralized Fiscal Control

Nevertheless, the reorganization movement has had a very substantial impact on day-to-day operations in higher education. By and large, this has come about as a result of the trend toward centralized fiscal control—a far more successful, though much less publicized, aspect of the reorganization movement in state government. Budgeting, auditing, and purchasing agencies have sprung up in state after state even while proposals for administrative consolidation were going down to defeat. What has been lost on one front has to some extent been retrieved on another.

For the creation of these instruments of central fiscal oversight has in fact represented something of a back-door approach to the objectives sought by administrative reorganization. Agencies that cannot be integrated through a formal process of consolidation can nevertheless be subject to a very close kind of coordination and control through supervision over the way in which they spend money. A most important development on this front has been the establishment of central budget offices in all parts of the country. For as one observer tells us:

> *The reforms of organization were never completely successful. Political pressures, tradition, and inertia kept many states from achieving the symmetry of organization postulated by theory. The goal of unified coordination through organization was seldom reached with the satisfactory results predicted by theory.*
>
> *The executive budget system was a different story. Operational differences, tradition, and inertia—all were split as if by a knife under the thrust of the executive budget.*[3]

And nowhere has the cutting edge of this knife been felt more keenly than in the area of higher education.

The Politics of Fiscal Control

Of course some of the same factors that impede proposals for administrative consolidation block or blunt the development of centralized fiscal controls. State legislatures can hardly be enthusiastic over establishment of fiscal agencies that enhance the ability of a governor to direct and control the entire range of activities under his jurisdiction. But legislatures are caught in a squeeze between mounting demands for public services and the unrelenting pressure that exists in all states to keep the costs of government down. Consequently, legislative support for the establishment of budgeting, purchasing, and other offices, has usually been forthcoming. And it has come largely in response to the belief that substantial economies will flow from the activities of these state offices of central management and fiscal control.

Once it has established these new agencies, the legislature ordinarily continues to support the growth of their power. Nearly every legislative biennium brings new laws extending centralized control over state administration. Characteristic illustrations include a recent Florida statute requiring the approval of the Budget Commission before hiring any state employee at a salary in excess of $10,000, and a law passed in Kentucky giving the Department of Finance virtually complete control over the location, design, and construction of all state buildings.

Today, of course, legislatures are also stepping out with their own instruments of control such as interim committees and legislative auditors. These agencies have two principal advantages from the legislative standpoint. First, they can oversee administration on an around-the-clock basis, whereas the legislature itself is ordinarily in session only for a comparatively brief period every other year. Second, and most important, these interim agencies owe their loyalty entirely to the legislature. For while in some states the budget officer can maintain close relations with the legislature and enjoy its confidence, in other parts of the country he is regarded as primarily a servant of the governor rather than the legislature. This lack of confidence in executive fiscal officials has a particular tendency to develop in states in which the legislature and the governor's office are controlled by different political parties. And where this cleavage exists colleges and universities are often caught in the crossfire between rival political camps.

But however the winds of state politics may blow, the swing toward overhead control of state administration is deeply imbedded in current trends in state politics and government. In consequence, institutions like state colleges and universities which stand out against this development inevitably cast themselves in the role of the underdog. A few decades ago the burden of proof would have been placed upon budget and other fiscal officials to justify the utility of these new controls. Today, officials in higher education are faced with the necessity of explaining why they should not be subject to closer administrative supervision.

The Shape of Things to Come

There can be little doubt that the move toward fiscal control will accelerate rather than slacken in years to come. Many states which already have the executive budget and other instruments of control are presently engaged in sharpening these toools. And where the trend toward centralization is still in its infancy, it may well move much farther in this direction. For there is a strong tendency for the states to imitate each other's innovations in the area of management practices—a tendency that receives strong reinforcement from organized associations of state officials. Through publication, annual meetings, and other means of communication, these organizations quickly spread the word from state to state about new devices and techniques of control.

Broadly stated, the emergence of agencies of central control has rarely occurred as the particular result, or discovery, of irregularities or abuses within the field of higher education itself. As a matter of fact, state officials will usually admit that these checks are less necessary in the case of colleges and universities than elsewhere in state government. For the prestige of higher education has generally been sufficient to attract men of great competence and integrity to its service. And this has meant that schools of higher learning have been less plagued by the fiscal irregularities and downright incompetence that have often prevailed in less fortunate areas of state administration.

But this does not mean that the state officials are willing that colleges and universities be entirely removed from the scope of centralized administrative oversight. Their reluctance to see such decentralization occur stems in part from their desire to preserve uniformity in state administrative practice. For at the back of their minds is the fear that any exemption from central control granted to institutions of higher education will constitute a precedent. And this precedent, once established, will lead to demands from other state agencies that they be accorded a smiliar privilege. State officials in Massachusetts, for example, will privately admit that the personnel controls formerly imposed over the university defeated the very purposes of an efficient recruitment system. Nevertheless, they are quite fearful that the recent enactment of the Freedom Bill relieving the university from these controls, will soon lead other state agencies to demand equal, and perhaps even greater, independence for themselves. It is, in short, a common view among state officials that the whole edifice of central administration will collapse if but one block is removed.

Moreover, while state officials will ordinarily grant that college officials are less prone to the fiscal irregularities that sometimes overtake administration in other areas of state government, there is widespread skepticism in various parts of the country as to the competence of the educator to handle business matters. This skepticism is based in good part on the stereotype of the academic man as an impractical sort of fellow who needs all the help he can get in "meeting the payroll." Whether this stereotype of the academic man is justified or not, it is largely irrelevant today when so many college administrators come from a business rather than an academic background. Man for man, the administrative experience of officials at leading universities would compare favorably with that of administrators in any other area.

Some pressure for extension of uniform controls over all state administration comes from lobbying activities of fiscal officers who are not at all averse to having their own power extended. But by far the most important element behind these controls is the mounting cost of state government. The postwar years have driven expenditures for state government from $7 billion in 1946 to more than $21 billion in 1956. During this same period, expenditures for higher education have also climbed at a rapid pace. In 1946, expenditures for state institutions of higher learning stood at $397,000,000, but by 1956 they had expanded to $1,678,000,000. In the face of this trend toward increased state expenditures, little difficulty is ordinarily encountered in winning broad public support for doubling the watch over state expenditures.

The Emerging Critique of Centralization

Within the world of public administration, the prevailing trend in recent decades has been to stress the advantages of concentrating authority at the summit of administrative power. Administrative centralization has been used as a cure for many of the difficulties that flow from a lack of coordination of the varied patterns of government activity in the modern state. And the establishment of agencies of central management and fiscal control has certainly done much to encourage a more rational allocation of the state's limited resources among the unlimited demands now made on the public treasury.

When this much has been said, however, it is equally true that "one good custom" can corrupt the world, and that carried too far, the pursuit of economy and efficiency through fiscal centralization quickly degenerates into little more than a fetish. Good government is more than a matter of tidy house-keeping. Budget and other fiscal officials can hardly be expected to know more about welfare, education, or highway administration than the officials in charge of those activities. And a system under which all significant administrative decisions must be channeled through an overhead fiscal office for approval, is perfectly designed to stifle initiative and responsibility and dampen enthusiasm among the operating agencies of government.

For precisely these reasons, more and more students of the administrative process are beginning to suggest that in the name of efficiency itself a halt must at some point be called to the trend toward administrative centralization. While it is only recently that this view has gained appreciable strength, its roots reach back into the very beginning of the reorganization movement. As early as 1922 Francis W. Coker denounced what he called "dogmas of administrative reform" by pointing out that "there is a vast amount of useful coordination that can be accomplished in our state administration without making too much of a fetish of the principle of one-man responsibility and control."[4]

Coker's criticism was prompted by an Ohio reorganization act which in his view revealed an unwarranted preference for concentration of executive power. For him, there were obvious advantages to a system of decentralized administration which proposals for reorganization, current at that time, failed to recognize. He noted that a decentralized administration secured "continuity of policy," helped establish "customs and traditions of non-interference by periodically changing political officers," elicited the participation of "disinterested citizens serving on unpaid boards," placed legal authority and responsibility in the officials "most likely to develop a sense of professional responsibility and pride" in their work, and did not extend the power of any official "beyond the limits" of his administrative competence.[5] Coker's last suggestion, that excessive centralization overloads administrative circuits at the top level, has surged to the fore in recent years.

Over the years, new dissents to prevailing theories of administrative centralization have sprung from several quarters. During the Ttwenties and the Thirties, W. H. Edwards published a number of articles critical of the tenets by which the reorganization movement was then nourished. Later (1939) Charles Hyneman struck out at the assumptions underlying current reorganization plans in an article bearing the suggestive title, "Administrativee Reorganization: An Adventure into Science and Theology." And in a recent discussion of trends in state reorganization, John A. Perkins suggests that "'taken function by function, the services of state government are more often than not carried on quite satisfactorily, in spite of their not being grouped or related properly to each other and to the chief executive. . . . Intimate acquaintance with state administrative activities can dull the enthusiasm for reorganization of even a doctrinaire political scientist."[6]

Curiously enough, the most challenging criticisms of administrative reorganization have recently come from central administrators themselves. Professional personnel administrators have been particularly vehement in their insistence on the need to decentralize responsibility for recruitment and other personnel functions to the line agencies of government. The central personnel agency is beginning to lose much of the luster it once gained in delivering the public service from the evils of "spoils." For there is now impressive evidence that agencies such as TVA were much more successful in attracting superior personnel when they were freed from the cumbersome restrictions of central personnel controls. Here, as elsewhere, centralization has reached a point of diminishing returns, and the direction of change has begun to reverse itself.

Summary

Up until recent times, state government was characterized by a high degree of dispersion of authority in its operations. Activities like welfare, education, highways, and public health were administered in virtual isolation from each other. Over the years the conviction developed that this system of fragmented administration made for expensive government. It did so because it allowed some state agencies to spend more extravagantly than others and did nothing to prevent duplication of facilities and even dishonesty in operations. And it was also felt that the development of instruments of central observation and control would provide a means by which demands for financial support from each state agency could be objectively appraised and balanced against the fiscal needs of other governmental activities.

On this set of beliefs the "efficiency and economy" movement strode into state politics. Its primary objective has been to establish agencies of management and fiscal control that will help plan and then police the operations of every state agency and prevent extravagance and irregularities in the management of the state's business. Throughout each succeeding decade of this century the strength of this movement has continued to grow. And there can be no doubt that the strong public support it has received has been fed in good part by the mounting costs of higher education along with all other state activities.

It is important to recognize that budget officers, auditors, purchasing agents, and other state officials do have a strong rationale and justification for their contemporary role in state government. It would be folly for anyone, least of all educational administrators, to overlook the inefficiencies and abuses in traditional areas of state administration that have brought these instruments of central inspection and control. Behind each lies a long history of scandal or mismanagement in such matters as the handling of contracts or the disposition of the state's resources. There is, then, good reason for keeping a close watch over the way in which the state's funds are handled. Sentiment for doing so is especially strong among taxpayer and business groups, which tend to line up behind every administrative device and development that offers the hope of saving money.

Elsewhere the efficiency and economy movement has won many friends in both the executive and legislative branches of government. Governors in particular have long found the scattering of authority in state administration a handicap in their efforts to carry out their own personal or party platforms. They have come to look upon the establishment of instruments of central direction and control as steps by which their leadership in state government can be rendered more effective. Consequently, chief executives have proposed and supported a study of state administration by a variety of so-called "little Hoover Commissions." Inevitably, each of these groups returns recommendations designed to integrate all state activities under a web of centralized control that will shore up and extend gubernatorial power.

On the horizon of state administration today, there is a dawning recognition that while sprawling decentralization has been the problem of the past, excessive centralization will be the problem of the future. Surely there is widespread appreciation of the gains that have been won through the establishment of instruments of central oversight. And there is considerable agreement that innovations like the executive budget are here to stay. But the burgeoning tendency of over-zealous central offices to run rather than serve all state activties, prompts a growing concern lest the "architects of orderliness" sap the vitality and creative initiative of the very agencies that render the services which state government exists to perform.

Notes

[1] Dwight Waldo, *The Administrative State* (New York: The Ronald Press, 1948), p. 156.

[2] Karl A. Bosworth, "The Politics of Management Improvement in the States," *American Political Science Review*, XLVII (1955), p. 84.

[3] Leo F. Redfern, "State Budgets and State Universities in New England" (unpublished Ph.D. dissertation, Harvard University, September 1957), pp. 101-102.

[4] F. W. Coker, "Dogmas of Administrative Reform," *American Political Science Review*, XVI (1922), p. 411.

[5] Ibid., pp. 410-11.

[6] John A. Perkins, "Reflections on State Reorganizations," *American Political Science Review*, XLV (1951), pp,. 509-10.

Legislative Control of Higher Education

Legislators consider themselves part of the most democractic and representative branch of state government. Like the governor, they are directly elected by the voters, but their individual constituencies are smaller, and members of the lower house of many legislatures serve a shorter term than the governor's. When citizens want to influence state policy, they most likely begin by attempting to influence their legislators.

In the article on university lobbying, John Hicks states that legislators "represent extremely well the wishes and feelings of their constituencies." A university president once made the same point a bit differently when he said, "I always assume that when universities are in trouble with the legislature, they are in trouble with the people." Legislators have a keen interest in their state system of higher education because the people they represent—alumni, students, parents, taxpayers—have such an interest.

As with the governor, legislators' interests in university policy may at times clash with university officials' desire to maintain maximum independence. Legislatures may get involved in decisions on location of a new campus (or deciding which existing one to close), identification of institutions to have graduate programs, tenure policy, admissions policy for out-of-state students, or faculty work load. If such activities go too far, university representatives will resist vigorously while at the same time remembering that the legislature is ultimately the body that will act on its budget and other items of vital interest to higher education.

The Eulau and Quinley article provides an overview of the attitudes of legislators toward the academic community. It is encouraging that while legislators have concerns about their universities, most also have a sense of confidence and pride in them.

The articles by Hicks and Angel address practical issues facing those who speak for universities before legislative bodies, governors, or other state agencies. Hicks served as major university spokesman for several years, and Angel has the unique background of having served as both legislator and college president. Jones presents an analysis of state politics in the 1980s and suggests ways in which universities should respond in this new political environment.

7. Legislators and Academicians
Heinz Eulau/Harold Quinley

The faculty are an integral part of higher education. They provide the majority of teaching instruction, serve as formal and informal counselors to students, and share in the governing of educational institutions. Colleges and universities are judged primarily upon the quality of their faculties. Yet, although money may attract highly qualified individuals, a large budget cannot in itself guarantee that a school will become a leader in the educational field. How a state goes about recruiting and retaining faculty is thus of utmost importance to the fulfillment of its educational goals.

State legislatures, of course, play a crucial role in this process. Through the allocation of state funds, they are able to determine—directly or indirectly—the level of faculty salaries in their states and the amount of money available for such additional attractions as research and graduate studies. Through their ability to pass legislation regulating faculty and student conduct, they are in a position to influence the academic atmosphere and attractiveness of state colleges and universities. A hostile legislature which requires loyalty oaths, investigates campus affairs, and brings political pressures to bear upon trustees and administrators can be as much of a handicap in attracting faculty as low salary schedules.

There are, it would appear, a number of reasons to expect conflict between legislators and faculty members. In the first place, legislators must allocate funds for a variety of state agencies and employees. Since higher education accounts for a large proportion of the states' nondedicated funds, state officials are likely to be more concerned with questions of economy and efficiency than are academicians. Secondly, state legislators are directly accountable to the electorate, a burden which college professors do not share. The electorate is frequently more critical of higher education than state officials—who are themselves predominantly college educated—and often exerts strong pressures upon them to regulate university affairs. Campus unrest is one area in which the public is apparently more critical than are state officials, and more supportive of punitive legislation. Faculty members themselves, finally, are primarily

Heinz Eulau is a professor of political science at Stanford University. Harold Quinley was a postdoctoral fellow at the University of California-Berkeley at the time this study was completed.

responsive to and regulated by professional norms and rewards. Few laymen can be expected to appreciate the need for academic research and publication; fewer still the extent to which academic success is judged on these grounds. To the outsider, the primary task of the professor is likely to be seen as providing classroom instruction, not as establishing a professional reputation.

Thus a great potential for conflict exists between state legislators and the faculty of state colleges and universities. The former are responsive to what they consider their states' needs—education being only one—and are highly susceptible to public pressures. Faculty are responsive primarily to their profession and to their colleagues. When state legislators exercise their authority over faculty members, they are likely to do so on the basis of a different set of perceptions and a different set of priorities. State leaders' perceptions of four such areas of potential conflict—attracting and retaining faculty, faculty salaries, faculty work loads, and faculty participation in public affairs—are the subject of this chapter. As will be seen, the opinions of state legislators and executives are indeed different from those commonly expressed by academic personnel.

Attracting and Retaining Faculty

Most state leaders indicated a high degree of pride and satisfaction in their own faculties. The majority of legislators reported that their states were doing an excellent job of attracting and retaining faculty and would do so in the future. Typical of their replies were:

Yes, I think we do {retain a good faculty}, and we underpay them a little bit. And considering that fact, I think we do a remarkably good job of retaining them. We have a lot of dedicated faculty.

Frankly, I am amazed how well we have done when you consider our faculty salaries, how near on the fringe we have been. I am amazed how well we have done.

If we consider the doctor's degree any gauge at all in comparing the institutions in Texas with those in Louisiana, Oklahoma, Arkansas, right on across the East Coast, I don't recall more than two or three universities and colleges who have higher standards of instructors than we have right here in Texas.

The most notable expressions of dissatisfaction were found among the California respondents—a number of whom felt that the state's ability to attract good professors had declined. Several doubted whether California was doing as well as it should or as well as it had in the past. As one official pointed out: "Other states are recruiting in California now. . . . Very few people were previously recruiting in California because no one left the state." The principal reasons cited for California's declining position were: (1) that faculty salaries were no longer sufficiently competitive with other states, (2) that campus disruptions and attacks by the state administration upon campus autonomy had made California less attractive to first-rate professors, and (3) that the emphasis on publication as a prerequisite for advancement had been carried too far in the state.

Although legislators sometimes disagreed among themselves on how well their respective states were faring in academic competition, most felt that high salaries were the most important single factor in their relative success or lack of it. A number of officials said their states were more successful in recruiting faculty than they had been in the past because of salary increases. Such a position, for example, was taken by a number of Louisiana respondents. Others felt that their states were losing out because of their low salary levels. "There is a shortage of top-grade instructors," an Iowa legislator asserted. "You've got to raise salaries and appropriations to keep people." A Kansas official similarly thought that his state was having difficulty retaining faculty because of its low salaries:

> *It's very difficult to retain individuals in the state because of salary. The competition is very great for academic personnel. . . . If we're going to get some of these better people—and I don't think publishing is necessarily a criterion for better people—I think we're going to have to pay more money.*

Most other factors were considered as secondary to salaries. Many officials felt that there was little the state could do to reduce faculty mobility; faculty members achieved professional recognition, they pointed out, by moving from school to school. Additional factors mentioned included research opportunities, tenure policies, an overemphasis upon research, and the academic environment of a state. Of these probably the last was the most important. A Texan explained what he thought was his state's relative lack of success in retaining faculty:

> *We are not maintaining the academic environment in the state that we ought to be. We are not encouraging freedom of expression on the part of our faculty members. We are imposing too many restrictions and regulations on what an individual faculty member can do or say. . . . I think that he*

ought to be judged as a teacher and as a scholar rather than on his political opinions.

And I think that we judge very strongly. We judge our faculty at our Texas universities a great deal on what they seem to think and the political nature of what they are teaching.

The Issue of Faculty Salaries

As noted, most respondents regarded high, competitive salaries as the most crucial factor in attracting and retaining faculty. When asked if faculty salaries in their states were adequate, however, they were far from unanimous in their opinions. They were about evenly divided between those who thought salaries were adequate, or even too high, and those who thought they were not adequate or might be too low.

Several legislators were ambivalent, failing to commit themselves one way or the other.

The respondents generally seemed to evaluate the "adequacy" of faculty salaries in their respective states in light of two criteria: first, were salaries competitive with those of other states and with industry and other professions? Were they high enough to attract and to retain the caliber of facculty the state needed? Second, were the faculty getting the amount of pay they deserved? Were they adequately paid for the amount of time and effort they put into teaching?

The variation in responses depended largely upon whether the legislators felt their states' salaries were sufficiently competitive and whether they felt the state was getting its money's worth. As will be seen below, many respondents wanted faculty members to spend a greater proportion of their time in the classroom.

Respondents in New York, Pennsylvania, Texas, and California were most likely to report that faculty salaries were too low. "Some professors are making pretty good money these days," a Pennsylvania legislator asserts, "but the pay isn't uniform and perhaps it should be increased." A New York official replied simply, "We've got to make up our minds that we have to pay these people enough to attract qualified people." Texans, eager to achieve a first-rate system of higher education, also tended to view salaries as too low. Two Texas legislators specified higher faculty salaries as the "number one" need in their state. As noted in the previous section, Californians were most likely to be dissatisfied with faculty salaries. Many felt that salary levels were primarily responsible for the state's recent inability to retain or attract top faculty, particularly in competition with New York. Several officials also complained about the salary differences between the state colleges and universities; salaries at the former, they thought were too low. "After visiting the campuses," one legislator answered, "I have no question in my mind that recruiting is difficult because our salaries now are not competitive, apparently, with many other comparable or even lesser institutions."

About an equal number of respondents thought faculty salaries were adequate or too high. Most of these respondents pointed out that the faculty received many fringe benefits in addition to their salaries and frequently obtained outside income from research grants, publications, and consultation. "They are all doing consulting for one or another foundation or business or something else," one official responded, "and as a consequence I don't attach that much significance to salaries per se." An Iowa Senator said:

Well, compared to other salaries in the Iowa economy and in the national economy, I think the faculties in our state institutions are doing quite well. The public isn't aware . . . and other government authorities in Iowa aren't aware of some of the benefits . . . you people on the faculty enjoy. . . . By and large, I think, for the hours spent, you're pretty well paid when you consider the benefits. Many of you do outside research work in one thing or another.

"It's a pretty nice life in many ways," he concluded. "Nice atmosphere, a lot of cultural advantages, and so on." A New York legislator also thought that additional compensation was readily available to the resourceful faculty member:

Well, as I see it, and again this I don't know in depth, but as I see it, any resourceful academician today can make a very good livelihood in academic life. I think we are paying a fairly good base. . . . There is such tremendous opportunity now beyond income from the universities themselves in the very thing that you are doing, the study commission, the innumerable study commissions.

A California legislator called the university "derelict" in its presentation of salary figures to the legislature.

I think the University has been derelict in the matter of free disclosure of information to the Ways and Means Committee and the Assembly. They have always given us the impression that faculty salaries are too low. But they never take into account—at least they don't tell us—about the outside in-

come of faculty members. Most of you guys are going off in all directions making money.

Faculty members, he charged, were "using the best tax-supported higher education facilities in the country" for their private use. "You're not teaching the kids well enough," he told his academic interviewer. "You're not around for talking to them, but you can use your offices and your libraries and your labs to make all kinds of money."

Whether or not they thought faculty salaries adequate, most respondents felt they would continue to increase. Such increases, most believed, would be necessary if their states were to remain competitive and if faculty salaries were to keep up with the cost of living. At least two legislators, however, were critical of the procedure by which faculty members bargained for higher salaries. The most outspoken of the two, a California Senator, called the process the "greatest and most fascinating conspiracy in combination in the restraint of trade that has ever come upon the face of the earth":

> Salaries in California may be too low in competition with salaries in New York, which got high because of New York, which boosted salaries in California.... If that little game of playing both ends against the middle hadn't gotten so far ahead, faculty salaries might now be twice what would {normally} be needed to pick the top men.

An Illinois assemblyman described the process similarly but was less disturbed by it:

> The method that's used in the education field ... is ... if they get a pay increase in Illinois, they wire their brothers in Lansing and say, "Look, we got a pay increase." Then they say, "Hey, Illinois is way above our standards" ... and everybody plays leapfrog.

"Of course," he continued, "teachers have been in great demand, and if you believe in free enterprise as I do, it seems to me that you have to believe that we should meet the going market price for them."

The Issue of Faculty Work Load

"Well, of course, everybody feels that they don't work hard enough." A New York Assemblyman spoke for many respondents when he made this statement. When asked how they felt about faculty work loads, the majority of state officials replied that they were too low; most felt that college professors led "a pretty soft life." The rare legislators who replied that faculty members were overburdened were often themselves present or former members of the academic community.

Typically, legislators asserted that faculty had a great deal of assistance in their teaching duties and apparently had a large amount of time to pursue their "own affairs." Many officials equated teaching hours with work hours, and few regarded research as a part of the college professor's required duties. Representative answers to this question were:

To my knowledge—and from the information I have—I don't think that very many of them are overworked.

From what I know about it, I think that their work load is about right because they have assistants to do most of their work—assistants, clerks, or whatever you want to call them.

I think we're doing a fair job here. I don't think that any of them are complaining too severely about work load or extra work assigned to them. At least it has not come to my attention.

I don't hear a lot of complaints from my sources in the faculty locker room. At least they still have time to get over and play ball and squash. . . . Even the ones who want to publish seem to have time to do this.

It was clear that most state officials considered the proper role of the faculty members to be that of "teacher" or "counselor." The majority did not feel that research was a legitimate or desirable part of the role. Few had any idea that publication was often a requirement of tenure. The most frequently voiced criticism of faculty members was that they were spending too much time in "personal" or "outside" activities—by which the respondents meant research endeavors—and too little time in the classroom. A California official said that such an image of faculty members was the predominant one among legislators. A second Californian indicated that the typical legislative evaluation of the faculty work load was that it was "lax." If it weren't, he reasoned, professors could not be "out leading demonstrations." He went on to voice another frequently heard complaint: "In general, legislators don't like the high number of teaching assistants that are used, instead of students facing bona fide faculty persons."

Such remarks about the use of graduate students as teaching assistants were frequent. A Kansas legislator pointed out that from his own experience in college, the "actual teaching frequently is not done by the professor. . . . The job is given to some graduate student, while [the professor] does research or goes out on some advisory project." A second official said:

> I think the work load is too low. I really do, and I think we've gone overboard in what teaching loads we've let them pressure us into believing that they ought to have.... My inclination is that as soon as those people finish a class, they're off that campus as fast as they can go and back home writing a book or doing some research or something else. Or carrying on some other moonlighting job.

A number of respondents felt that some way should be found to reward those engaged in teaching more than they presently are. "They should be paid enough money," as one official asserted, "to keep them in the classrooms." A California Assemblyman asserted that he spoke for the entire legislature in his state in arguing that "good teachers"—those who spend time in the classroom rather than doing research—should be better rewarded. A Kansas legislator made a similar distinction between "working teachers" and "professors." The former, he thought, were not adequately paid.

Not surprisingly, legislators with academic backgrounds tended to be less critical. Many of the state leaders who indicated that faculty work loads were high had themselves been faculty members. Among these was a Kansas legislator who served on the faculty of a junior college. He claimed that the faculty worked harder than most legislators realized and that teaching involved much more than the number of hours spent in front of a class:

> My brother teaches mathematics ... and ... he seems to think ... that a 9- or a 12-hour load is a pretty good load when you have a lot of preparations in higher mathematics... ..I know at ... the graduate level, we are expected to do more research. You are committed to reading more term papers and giving guidance to students on research projects.... Really when you're just talking about a 12-hour work load, you're just talking about part of your job that you have in teaching.

A California legislator, a former college teacher with many contacts at the University of California, said:

> I think the state colleges will find it more and more difficult to compete with institutions of higher education in other states which are comparable because in California the state college teaching load is pretty high. But the members of the Legislature here, I'm convinced, are not of that opinion at

all, and I think they believe that state college faculty should spend more time in the classrooms. . . . They are not disposed to a program of research, even limited research.

The most sympathetic response came from a New York legislator who advocated that faculty be "given a lot more credit than they are given." He felt they should have sufficient time to do independent research and said, "If the individual faculty member is so loaded down that he has not time for research, something is wrong."

Faculty Participation in Public Affairs

"What is your opinion about faculty participation in public affairs?" the respondents were asked. "Should they participate or stay out?"

They invariably replied that faculty members should become involved in public affairs. The faculty, they asserted, are citizens and like every citizen, have the right and duty to participate. A number of respondents went even further and declared that faculty members—by virtue of their superior education and intelligence—have a particular duty to contribute to society through public involvement.

At issue in these responses, as might be expected, was the officials' definition of "public affairs." Far from advocating that professors be political activists, most legislators defined the proper public role of faculty members in narrow, conventional terms. Participation in such activities as civic clubs, Boy Scout and Girl Scout troops, the Red Cross, service clubs, and the chamber of commerce were strongly urged. Participation in antiwar activities, radical organizations, and often even partisan campaigns was discouraged. State leaders, in other words, would largely limit the role of faculty members to social-service organizations. Very few were willing to tolerate, much less encourage, faculty participation in unconventional activities. Many indicated that it was proper for college professors to engage in partisan politics, but those who approved of such practices frequently cautioned the faculty to be careful not to associate their university with their private activities.

A typical response was that of a Texas senator. "I think that they ought to be allowed to participate just like any other citizen," he declared. "Just because they are faculty, you shouldn't put a muzzle on them. They are citizens." A New York legislator took a similar position: "I am definitely opposed to the idea of their staying out. I don't think they should be any different than anyone else.

Whether they are professors or workingmen, they should participate." Others emphasized the "responsibility" of faculty members to engage in such activities by virtue of their positions as educators. "They're deeply involved in public affairs by being in there," a California Assemblyman asserted, "and by not taking an active part then I think they're evading their responsibility." A Kentucky senator admitted that "some faculty members . . . say things I wish they wouldn't." But, he continued, "they'd better participate in the public affairs because, after all, they are part of the brainpower in the state."

An Illinois legislator asserted:

> They should participate in many more areas than they do. I think that the faculty have a unique contribution that they could make, and many of them are not doing it. . . . If they would take a much more active part in the Rotary and Kiwanis and Lions and other areas—chamber of commerce, junior chamber of commerce, and so forth—the people downtown would see they they really were human.

A Texas legislator thought that college professors should become actively involved in civic affairs so as to upgrade the community. An Iowa Asemblyman differentiated between involvement in peace rallies and Boy Scout and Girl Scout troops, condemning the former and endorsing the latter.

> I'm of the strong opinion that they must become involved because, by nature, they are knowledgeable people. . . . Because of this, they have a leadership role and should exercise that in public affairs. Unfortunately, the . . . ones that we hear about are those who make the headlines because of peace rallies and so forth. This is not the type of involvement that I refer to . . . We have professors who serve as advisers to Boy Scout troops and Girl Scout troops and so forth.

Not all state officials would limit the faculty's role in public affairs to participation in civic clubs or organizations. A large number, probably the majority of the respondents, would allow them to participate in partisan politics as well. A few legislators criticized college professors for their naive and arrogant attitudes toward politics and the political process and advocated that they should become engaged in partisan politics to "find out what it was really like." A New York Assemblyman argued that educators did not know enough about politics and suggested that they obtain an education by running for public office. "I think it would be an eye opener for some of them," he asserted. "I think they have no conception, really, of . . . public office."

A New York senator was especially critical. There was, he felt, a great deal of snobbery among academicians about the political process. He went on to argue that one must know how to solve problems practically as well as intellectually or theoretically. A California senator said:

> *You know, the thing that really amuses me, the very guy who sits down there before 30, 40, 50, a hundred kids and talks about political science has a tremendous contempt for the system. And I think this is bad. Because his very existence, his very freedom, depends on legislation or lack of it. And here he has a tremendous contempt; he ridicules politics and politicians all through his lectures. He is so far removed from the reality of life politically that to me it is just fantastic.*

A Kansas legislator approved of partisan activities but said college professors should not "run for public office on the state's time." A Texas official said:

> *I favor participation if they want to. I don't think they should be forced to. I think that if they are able to divorce themselves from their educational institutions and participate in public affairs on an individual basis, there should be no basic restrictions.*

A New York assemblyman took a similar position:

> *As individuals, I think they certainly have the right to. I think they have an obligation, as far as they can, to divorce themselves from projecting the image that this is the faculty position or that it is the university position. I guess I have a negative reaction to the State University faculty committee on this or that when it is getting out of the educational field.*

Many respondents, as might be expected, condemned faculty involvement in radical or militant activities. The more conservative legislators frequently included college professors in their denunciation of student activism, while others argued that faculty members were hurting their own institutions by engaging in certain forms of behavior. A California official probably spoke for many when he asserted:

> *When they get involved with the militants, when they get in with the agitators, they tear down their image. I think that now all professors are suspect by the people, even the good ones. People are losing their confidence in the University.*

While none of the respondents suggested that legislation should be passed restricting the activities of professors, it was clear that the majority were critical of militant faculty behavior. The reaction of public officials to faculty activism was thus similar to their reaction toward student activism: they strongly disapproved of the conduct but did not want to involve the legislature in the situation.

Conclusion

It is apparent that state officials' perceptions of faculty members are highly colored by their own positions and that their views are frequently in conflict with the prevailing opinion of academia. Most state leaders exhibited a good deal of pride in their own faculties and anticipated that their states would attract competent faculty personnel in the future. The only major exception was in California where a number of respondents believed that their state was losing its competitive edge. At the same time the state officials were split on the question of salaries. About half thought they were adequate or too high, about half that they were too low. Regardless of their position on this question, however, almost all respondents said that faculty salaries were the major means to attract top personnel and that they would go up in the future.

The contrasting perceptions of public officials and college professors were most apparent on the issues of faculty work load and involvement in public affairs. Few legislators or executives considered research to be a necessary part of the academic role. Most thought that faculty should spend most or all of their time in the classroom, and many equated work load with classroom teaching hours. Almost all state leaders, as a result, felt that the faculty work load was too low; they considered research and publication to be a part of the professor's "outside" or "personal" activities. Many of those who argued that the faculty were well compensated pointed to the additional funds which they often received for these outside activities.

Faculty participation in public affairs was favored by most officials. It was apparent from their responses, however, that their definition of public affairs was a limited one. Many urged the faculty to become more active in civic and community organizations. Those who approved of their participation in partisan politics often asserted that they should divorce themselves from the university in radical or militant activities. No direct question was asked on this last issue, but many officials volunteered their views on the matter anyway.

8. Lobbying for Limited Resources
John W. Hicks

No single approach to lobbying can be guaranteed successful for all time for all people. As is the case in many other human activities, however, there are certain general principles which, if applied, will increase the probability of success. I will limit my comments to lobbying at the state level, since that is where we in the public institutions get the bulk of our basic support, and where we can probably have the most impact either as individual institutions or as systems of institutions. In fact, current trends with respect to revenue sharing would indicate that lobbying at the state level will be even more important in the future.

The most important basic principles are:

1. Lobbying is an unglamorous, pedestrian job that consists of day-to-day, year-by-year nurturing of attitudes held by human beings with respect to higher education and the institutions which provide it.

2. In any state, a few key leaders make the basic decision as to how much will be appropriated for higher education. The lobbyist should concentrate on developing their long-range understanding. He or she should not waste too much time on an obscure freshman representative who is a member of the Committees on Veterans Affairs and Ditches and Drains. The really vital people are the governor, his or her fiscal staff, and a dozen key legislators. While concentrating on them, the lobbyist must be nice to everyone.

3. In the long run, the way an institution serves is its greatest selling point. For this there is no substitute.

4. Integrity and accountability are essential in lobbying. This is not a moral judgment, but a pragmatic one. A lobbyist caught in a lie loses effectiveness. A public institution must be even 1000 percent accountable. There are no inappropriate questions that can be asked by a legislator about a public institution. There are stupid questions, but even these must be answered intelligently and politely.

5. Most legislators and public officials do not have time to read long, involved treatises on higher education, nor are they easily

---

John W. Hicks served many years as assistant to the president of Purdue University. In that position he had primary responsibility for state relations for the university.

influenced by slick-gimmick publications or fancy slide shows. They do, however, need a few key facts and catchwords to orient their thinking.

6. Faculty members are usually ineffective lobbyists and faculty committees even less useful in lobbying than for most other purposes.

7. Students, properly applied, can be very useful. They should be themselves, and concentrate on their own senators and representatives on a one-to-one basis when they are home on vacation or weekends. They should confine their efforts to explaining why it is important to them to have a first class education at a reasonable cost. If 10 percent of our students were to do just this, the rest of us would no longer be needed. But, of course, they never will.

8. The purpose of a college or university is to disseminate and accumulate knowledge. No public institution should ever become involved, as an institution, in any public-policy issue not directly related to higher education. Students and faculty members, of course, are also citizens, and may pursue any cause they wish, but not in the name of the institution. The institution itself should remain neutral in this respect, virtuous or popular as the cause may be. Always remember that in Hitler's Germany persecution of Jews became a "virtuous and popular" cause.

9. The university president is a key figure in lobbying. He or she should develop a personal style and stick to it, avoid overexposure, and present an aura of integrity and sincerity—in fact, appear a bit larger than life. Presidents should never engage in half-truths or name calling. Legislators would like them to wear a halo. They should try with all their might to do so.

If all of these nine points are followed, can successful lobbying be guaranteed? Of course not. So much depends on the time and the place. During the honeymoon period of the mid-1950s to the mid-1960s, almost any lobbying tactics worked, at least in the short run. If a state is broke and enrollments are declining, even the most brilliant tactician will fail. But over the long run, on a kind of market-averaging basis, these considerations are important.

Four factors are our allies in lobbying for funds for higher education. First, nearly all people are concerned about their own children's future and also about youth in general. Second, despite everything, we have tremendous faith in education in America. Third, our economy and our standard of living are still growing. And fourth, it can be demonstrated that there is a positive correlation between educational opportunity and economic development and social mobility.

These four factors also guide us in deciding what is most salable. Honest data indicating increasing enrollments almost always bring more money. This is one of the reasons for the long post-World War II honeymoon for higher education, and also one of the reasons that the honeymoon is over. Data concerning inflation and unavoidable cost increases usually meet with a sympathetic hearing. People who work for a living are also aware of these costs increases and know they must be met. Increased funds to provide for academically disadvantaged students—students who previously did not go to college—are currently in favor if described properly. Programs that will increase the economic productivity of the state can often be sold and will produce additional appropriations. And currently there is interest in health-related and environmental areas.

The most difficult thing of all to sell is quality. There has always been, in public education in the United States, a strong equalitarian tendency. On balance this is probably good, but it causes difficulties for those institutions which want to consider themselves elite and to be supported by the public accordingly.

Perhaps of equal importance to the things that may be useful in selling an institution's appropriations request are the things that are counterproductive. The most important of these is criticism of a sister institution. Many times one is tempted to make invidious comparisons between one's own institution and another, to prove such things as greater efficiency, or more careful management. The aim, of course, is always to get more funds at the expense of the other school. The result, at least in the long run, is to undermine total confidence in higher education, and this probably will result in less money for all institutions.

Tearing down a sister institution usually brings retaliation, and no one is perfect enough to be without faults that can be criticized. But even if there be no retaliation, the fault pointed out in the sister institution will usually also be attributed to your own. Legislators and the public have a bad habit of generalizing about colleges and universities. This habit was especially evident during the days of campus unrest. When the media blessed us with exaggerated coverage of sit-ins on campuses several states away, many people thought all campuses were in turmoil and castigated us accordingly.

Other things probably not helpful in seeking financial support are: (1) tearful revelations about how legislators do not understand the educational process or the sensitiveness of professors; (2) discourses on faculty rights and prerogatives and the place of the faculty in university governance; (3) tirades against the federal government for its cutbacks in research support; (4) relevations of the evils of politics, the business community, organized labor and current society in general, with the university as the last virtuous bulwark against chaos.

The vast majority (more than 90 percent) of legislators and elected public officials are honest, decent citizens trying to do their best for the people they represent. My experience shows that state legislators represent extremely well the wishes and feelings of their constituencies. Most of them believe strongly in education and in the opportunity for young people to get an education.

9. How to Play the State Capitol Game
Dan Angel

Not too long ago, a group of educational administrators became incensed with pending legislation that would sharply reduce state financial support. They decided to march on their state capitol to tell their legislators exactly what they thought of the proposed action. Unfortunately, although more than fifty leaders from throughout the state made the trip, not one of them saw a state legislator. Why? Because the legislature was not in session that Friday!

Recently in Erehwon, U.S.A., a college president received some bad news in his daily mail. A bill was pending final floor action in the state senate that would curtail his institution's decision-making power and center it in the state capitol. President "Leave-me-alone-and-let-me-function" decided that it was time to get in touch with his state legislators. He inquired of people in his office as to just who his legislators were so that he could contact them.

How would you evaluate his potential for success?

The above examples are not atypical. The trend has been for more policy-making decisions to come down from the state capitol, and for administrators and trustees at the institutions to live with the consequences. This is not our only choice. We don't have to be bystanders. Our academic bent might be to remain legislative isolationists, but that is simply not a feasible course of action in the 1980s. I would counsel all chief administrative officers and trustees to view legislative lobbying as a desirable, necessary three-dimensional process. It involves knowledge of the legislative decision process, familiarity with the players and detailed knowledge of the issues.

The Process

In order to work within the legislative framework, administrators and trustees must concern themselves with the following five process essentials: key calendar dates, specific committee structures, the chairman's power, the party in control, and the flow of legislation.

Dan Angel has seen university-state relations from both sides. He served as a member of the House of Representatives for the Michigan legislature and subsequently became president of Citrus College in California.

Rule One: Know when to spend time. Ordinarily the legislature will work by standing rules, or by resolution establishing a timetable for specific action. For instance, all bills must be originated in the House or Senate by May 1. Typically, such regulations will provide for final action in one house or the other and also final action by policy or financial committees. This is baseline information that should be reviewed before planning any lobbying activities.

Friends

Rule Two: Know where to spend time. The size of most legislative bodies prevents working with all legislators intimately. Your task will be considerably improved if you isolate the Educational Policy Committee and the committee or subcommittee that handles appropriation decisions affecting your institution. Considering the fact that most states have a bicameral legislature, this should reduce the number of working contacts to twenty or so. In some instances, you may easily establish who actually has power and who does not, and work with only a subcommittee or even one member of a subcommittee.

Rule Three: Know with whom to spend time. The chairperson is extremely influential. This is evident from the fact that he or she was picked by the speaker or leader of the respective house for that position and, therefore, has some clout. A chairperson decides when, what, and if a particular bill will come before the committee. In some cases the vice chairman, key advisor, or staff should also be studied for their influence. Largely, they can determine whether a bill ever sees the light of day and how it will fare when it does. Good relationships with the chairperson can be an immense step forward in terms of getting policy or finances you desire.

Rule Four: Know with which political party to spend your time. It obviously does you much good to work with the majority party since that is what you will need for a policy or finance decision in the end. If one party controls the legislature by a two-to-one majority, then this is where you should spend your time. On the other hand, if the majority is a slim one, you will have to spend time with both minority and majority parties. Also, remember that party control can change with any given election and it is not a bad idea to pay some attention to the minority leadership—even if they are heavily outnumbered.

Scheduling

Rule Five: Be aware of the ebb and flow of the legislative schedule. A typical legislature has both unvelievably busy and unbelievably slow action sequences. Ordinarily, a legislative year begins like molasses in January and expedites to the explosion of thousands of firecrackers around the Fourth of July. Whereas a legislator may have time to chat and lunch with you earlier in the year, he's unlikely to have that kind of time as June and July descend and critical decisions must be made instantaneously. Get your oar in early when there is calm water in the river!

Also, there is a certain sequence and normal process to the flow of legislative consideration. Ordinarily, a bill is reviewed first by a content committee, next by an appropriations committee or a subcommittee, and only then is it ready for floor action by one house. Then the whole process starts over again in the other chamber. Any deviations between these groups after a bill is passed are usually handled by a conference committee composed of only a handful of individuals from both houses. Early in the process it is most helpful to identify the likely conference committee members, because in reality these six individuals will probably dictate the final outcome.

The Players

Rule One: Remember that legislators are people, too. The message here is that legislators have wants and needs as do people in all walks of life. They expect to be treated in a humane fashion while discussing state policy. Don't neglect social amenities or common courtesy.

Rule Two: There is no excuse for not knowing your own legislators well. It might be helpful to lay out an "Identification Continuum." Begin with making an informal acquaintance, then share some social occasions, and finally arrange for an informal informational session. Only after this continuum has been exhausted should you consider a hard-sell, a justification confrontation regarding a vote that the legislator cast, or an outright rebuff, verbal or written. While considering the latter course, remember, too, that it is more important to win the war than a particular battle over one bill that displeases you!

If you are to understand the players, you will need to begin by knowing the legislator's specific background. What has he/she done? What kind of educational training? What community involvement? What groups supported him during his campaign? Where did she get her campaign financing? What are some of her particular interests? What expertise does the individual have?

Does the individual work from a consistent base philosophy or is she issues-oriented?

Other questions in player dynamics concern positions of formal leadership, individual peeves, idiosyncrasies, and family and home-life considerations. Much of this data is available through the House or Senate clerk's office, the document room, the local newspaper, or handouts provided by the legislator's staff for public relations purposes.

Rule Three is a simple fact: Politicians are individuals with a better-than-average ego. Cater to it. Legislators are always running, either for reelection or for higher office! This can be useful to you because you can get them before groups, provide news stories, invite them to write articles in your inhouse publication or otherwise be of assistance in gaining exposure. You might find, to your surprise, that an individual who has been rather faint in prior commitments you favor suddenly becomes a leader.

The Issues

The first rule concerning issues is one that I learned early as a member of the Michigan House Higher Education Committee. The committee had invited several college presidents to come and testify regarding a particular bill. The interested legislators pursued several questions and to our displeasure some of them could not be answered in even general terms.

Rule One: Be well informed on all educational issues on which you attempt to lobby. Furthermore, expect related issues to come into the conversation and be able to respond to those as well. Know your budget, know their budget, and know how the two connect in specifics. Much of this information can be obtained by getting a copy of the Legislative Analysis of each bill that comes before a committee or up for a floor vote.

Rule Two is to be prepared to speak when the legislator or legislators are ready to listen. Because of the large number of issues which they must attend to, your particular interest may get lost in the shuffle and may not seem paramount in their mind at the same time it is in yours.

Rule Three. Know what you want to accomplish before going in. What do you want from the legislator? Do you simply want him to be better informed? Are you expecting a commitment? Do you want a vote? Are you after a public statement? Do you want him to lobby other legislators? Or do you want him to lead the floor fight?

Rule Four. Be patient. Let the legislator identify his or her problems with the bill under discussion, or with the position that you are advocating. If you allow the legislator to tell you why he or she can't do what you want, you may be able to respond specifically to those concerns and show that there really are no significant problems as a result or that alternatives are more hazardous than your course of action.

Rule Five. Be straightforward. Do not attempt to stretch the truth. (This often has a boomerang effect.) Instead, document your case with whatever hard data and supporting evidence you can.

Rule Six. Remember, your job is to persuade. You will, therefore, have to discuss need, the particular plan, and advantages both to you and the legislator.

Rule Seven. Don't expect to get everything you want at once. Plan a campaign to get your idea across. In addition, one semicommitment should not be relied on too heavily. You will have to recheck your commitments from time to time. Circumstances and positions change with or without the possibility of numerous amendments. Legislation is an extremely time-consuming process.

Rule Eight. Remember that logic does not always win the day, but a majority vote does. Work on your commitments and try to get the magic number of votes plus a few.

The Executive Office

Don't stop with the legislature. The governor initiates the original budget, has major influence in the development of both policy and budget, and finally has veto power.

My advice in dealing with the executive office is threefold:

1. Your goal should be to have first-name identification with the governor and the people surrounding him, including key staff, secondary staff, and secretarial support staff.

2. Remember that access to key staff is always important, but even more important when dealing with the executive office. It is extremely unlikely that you will be able to call or speak with the governor on a frequent basis (if you attempt to do this too much you will find that you lose access to him). It's much more likely that you can develop close ties along the same legislative identification continuum with executive office staff (particularly in the finance and educational areas).

3. Don't forget your group contacts. The executive office, as well as the legislature, is much more impressed with a statewide organizational spokesman than with a single district spokesman and with a large district spokesman rather than a small district

spokesman; in general, the larger the number he or she represents, the more powerful the player.

Summary

The trend nationally is for more and more dollars to be forthcoming from state fiscal coffers. In addition, there is no question that state policy intervention is increasing.

In days of old it may not have been necessary to lobby the legislature and the executive office. Today it is not only good advice to lobby; it is a matter of survival.

My final word: remember that your job is continually building ethos. Don't cash in prematurely, and when you do, be sure you have several well-earned chips in hand!

10. Public Universities and the New State Politics
E. Terrence Jones

State politics have been changing dramatically during the past decade, and many public colleges and universities are losing ground because they are playing the 1980s game by 1960s rules. If higher education is to maintain and increase its financial support from state budgets, it must revamp its political efforts. Changes in state politics require changes in university lobbying practices: there are more effective ways for public higher eduction to make its case. Although the following discussion pertains most directly to institutions that receive substantial support from state revenues, it also applies to private colleges and universities. As more states have adopted programs for assisting private higher education, the distinction between public and private has become more a continuum than a chasm.

The New state Politics

Five changes in state politics are especially relevant for public universities; resources are scarcer, responsibilities are greater, citizens are less supportive of government, referenda are more frequently used to make major policy decisions, and interest group and campaign technology has become more complex.

States have less spending power for several reasons. First, the national economy is less productive, and real growth requires higher productivity. Second, revenue systems in most states do not keep pace with inflation; neither the sales tax nor the property tax are well suited to cope with rapid price increases, and most state income tax rate structures are not highly progressive. As a result, typically only states with major energy resources and accompanying severance taxes have done well during the past decade. Third, almost one-half of the states have passed some type of fiscal limitation measure during the 1970s. The net effect of these actions has been to impose yet another constraint on state revenue growth. Fourth, federal assistance has declined. The most flexible aid—state general revenue-sharing—was eliminated, and other grant programs have been reduced.

E. Terrence Jones is dean of the College of Arts and Sciences at the University of Missouri-St. Louis. Prior to assuming the deanship, he was a professor of political science there.

At the same time that states have less to spend, they have more to do. Since the early 1970s, successive national administrations have tried to unload greater portions of the domestic policy burden on state and local governments. The Reagan Administration is trying to accelerate this trend through its increased use of block grants and, unlike its predecessors, has decidedly favored giving responsibility to state governments rather than local jurisdictions. The larger cities, many of which had become financial wards of Washington, have now been encouraged to bring their needs to the states.

During the 1970s, all the leading national public opinion surveys reflected a growing disillusionment with government. People are more cynical about government practices and less confident about government effectiveness. The last two presidents, Carter and Reagan, won election by capitalizing on these sentiments. Although much of this decline can be traced to national events (most notably, Vietnam and Watergate), state governments suffer from the attitudinal fallout. The general public does not always distinguish among levels and types of governments; hence, if one, especially the most visible, falters, then the public image of all is affected.

An increasing number of state policy decisions are being made at the ballot box rather than in the state capital. Although various referenda and initiative provisions have long been part of the legal apparatus in many states (forty-nine require elections for constitutional amendments and thirty-nine make them available for non-constitutional use), in recent times their prominence has grown. The reasons for this rise are many, but a primary one is the tendency for state legislators to avoid the more-responsibility-but-fewer-resources dilemma by (in the name of encouraging democratic participation) passing the buck to the electorate.

High technology has come late to politics, but it is now practiced widely and well. Interest groups and campaign organizations have largely abandoned nineteenth-century techniques for assessing and influencing citizen opinion and have embraced twentieth-century methods. Today's lobbying tool kit includes sample surveys, focus groups interviews, targeted direct mail lists, multimedia advertising campaigns, and telephone banks.

The Old Style of University Lobbying

Past and present attempts by public colleges and universities to influence state policy making have had a narrow focus, have been conducted largely on a go-it-alone basis, have geographically centered on the state capital, and have involved relatively few university officials.

Each institution's lobbying efforts have focused almost exclusively on higher education regulatory and budgetary policy. On some occasions, a college or university concentrates solely on its own budget and even ignore the more general issues of postsecondary schooling. Higher education typically remains silent on other public policy matters—even when they might have profound long-term effects on its future.

Individual public colleges and universities rarely band together at the state level in attempts to achieve some mutual policy objective. (At the national level, of course, higher education is much more coalitional.) Occasionally, public higher education might engage in some coordinated efforts and, even less frequently, colleges and universities might work with elementary and secondary schools or private colleges. Links with noneducational interests are extremely rare.

The targets of most public college and university lobbying are found in the state capitals. The governor and the legislative leadership receive special treatment, and the other elected representatives are also courted. As state higher eduction agencies have been established and their regulatory role has grown, their professional staff has also been frequently visited.

Only a handful of university officials are actively engaged in delivering higher education's policy message to state government. The lobbying cast typically includes a few governmental relations specialists, the chief executive officer, and, occasionally, a few other university staff members who have special access to key legislators. (Deans of agriculture tend to be overrepresented in this latter group.)

The New Style of University Lobbying

One can question whether public higher education's prevailing procedures for influencing state policy making were ever the most effective arrangement. But given the past decade's dramatic changes on state politics, they certainly are now outmoded. Although they need not be replaced (it will always be highly beneficial, for example, for an institution's head to be on friendly terms with the governor), they should be drastically extended and revised. Public higher education needs to take an interest in additional policy areas, be more willing to participate in coalitions, be more active in influencing attitudes throughout the state, and involve more segments of the campus community in lobbying.

Higher education appropriations do not exist in a policy vacuum. If public colleges and universities are to receive adequate state funding in an area of scarce resources and increasing demands, they must be as concerned about the size of the total revenue pie as they are about the proportion of their individual slice. For any state agency, practicing status quo politics probably means accepting a fixed fraction of a shrinking whole. Public higher education, then, must direct some of its political attention to policies aimed at increasing state revenues. Such efforts might include changing the tax structure or stimulating economic development.

In both areas, universities can enter the policy process at several points, although the earlier the participation the greater likelihood of success. Top university officials, board members, and key alumni can help get an issue on the policy agenda by making speeches calling for a "fresh look" at the state tax system or addressing the need for a coordinated economic development program. Faculty research can help define the problem (whoever formulates the question has a substantial influence on the content of the answer), and faculty members can work with others (such as legislative staff members) in preparing policy alternatives. Once proposals have reached the legislative arena, student groups and alumni organizations can join with the university leaders in urging their adoption.

As public higher education broadens its policy interests, it must also seek new political allies. It is highly unlikely that any single interest group can unilaterally produce major shifts in state policy making. Although coalitions escalate the bargaining that must be done (the members, after all, rarely have identical goals, and each wishes to gain more from the coalition than it gives), they are an essential element in accomplishing significant changes in any decentralized policy. State political structures favor the status quo, and it typically requires a supramajority to overcome policy inertia. Although universities have occasionally been members of ad hoc coalitions formed to sponsor a specific proposal, they have not forged more permanent linkages with compatible interest groups.

Not only should public higher education participate in such coalitions, but in the 1980s it should take the initiative in bringing together groups that oppose the recent shrinkage in state financing and support the need for increased public involvement. Public colleges and universities have much to offer such a coalition: prestige, intellectual resources, organizational continuity, and a large membership. Potential noneducational coalition partners include users of other state services (such as families of mental health patients), suppliers of state goods (such as concrete producers), industries dependent on state facilities (such as trucking), professional associations having large state employee memberships (such as social workers), groups highly dependent on government services (such as senior citizens), and organizations sharing similar social values (such as environmentalists and private higher education). The membership in a coalition must be tailored to each state's political setting. Higher education might have long, cordial relationships with certain groups in some states but not in others. In addition, in the search for allies it must be remembered that the maxim "the enemy of my enemy is my friend" often inhibits otherwise sensible alliances.

In public higher education lobbying, a straight line is not always the shortest distance between two point. Just because a university president or governmental relations specialist has an inside track to the governor or the key legislators does not necessarily mean that success is guaranteed. One increasingly common response to university appeals for more state support is that although state elected officials realize that public higher education has a valid case for greater assistance, their constituencies do not agree. Most governors and legislators sense the increased cynicism about government and translate it into a belief that promoting larger allocations for higher education is not politically wise.

The problem, then, is not so much persuading the state officials that higher education needs more money as it is convincing them that it makes *political sense* to increase support for public colleges and universities. To overcome this obstacle, higher education must either alter state officials' perceptions of public opinion or, if the governors and legislators have a roughly accurate assessment of citizens' attitudes, convince those citizens to change their opinions and then tell the elected officials that they now endorse the notion of more tax dollars for public higher education.

This latter approach calls for universities and colleges to apply the new political technology systematically and persistently. The state's electorate must be divided into relevant segments (such as opinion leaders, frequent voters); each segment should be surveyed about its attitudes, beliefs, and opinions regarding public higher education; an appropriate educational campaign using multiple channels of communication should be devised for each electorate segment; and periodic surveys should be conducted to assess the effectiveness of the educational campaigns and to make appropriate adjustments. Such an ongoing process identifies public higher education's supporters and opponents, tells higher education how to increase its friends and decrease its enemies, and provides the basis both for conducting lobbying efforts and for planning referenda campaigns.

Public universities and colleges need to involve more of their community in their lobbying efforts. To do this, university officials must first make the case for more support among alumni, faculty and staff members, and students. Unless the overwhelming majority of the campus community understands and endorses higher education's policy requests, they will not be effective advocates. And, of course, each of these groups is more likely to work for policies when they or their representatives played some part in their formulation. Efforts to mobilize a wider share of the university community in lobbying will encounter some obstacles. For example, because presidents and chancellors have often acted as if making higher education's case were their exclusive responsibility, some faculty and staff members might initially regard an invitation to join the political persuasion process as an administrative attempt to enlist others to do the dirty work. Still others might consider it beneath their professional dignity to spend precious time telling the world beyond the campus to do what it should already knows to be right and proper.

To the extent that campus groups deliver higher education's messages, they constitute a significant force. In the typical midwestern state, for example, public higher education students are 3 to 5 percent of the electorate, faculty and staff members are another .5 to 1 percent, and alumni of the state's public four-year institutions are an additional 6 to 8 percent. If parents of recent, present, and prospective public higher education students are included in the total, more than one-fourth of the eligible voters have a close link to a state's public colleges and universities. Moreover, because persons with more education are more likely to vote, these percentages undoubtedly understate higher education's share of the electorate.

Costs and Risks

The new university lobbying might be better, but it will not be cheaper. It requires more planning and involvement by top administrators, more coordination by governmental relations staff, more and better internal and external communications, and more information gathering.

The new approach requires that higher education speak to an entire state. To be successful, the communication must be carefully planned and consistently executed. If public universities and colleges have not gotten their act together before they go on the road, the result will be chaos. In addition, any audience is apt to give more attention to an institution's message if it is delivered by the person in charge. Consequently, both as managers and as spokespersons, chancellors and presidents must spend more of their scarce time planning and implementing their institution's programs.

Because the new university lobbying involves a much larger cast both inside and outside the institution, more work will be needed to coordinate everyone's actions. Universities are highly decentralized organizations, and it requires considerable effort to know who is doing what, when, and where. Other potential coalition partners must be identified, courted, and, once included, consulted. Accordingly, an institution's governmental relations operation must add staff members whose principal function is campaign coordination rather than legislative contact. If and when more state institutions begin to develop and implement this new lobbying style, care must be taken to learn from the experiences of others. States have traditionally served as public policy laboratories, and each initiative should be treated as an important experiment. Therefore, some staff time should be devoted to monitoring efforts in other states, and there should be more active exchanges of information among state relations specialists.

Targeted communications to diverse audiences are central to the new university lobbying. Most campuses are already experienced in preparing materials for students, faculty members, and alumni. What these messages typically need to be more effective lobbying tools is tighter coordination rather than higher quality. All too often, in part because different offices are responsible, these internal communications are not coordinated to produce a unified effort—namely, a change in attitudes or actions. Although they may and usually should employ different techniques and examples, internal publications should deliver essentially the same message. In addition, the increased emphasis on off-campus communications makes it necessary for the university to improve its capacity to design and produce direct mail and mass media materials. In many cases, the talent and skills are already present among the campus faculty or staff. In other instances, they must be acquired off campus.

Having accurate and timely information about the opinions of the key groups in the state's political process is essential for designing, implementing, and adapting higher education's efforts to garner more support. Such data are needed both to plan future campaigns and to assess past efforts. Hence, alumni, faculty and staff members, students, and key citizens should be polled at least annually. Although sample surveys can be expensive, using on-campus survey experts can significantly lower the cost.

Finally, any university or college employing the new university lobbying system runs the risk of losing its above-the-fray image. Education, in general, and public higher education, in particular, often claim to be nonpolitical. From an analytical perspective, such an assertion is nonsense: how much is spent on education and what is taught are both sources of societal conflict and, thus, must be resolved, at least temporarily, through the political process. But from a tactical standpoint, this apparent neutrality has its uses. Within the American setting, those who are unalloyed political participants are supposedly sullied by the experience. Appearing to be impartial while pursuing one's interests can often provide a distinct advantage.

Thus the *new* style of university lobbying should not be labeled as such. It is, more precisely, an organized effort both to understand better what the state thinks about higher education and to explain more effectively academe's contribution to the polity. Thus, emphasizing the distinction between lobbying and educating is not wise strategy. Those in higher education believe fervently in its crucial role in human development, and it is their obligation to employ the most effective techniques to explain its importance to everyone in a democratic society. As Clodus R. Smith, Cleveland State University's vice president for university relations, has written,

> *It is a democratic imperative that social institutions be bonded to the people. The acceptance and support of a state system of higher education ultimately rest with the people it serves. . . . Communication and participation with citizens are civic responsibilities that cannot be left to chance.*

Universities, Budgets, and Dollars

No discussion of higher education politics would be complete without some attention to the financing of colleges and universities. Today over 75 percent of college students are enrolled in public colleges and universities, funded primarily with state tax dollars. After a period of relatively rapid budget growth in the 1960s, universities found themselves facing stable or shrinking budgets in much of the 1970s. That fact, coupled with the inflation of the 1970s, presented them with a period of severe budget stringency.

The rapid growth of federal aid to higher education during that decade provided some relief from these problems. While most of the federal dollars flowed to students in the form of grants and loans rather than to the institutions, many of the dollars ultimately reached universities and colleges in the form of tuition and fee payments, dormitory rents, and so on.

The question of who should pay for higher education is not just a budgetary issue. It strikes at the heart of debates on public policy in this country and raises the basic question of the role of higher education in society. It has been widely believed that a major portion of the support for public colleges and universities should come from tax sources in order to keep tuition as low as possible. Advocates of this view contend that the low tuition policy is the best way to ensure wide access to higher education, thereby allowing universities to be vehicles of upward economic and social mobility for those in middle- and low-income families.

Supporters of this view also point out that society as a whole benefits from a strong system of higher education. If the students themselves were the only beneficiaries, so this reasoning goes, then perhaps they should pay the entire cost of a college education. But this is not the case. Everyone, even those who never attended college, benefits from living in a society of educated teachers, attorneys, social workers, architects, and citizens and can, therefore, justifiably be called on to help support higher education.

The question of how much of the cost should be paid by the individual student and how much by the larger society stimulates continuing debate. Officials of private colleges and universities worry that the different tuition levels between public and private institutions may cause many students to make a college choice for other than academic reasons.

The first two chapters in this section are written by authors Chambers and Ostar, who are strong advocates of having most of the cost of higher education at public institutions provided by state or federal funds. Chambers presents an optimistic view of the long term prospects for public funding of higher education. Ostar effectively states the case for keeping tuition levels as low as possible.

Cyert offers a much more sober view of the financial condition of higher education, discussing the problems of university administrators in responding to stable or declining enrollment or budget situations.

One of the continuing concerns of students of higher education is how, and to what extent, tax funds should be used to support private (some prefer the term "independent") institutions. Two views on this question are presented in the articles by Muller and Priest. The article by Rhodes identifies a series of policy questions that must be resolved if both sectors of higher education are to remain healthy and serve their students effectively.

11. Long-Term Expectations for Financing Higher Education
M. M. Chambers

Higher education, in recognizable form, has a history of more than two thousand years in the Western World, to say nothing of the ancient East. It is a permanent human institution.

A long-term trend may be measured in centuries or millennia rather than in years or decades. In the United States, no state university existed until the late 1780s and early 1790s, and the handful that came into being were little-understood, precarious enterprises for half a century after that. At the turn of the twentieth century, there were only 275,000 students in all universities and colleges of all types in this country; three-quarters of a century later the number had approached twelve million. Always, up to 1950, the numbers enrolled in private colleges exceeded or at least equaled those in public institutions of higher education. Since then, both sectors have grown—the public about twice as fast as the private—so that the ratio of public to private now approaches 80:20.

In 1950, an estimate of the number of all university-level students in the whole world was about five million; in 1975, it was forty million (UNESCO estimate). The rate of growth of higher education surpasses that of the fabled and feared explosion of population.

At what century or year and with which of the scores of pertinent themes does a discussion begin of long-term trends in financing higher education? It seems futile to aim for a point in history that would antedate any sense of crisis, for the adage that "no college ever has enough money" is true. Even the 1960s in the United States, now sometimes erroneously characterized as a halcyon period of astronomic growth and booming prosperity for higher education, was in fact a time of growing pains generated largely by insufficient resources to serve optimally the increasing influx of students—which is just another way of saying financial austerity.

The colleges and universities has overcome a somewhat similar difficulty during the "veterans' bulge" a decade and a half earlier; and, by the way, the Calamity Janes of the day had predicted

---

M. M. Chambers has been a professor of higher education at Illinois State University. He is well known for his periodical studies of state financial support for higher education, published each year by the National Association of State Universities and Land-Grant Colleges.

that as soon as the enrollment of veterans tapered off, total enrollments would decline catastrophically—a phenomenon that did not occur.

Historical Context

The fragmentary statistics mentioned above do not convey much meaning except when conjoined with knowledge of the conditions of living and working as they prevailed for different classes of people at the time. At any time, the intimate connection between the status of higher education and the socioeconomic aspects of life is apparent.

It is a great error to base enrollment projections solely on birth rates of twenty years earlier. The invalidation of such predictions by recent and current gains in increasing access for women, blacks and persons of all minority races and nationalities, persons of all ages above eighteen, part-time students (who were once little tolerated, if at all), disadvantaged persons, handicapped financially or physically, has become so self-evident that it will not be examined here. It is, and ought to be, common knowledge that such advances, once made, are never wholly lost, though they may occasionally incur small temporary setbacks.

Universal Higher Education

About 7.2 percent of California's 23.5 million people are engaged as students in higher education. The average for all fifty states is near 5 percent. In some states, including a few of the most populous, the percentage is well below 4. It is not easy to believe, in the light of the expansive changes in higher education now in progress, that the contiguous and similarly populous, urbanized, and industrial states of New York and Pennsylvania will continue forever to have, respectively, 5.4 and 3.9 percent of their people engaged as students. This means that the nation is willing to see one state benefit to a much lesser extent from higher education than another in similar circumstances—a doctrine now passing into limbo with the idea that the nation should do nothing to better the condition of a member of a race or sex or unjustly disadvantaged class deprived of fair opportunity. The people of this nation will advance together, not by any race, class, or section over another. That is the basic reason underlying the vast complex of federal governmental activities, which is temporarily unpopular but will not disappear.

Federal support for higher education seems about to decline somewhat from its peak of $18 billion a few years ago, and as compared with a nationwide total of $21 billion appropriated by the fifty state legislatures for fiscal year 1981.[1]

More impressive reasons for eventual great expansion of higher education are in the numerous well-reasoned books and papers published by Howard R. Bowen of the Claremont Graduate School in California and some of his associates, particularly *Investment in Learning: Individual and Social Value of American Higher Education,* which convincingly sets forth at length the case for the indispensable advantages to the whole national society that will come from more and better education for more people.[2]

A 1980 publication prepared by Carol Fances, former chief economist of the American Council on Education, *College Enrollment Trends: Testing the Conventional Wisdom Against the Facts,* introduces a cool and reasonable note of sanity into that very fallible field.[3] The final report of the Carnegie Council on Policy Studies in Higher Education, *Three Thousand Futures: The Next Twenty Years for Higher Education,* provides lengthy consideration of large numbers of possible forthcoming changes, but treats them as speculative, and does not dispel the aura of dispirited pessimism that has been an incubus for a full decade.[4]

The Future of National Support

Nearly a decade of accelerating rates of inflation of prices and wages, complicated by an alleged energy shortage, accompanied by recurrently threatened economic recessions of varying severity, and topped off by an overlong and overheated two-year national political campaign ending with the election of an avowedly right-wing national administration taking office in January 1981, continued a situation of unusual economic uncertainty. The new administration received a generally amiable "honeymoon" during the early months of 1981; but since it did not have full partisan control of the Congress, considerable doubt persisted as to whether it would be able to obtain enactment of a program of legislation that would put in place some ultraconservative measures, principal among which were large reductions of federal spending (except substantial increases for the Department of Defense), and drastic decreases in federal income tax rates (originally requested at 10 percent per year for three successive years).

Admittedly several years will be required to determine whether, if fully enacted, the right-wing economic plan will bring about the desired effects, and how strong a hold the ultraconservative political philosophy may have on the public in general. This gives reason to suppose that for the ensuring few years there may be some decline, or at least a leveling-off tendency, in financial support of higher education from the federal government.

Even if this eventuates, it is very doubtful that higher education should be thought of as facing any permanent shrinking of its scope or of its support from the national government. Eventual increase is likely because the long-continued and persisting concentration of industry and power in few hands makes it impracticable for smaller units of government (including the states) to devise and operate revenue systems production enough to provide full support for their own public services, including education. That day is already long past. The exercise of the taxing power is gradually pushed upward to the larger units of government. In the long future, then, as the public services expand as they are sure to do, it is practically certain that large proportions of their support will come from the national government. That the process will be better administered than at present, with less voluminous regulation, may be hoped and expected; but come it must, for reasons already visible. Take the long view (no one knows precisely how long) and feel sure that one day the higher education enterprise will be much larger in scope than it is now, and that more of its support will come from national revenues, both absolutely and relatively.

The Philosophical Basis of Higher Education Policy

To see the issues clearly, one must ponder some basic concepts. Is higher education solely for the purpose of aggrandizing the individual student and his or her family, and if so, should it be privately bought and paid for in full as a private investment, as a house or an appliance or a vehicle or other "durable goods" is purchased?

Or is higher education chiefly or wholly for the benefit of the whole society, and if so, should the facilities be provided by governmental units as a productive investment of public funds, with all students regarded as performing a public service, for which they are entitled to receive free tuition?

Learned economists have sometimes argued as to what exact fraction of the total benefits of higher education accrues to the student, and what to the public. This is largely futile, because there is so much overlapping as to make the question virtually insoluble. Often economists ignore the public benefits, saying they are "doubtful" or "hard to calculate." This is avoiding the nucleus of the problem.

These views are of long-term significance. They lurk, often unnoticed or unmentioned, at the heart of the myriad of more specific and more ephemeral questions and issues that beset citizens and legislators.

Avoiding Disorganization and Fragmentation

The current multiplicity of federal programs financially aiding higher education directly and indirectly is a latter-day outgrowth, in part of compromise of differing older notions of how government should perform its functions. The firmly rooted idea that in general (except perhaps in emergencies calling for hasty and huge-scale production of weaponry and munitions in time of war or impending war) public services are better performed directly rather than vicariously by making grants or contracts with private grantees or contractors, was negated by court decisions holding that scholarship money is primarily an aid to the student rather than a subsidy to the college, opening the way for the large and varied complex of student grants and loans. In similar manner, the interest of the federal government in science and technology has become so great that it wants much more research done than it is able to perform with its own personnel and facilities, and it deals with the universities, public and private, as surrogates whom it adjudges most capable of doing the job. This produces the large system of categorical grants and contracts for research.

Over recent years both of the forgoing complexes of programs have come to be regarded more as outright support of universities and colleges than as mechanisms for the purchase of essential governmental services, both in the popular mind and in many professional minds. All such systems have a strong tendency to grow in size and complexity and a seemingly inescapable proclivity to annoy their clienteles and the public with redundant red tape and rigid bureaucracy. There is a regularly recurrent necessity of simplification of the processes, enlivening of communication with the public, and streamlining of the organizations.

What about Institutional Grants?

One proposal advanced from the University of Minnesota a few years ago would have amounted to a supplement rather than a substitute for the current programs of federal aid, though it might in the long run supplant some of them to the advantage of higher education and the public. In short, it would have Congress make an appropriation annually to every reputable university or college in the United States, public or private nonprofit, of an amount equal to a specified minor percentage of its average total annual operating expenses over the immediately preceding three years. Each institution would have full discretion as to the use of the money for any or all of its educational purposes.[5]

This would probably have the merit of a tendency to restore eroded institutional autonomy, and in accomplishing a small decentralization of power from apoplectic Washington. Five percent of the average annual operating expenses over a period of three years might add up to an appropriation of some $6 billion annually. The idea of straightening the channel from Congress to the colleges has its attractions and should be kept in mind and thought about for the day when the productivity and morale of the nation have been improved and the recognition returns that expansion of higher education should have high priority.

The States Retain the Primary Role for the Present

Each of the fifty states has an ongoing system of higher education including a network of public institutions of character and scope approximately appropriate to the population and resources of the state, plus a complement of private colleges. There is immense variation among the states: Wyoming, smallest in populations, has one state university, seven community colleges, and no private college at all. By contrast, the five East North Central States—Wisconsin, Michigan, Illinois, Indiana, and Ohio collectively have 41 million people and seven of the world's best-known state universities, some sixty other state colleges of direct types, sixteen private universities, many private colleges, and 200 public two-year colleges.

Collectively, the fifty state legislatures have long been the principal single source of tax support for all higher education. Whoever said they "can look to a proud past and a glorious future" in this field did not exaggerate.

State and Local Tax Revolt is a Paper Tiger

Apart from the recent and current debates and developments regarding federal taxation, the "tax revolt" that was alleged to have followed the adoption of California's Proposition 13 in 1978 has thus far not materialized. In the elections of 1980, another initiative in California, intended to reduce state income taxes drastically, was heavily defeated at the polls. A somewhat analogous measure in Michigan was also voted down by a large majority. Measures of the same ilk were defeated in half a dozen other states. There is very little evidence that state taxpayers are about to abandon their support of state and local governments and public services, including higher education.

Based on analysis of state appropriations for annual operating expenses of higher education in each of the fifty states for twenty-three consecutive years, the persistence with which state tax support has been maintained, not only through the 1960s, but also through the 1970s and early '80s, is impressive. It is true that rising inflation has tended to spoil the picture increasingly during the most recent seven or eight years; but, taking the fifty states as a whole, the weighted averages gains over successive two-year periods have continued at or above 20 percent, reaching 28 percent for fiscal 1976. These rates of gain have consistently been above the rates of inflation by any reasonable calculation.

In a small minority of states, chiefly in the Northeast, there have been recent small and temporary declines; but instances wherein any entire state system received less state tax support than in a previous year are extremely rare. In absolute figures, the national aggregate of state appropriations for annual operating expenses of higher education rose from $6.1 billion for fiscal 1970 to $19 billion for 1980 and $21 billion for 1981.

The figure of 1971 ($7 billion) was tripled by 1981.[6]

State Revenue Systems will be Improved

Some relative advances in the productivity and justice of state and local taxing schemes have been made in recent years, but they continue to be largely regressive and slow to change. Some forty-six states now apparently have some form of state income tax, but half a dozen of them cling to the flat rate or nongraduated form, some at an astonishingly low rate; and of the four states having no income tax of any kind, two are among the ten most populous in the nation—Texas and Florida—both big beneficiaries of the population movement into the Sun Belt.

There is much room for improvement in the structuring of graduated income tax rates to fit both the changing economic conditions of the people and the relatively low-rate niche in the total scene open to occupation by the states without politically unacceptable overlapping of the turf of the federal income taxes, individual and corporate. Since the state governments have recently shown a tendency toward somewhat better than usual efforts to perform their fiscal responsibilities to support public services, there is reason to expect that many of the glaring holes in their state revenue systems may be plugged, especially after emergence begins from the depressing condition of extreme economic and political uncertainty that has prevailed for several years.

Before 1967, when Illinois first adopted a fairly productive state income tax which now brings in over a billion dollars a year, and thereby saved the state from financial catastrophe, this step had been blocked for more than a generation mainly by conservative lawyers who squelched every advocacy by solemnly wagging a finger and groaning, "An income tax would probably be unconstitutional in Illinois."

Many well-meaning people believe that above all a state tax system should be stable; and there is some merit in stability, but it should not be adhered to in defiance of demographic and technological change until it brings the entire social organism to a halt. The most recent half century of our history has taught that lesson; and it cannot be ignored.

Let those who feel keenly the heat of controversy over budgets for the immediately ensuing year preoccupy themselves with that political battle if that is their own individual choice, or their duty as they see it. But it ill befits a great profession or an intelligent public to be forever intensely obsessed with "the current crisis" with never a look forward or backward over more than a few months or years. This is a kind of temporal provincialism that matches the space-provincialism demonstrated by the person who thinks only of one institution or one university system or one state or one region, with only cursory attention or none at all to comparable conditions in the larger cosmos around it. We need to have more people thinking about the finance of higher education, and in longer perspectives and broader purviews. This is coming, but slowly.

Private Sources of Support

Tuition fees and all other charges paid by students are no part of tax support. Nor are bonds issued by the institution to finance income-producing facilities. The other principal private sources of income are gifts from individuals and private foundations, and endownment earnings derived from accumulated funds. The overall proportion of current annual costs of operation of all higher education, as between the public and private sources, is about forty public and sixty private, if a reasonable accounting of the students' sacrifice of time and earning-power is included, as it should be, as a segment of the cost defrayed by private individuals.

At this time, while economic uncertainty persists, look at a few long, slow trends in contrast to comparatively trivial, immediate, year-to-year changes: with the massive shift of students from the private to the public sector which has already occurred over thirty years, steps have been taken a decade or more ago by many states to keep the private colleges operating at or near capacity—direct appropriations of state tax funds to private institutions as in New York, Pennsylvania, and few other states; state scholarship systems that usually favor private colleges, in a majority of the states; likewise the several large federal student aid programs.

Private nonprofit universities and colleges will continue to receive many other favors from both state and federal governments for at least another generation, and probably indefinitely. Few private charitable institutions will disappear; and their present share of total enrollment (about 20 percent) may not decline much further. Many powerful factors: religious leanings, ties of family and friendship, tradition and others, as well as prestige and supposed superiority and autonomy, will continue to attract their clienteles. The same factors and others will move private donors to maintain and to increase the level of their gifts. Private gifts as a minor factor in the support of public institutions are increasing and will continue to grow.

The Broad Outlook

For all higher education, no pinnacle has been reached. The road ahead is unlikely to lead downward, though there may be occasional temporary setbacks. The prospect over the ensuing generation is that, no matter how soon or by what measures the frightening uncertainties of the national and international scene come to be solved or mitigated, a growing and improving higher education enterprise will continue to be an indispensable component of an advancing civilization. It is and will be indeed, a prime mover in such an advance.

Notes

[1] The figure for the aggregate appropriations by the fity states is from *Appropriations of State Tax Funds for Operating Expenses of Higher Education, 1980-1981* (Washington: National Association of State Universities and Land-Grant Colleges, 1981), p. 24.

[2] Howard R. Bowen et al., *Investment in Learning: the Individual and Social Value of American Higher Education* (San Francisco: Jossey-Bass, 1978), p. 507.

[3] Carol Frances, for the Association Council for Policy Studies and Research, *College Enrollment Trends: Testing the Conventional Wisdom Against the Facts* (Washington: American Council on Education, 1980), p. 73.

[4] Carnegie Council on Policy Studies in Higher Education, *Three Thousand Futures: The Next Twenty Years for Higher Education* (San Francisco: Jossey-Bass, 1980), p. 439.

[5] William H. Young and Robert Taylor, *An Opportunity for a Major American Advance through Higher Eucation* (Madison: University of Wisconsin, 1967), p. 32.

[6] Data collected by M. M. Chambers and circulated from Illinois State University, Normal, IL 61761, in small monthly reports under the title *Grapevine*. Annual fifty-state summaries appear each autumn in the *Chronicle of Higher Education*.

[7] Data from *The Book of the States, 1980-81* (Lexington, KY: Council of State Governments, 1980), p. 679.

12. State Tuition Policies and Public Higher Education
Allan W. Ostar

Who should assume the major share of the costs of public higher education? Individual students and their families? Or society as a whole?

No single issue is more vexing to relationships between state governments and public colleges and universities. Periodically, it pits state legislators against governors, governing boards of segments of public postsecondary education against statewide regulatory boards or against one another, public colleges against private ones, economists against economists, philosphers against philosophers, states against federal government, taxpayers against taxpayers, and sometimes even generation against generation.

Though an issue fraught with social, cultural, and economic implications that penetrate the very heart of the true purposes of higher education in a democratic society, it is essentially *political* in nature. And it is an ongoing issue that relentlessly caroms from one state or region to another and back again—each time in a changed context. But the fundamental question never seems fully resolved to everyone's satisfaction; consequently, it appears destined to keep resurfacing on the national public-policy agenda.

Today, in the mid-1980s, after a lapse of over a half decade, the issue has returned. This time the "changed context" is the most dramatic and significant higher education has experienced since World War II: the federal government's share in financing the costs of attending college has begun to decline, thus abrogating policies that have guided every postwar administration from Truman through Carter. The decline in federal support will compel the states, for at least the balance of the decade, to assume even greater responsibility for the financing of higher education.

The approximately 1,500 public colleges and universities in the United States provide a diversity and freedom of choice unmatched in the world: distinguished research institutions, colleges and universities emphasizing high-quality education at the undergraduate and graduate levels, and community colleges offering a

---

Allan W. Ostar has been president of American Association of State Colleges and Universities since 1965. He is a nationally recognized spokesman for public higher education and was voted in a *Change* magazine poll as one of the forty-four most influential leaders in American higher education.

wide range of academic and occupational programs. They all share a common commitment to provide expanding educational opportunities for individuals of all ages and backgrounds and to serve the postsecondary learning needs of their states and communities. This commitment has meant hope and advancement for families in every corner of the land for over 150 years.

Americans built their public higher education institutions on the idea that it is in the national interest to have an educated populace. From the late 1940s to the early 1980s, the federal government sought to eliminate the barriers to full participation in higher education and provide all citizens the opportunity to obtain the education and training necessary to enrich their lives and society.

But the public policies that helped broaden educational opportunity in America had not only an ethical and moral base but a practical one as well. History demonstrates that educated people bring economic benefits to the communities and states in which they live: they get better jobs, earn higher wages, and pay more taxes. Although it is difficult to quantify all the social benefits of higher education, the results are evident: a highly educated, productive labor force; cures for formerly deadly diseases; longer lives; hybrid corn; semiconductors; a greater sharing of aesthetic and cultural values; cleaner, more effective local and state government; the wonders of high technology; and teachers to educate new generations of Americans. The list of social benefits accruing from an educated citizenry is endless. Most important, their participation in civic affairs is the wellspring of this nation's democracy.

Reflecting the fact that expanding educational opportunities yield benefits to society as well as individuals, public policies in most states—in some instances dating back to the late 1830s when the "normal schools" were founded—have sought *to keep tuition at state colleges and universities as low as possible.* Prior to World War II, most public postsecondary institutions, particularly those in the West, South, and Midwest (where there was a smaller concentration of independent colleges), kept tuitions at nominal levels; indeed, in a few states, charging tuition was forbidden by statute or constitutional mandate and, in others, laws required that it be kept minimal. In those days, the financing of a student's college education was primarily a parental responsibility often shared by students through part-time earnings. Although some scholarship and loan programs existed, they were not the prevalent or major forms of student support. "Working your way through college" was the most common type of student aid.

On the institutional side of the ledger, pre-World War II, the financing of state colleges and universities was the responsibility of "society," as represented by state governments; the federal government was scarcely involved at all. Tuitions at public institutions were kept low to encourage attendance of young men and women of all classes. The policy became an accepted political and social principle.

According to the low-tuition principle, while costs vary widely from state to state, tuition levels in the public sector should encourage, rather than deny, access to postsecondary education. It is based on the concept that society recognizes the fundamental values inherent in education and that national survival depends on the nourishment of those values. Accordingly, society should bear a part of the financial burden of a student's college education.

Keeping tuition levels low in public higher education constitutes, in effect, an intergenerational transfer of wealth. The parental generation pays, primarily through state taxes, for the education of young people who attend public postsecondary institutions. Then, members of the younger generation, as college graduates, enter the work force, earn income, quickly become taxpayers, and in their productive years pay, in turn, for the higher education of the next generation. The investment in education is thus constantly renewed: by paying taxes each generation accepts responsibility to increase educational opportunity for successive generations. The low-tuition principle that undergirds public higher education is viewed by most Americans as an extension of the free public elementary and secondary school system, an extension that becomes all the more necessary as America's technological and social complexity increases.

The Low-Tuition Principle's Early Beginnings

Immediately after World War II, the GI Bill brought millions of veterans to America's campuses, extending educational opportunities far beyond previous expectations. President Truman's Commission on Higher Education recommended in 1947 that it be national policy to provide two tuition-free years, and two Carnegie Commission studies—*The Capitol and the Campus* and *Higher Education: Who Benefits? Who Should Pay?*—have since advocated low or no tuition during the first two years of attendance at a public college. The rationale behind these recommendations was to provide equal access to postsecondary educational opportunities in order to secure a national intellectual resource necessary to the economic, social, and political well-being of the nation;s democracy—not as largesse from the American taxpayer. Low tuition, in this broad context, is considered an investment in political stability, human resources, economic growth, and the other beneficial by-products of a higher educational level.

Against the backdrop of the GI Bill and the advent of Sputnik in 1957, some dramatic changes occurred on the U.S. higher education landscape:

- Student grants based on financial need rather than scholarship became a staple in federal policy and common on both public and independent campuses, with financially disadvantaged students from low-income and middle-income families the chief beneficiaries.
- The use of federal loans to assist students in defraying college costs increased sharply.
- With the increasing number of married students, spouses became a major source of financial support for students.
- The federal government contributed to institutional development through a wide array of grants, contracts, and loans designated mainly for research, training, and buildings.
- Philanthropic foundations and industrial corporations became patrons of higher education, and colleges and universities became more aggressive and professional in their fund-raising campaigns.
- State and local governments greatly increased their appropriations to public colleges and universities, some states established scholarship and loan programs, and some made grants to private institutions.
- Legislatures and governing boards began raising tuition at state colleges and universities year after year as enrollments grew dramatically—a trend which, by the end of the 19602, began to alarm the leaders of public institutions, who saw the low-tuition principle eroding as the inflationary spiral started seriously to affect college costs.

A Payment Shift from State to Student

An extrapolation of such changes in the post-Sputnik era and into the 1980s reveals that the question of who should pay for public higher education, and how much, has taken on some new twists. First, college *loans* have become the new order of the day; increasingly, public policies at both the state and federal levels force students and their families to borrow substantial funds for college. The burden of paying public college costs is shifting more and more from the state (i.e., society-at-large) to the individual student and his or her family.

Emerging from this public-policy reversal (from grants-in-aid to loans) is *a debtor class of college graduates* saddled with the burden of college loan repayments and thus handicapped in their ability to purchase cars, insurance, homes, appliances, and so on. And with young married couples, more often than not, there are two college loans to be repaid, some spanning both undergraduate and graduate or professional school.

The loan phenomenon hasn't happened overnight, of course, and has been fueled over the years by many factors, including inflation, the job market, political trends, changes in social policies, and so on. When the National Defense Education Act was passed in 1958, making federally supported loans a part of the student financial aid package, the first executive officer of the National Association of State Universities and Land-Grant Colleges, Russell Thackrey, warned time and again that public higher education would rue the day because "the burden of paying the cost of going to college will inevitably shift from society to the individual—and the banks will love it."

His forecast, unfortunately, was right. Furthermore, legislators (including members of Congress) learned to love it, too: in recent years, "borrowing" has somehow come to sound better than "taxing" or "spending." This change in federal outlook has resulted in the rechanneling of funds once devoted to programs for helping needy students enter and remain in college, into expanding student loan programs. The College Board found that 80 percent of total student aid awarded in 1975-76 was in the form of grants, but in 1984-85 the figure had dropped to about 40-45 percent. In early 1985 the National Governors Conference took note of this serious trend toward imbalance and called for an increase in the percentage of student aid allocated to grants, and a corresponding decrease in support for student loan programs.

To redress the balance, Congress and the Executive Branch ultimately will need to make Pell Grants-in-Aid and Work-Study the primary means of federal student assistance and, as a matter of sound public policy, make loans the secondary means. At present, in the mid-1980s, there is no sign that the imbalance will be corrected quickly; effecting that change in national policy may take years.

But at the state level, at which continued expansion of higher education opportunities in the public-sector colleges can only be sustained by increased legislative appropriations and relatively low tuition levels, the case against increased reliance on loans to finance college education can be made more effectively. The academic community's natural allies in making that case are the leaders of the business community. They are the ones who depend on increased purchasing power for the success of their enterprises. Young college graduates are a primary business market—the principal target for the consumer goods and services the American economy turns out so abundantly.

That market, however, is not going to be such a "target of opportunity" for the business community when young adults enter the world of work saddled with debt—a debt, incidentally, that mounts each year as college costs soar in the public and private sectors. Business leaders have a stake in increased appropriations to state colleges and universities as a means of offsetting the trend toward individual and family borrowing to pay college costs.

When projections are made about what the effect of a "debtor class" of college students on the American economy and society generally, the picture is disconcerting. Undergraduate students in the late 1980s can easily accumulate up to $10,000 in debts over a four-year period, and if to that is added the debt burden from graduate or professional schools, the total can shoot up to $30,000 easily.

In addition, college loans can affect a student's career choice: the larger the debt, the bigger the student's financial bind, which can have a constricting effect on occupational decisions. Low-salaried professional positions such as teaching or journalism, for example, will prove far less appealing than the higher-salaried positions in business or engineering to someone who graduates from college owing $10,000 or more.

And what will be the effect on enrollment in America's graduate schools of public policies that force undergraduates to borrow their way through college? At a time when graduate school enrollments in some fields have already leveled off or started to decline, such policies will only compound the problem; college teaching as an attractive and rewarding profession will surely suffer. The nation risks sacrificing a significant portion of its intellectual capital.

Although student loan programs have clearly tipped the scales of responsibility for shouldering the costs of public higher education from society to the individual, the verdict still seems out on the impact of federally funded student grants-in-aid on that balance.

Specifically, since the advent of national student aid programs, the question is, does the availability of federal financial assistance induce tuition increases in both public and independent postsecondary institutions? Or, to put it another way, can colleges and universities "capture" more federal dollars in student aid by raising tuition levels, given the fact that the formula used by the Basic Educational Opportunity Grant (BEOG) to calculate the amount of aid a student in a state can receive is pegged to institutional tuition levels?

According to James Chrest, who served for several years as chairman of the House Education Committee of the Oregon legislature, the answer to the question is yes. In a critique of federal student aid policies that included a strong defense of the low-tuition principle, he said, "The BEOG program is an excellent example of how and why it is difficult for a state to establish a low tuition rate. There is an optimum tuition level whereby a state can receive more federal dollars for students if the tuition is set at a high rate. The maximum amount a student is eligible for from the federal government is based on the dollar tuition amount which the state determines." Thus, the effectiveness of federal student aid dollars is reduced because the program encourages states to raise tuition.

In the late 1970s and early 1980s, this was not theory but fact. In New York State, the Commissioner of Education and Deputy Commissioner for Higher and Professional Education used the existence of federal as well as state student aid as a rationalization for much higher tuition at the City University of New York. Without student aid, they said, the tuition increase "would not have been feasible." Similarly, at about the same time, Pennsylvania raised tuition at public institutions "in order," one official said, "to capture more BEOG dollars." Reports from other states, including Rhode Island, Vermont, and Wisconsin, indicated that other legislatures and governing boards were contemplating the same tactic.

American Association of State Colleges and Universities (AASCU) expressed strong public concern about this issue in 1979 and subsequently pointed out that federal student aid programs tended to spawn a false set of expectations from state officials about the relative impact of tuition levels and federal aid on student enrollments. A Tennessee study, AASCU pointed out, indicated that if tuition at the state university were raised $100, the average BEOG recipient would receive only about $26 additional student aid; most students would have to pay the full $100 increase. In other words, every dollar manipulated away from institutional and tuition support in the states does not buy a dollar's worth of educational opportunity from the federal government.

By the mid-1980s, partly because of expressed congressional interest in some form of higher education "cost containment" legislation, and partly because of growing reaction in some state legislatures against rising tuition levels at public colleges and universities, fewer states were resorting to the policy of increasing tuition rates to "capture" more federal student aid funds. Reports from the State Higher Education Executive Officers (SHEEO), the National Governors' Association, and the National Conference of State Legislatures reflected public concern that the individual's share in paying for the cost of attending a state college or uniterstiy not violate the historic low-tuition principle.

Shifting the Responsibility Back to the States

Cutbacks in student financial aid at the federal level, including the policy shift from grants-in-aid to loans, mean that, for the balance of the 1980s and on into the 1990s, the states will have to shoulder greatly increased responsibilities in expanding higher education opportunities for America's rapidly growing minority populations. In fact, by mid-1985, the nation faced new and serious problems in providing educational access for its minorities. In 1980, blacks and Hispanics constituted 18.1 percent of the total U.S. population, but by 2020 they are expected to represent 25-30 percent. Blacks and Hispanics are already seriously underrepresented in four-year and advanced-degree programs. Their progress toward achieving representation in postsecondary institutions reflective of their actual numbers stalled, if not suffered a setback, since the mid-1970s.

Commerce Department data show that the numbers of college-age Hispanic youths increased by 42 percent between 1975 and 1981, yet Education Department figures for that period show only a 21-percent increase in bachelor's degrees earned by Hispanic young people and only a 22-percent increase in the numbers receiving master's degrees. The same data show that the numbers of college-age black youths increased by 18 percent from 1975 to 1981, yet there was only a 2-percent increase in the number of black young people receiving bachelor's degrees and a 16-percent decrease in the number awarded master's degrees.

A survey of student aid recipients at public colleges and universities released by AASCU in spring 1985 revealed a sharp drop in minority students receiving student aid—down 12.4 percent in 1983-84 from 1981-82 levels. The total number of student aid recipients at public colleges during that period declined 2.3 percent while overall enrollment remained stable at 9.7 million. There was a 7-percent drop in student aid dollars—from $7.2 billion to $6.7 billion—and a 5.5-percent decline in the number of need-based grants.

Despite all the efforts made in the 1960s and 1970s, there seems to be less equity in the nation's postsecondary educational system in mid-1985 than there was in 1978. Although students from middle- and higher-income families are more likely to go to college in the late 1980s than there were in 1978, students from lower-income families aare less likely to attend. Because such a large proportion of the minority population is poor, college attendance is more difficult for minority students in the mid-1980s than it was a half decade ago. Thus, in general, minority families are less likely to be able to pay for a college education for their children; consequently black and Hispanic students must depend on financial aid, particularly grants, to a greater degree than others.

The net price of postsecondary education—that is, the out-of-pocket family contribution—increased by 11.8 percent between 1978 and 1983, after adjustment for inflation. Dependent individuals from families with incomes under $20,000 (adjusted for inflation) were less likely to be enrolled in 1982 than they were in 1978, while enrollment of dependent individuals with family incomes above $20,000 increased between the two years. While college costs have continued to climb for well over a decade, the type of financial aid the lowest-income students depend on the most—grants—has declined.

If, despite these data, state legislatures and public postsecondary governing boards were to turn their backs on the low-tuition principle in establishing substantially higher tuition levels at state colleges and universities, they would be closing the door to economic and social advancement to a significant and growing proportion of America's population, for of all the costs involved in attending college, tuition has been found to be most critical. In a large-scale study of "The Effects of Public Policies on the Demand for Higher Education," conducted in 1977 by John Bishop of the University of Wisconsin-Madison, the following findings were reported: "Tuition, high admission standards, foregone earnings, and travel and room and board costs are found to have a significant negative effect on attendance. The per dollar [negative] effect of tuition is larger than any other cost and is largest of all for low-income, middle ability students." Conversely, the study went on, "The primary determinants of the costs of college attendance turn out to be (1) the level of in-state tuition, (2) the distance from the student's high school to the nearest public institution, and (3) whether a student lives in a political jurisdiction with access to a low-tuition college."

Students in low-tuition states grow up assuming they can attend some form of higher education institution if they so desire. Students from high-tuition states grow up assuming that higher education as an option is not open to them. The higher proportion of students in low-tuition states going on to higher education in some form and the smaller proportion going on in the high-tuition states indicate the value of low-tuition as the most desirable form of financing public higher education, as well as the most effective in developing high educational aspirations and expectations among high school graduates.

Policy Issues

But as the costs of going to college continue to rise and cutbacks in federal student aid programs begin to take their toll on enrollments, state legislators, governors, and public postsecondary boards are being pressed to examine policy alternatives for establishing student charges at community colleges and state colleges and universities. Not only at issue is the question of what share of the cost of higher education should be borne by students, as opposed to that assumed by state and local government, but also the question of different charges for different students.

Several bases are commonly used by states in determining appropriate levels of student charges:

• a predetermined percentage of the cost of instruction in different types of institutions

• the academic level of students, such as lower division, upper division, or graduate

• treating tuition as another state revenue-generating device—a "user tax," in effect—to be employed in meeting budgetary shortfalls, as with the sales tax or other consumption taxes.

In addition, since the late 1970s, many states—most notably, New York—have studied the possibility of tying tuition levels to family income—that is, establishing a sliding-scale tuition policy based on an individual's ability to pay, with students from high-income families paying the highest rates and those from low-income families charged the least, or receiving grants-in-aid from state scholarship funds.

Currently, the cost-of-instruction method of setting tuition or required fees is used by seventeen states, including Arizona, Colorado, Florida, Kansas, Maine, Massachusetts, New Jersey, Ohio, Oklahoma, Oregon, Rhode Island, Virginia, Washington, and Wisconsin for all undergraduates and, in some instances, for graduate students. New Hampshire uses this method for nonresident students; Michigan and Minnesota use variations of it for setting both resident and nonresident student charges at some, but not all, of their public institutions; and at least six other states are considering adopting it.

In general, this method involves distinguishing between instruction-related costs and other costs, such as research and public services. Normally, instruction-related costs include both the direct cost of instruction and a pro-rated share of the costs for libraries, plant maintenance, and other institutional services. Computing these costs requires uniform accounting procedures at all of a state's public institutions and some agreed-upon procedures for assigning costs. Such a consensus is extremely difficult to achieve, however, even in a state with only a few public institutions of higher education; furthermore, the costs of securing the needed data increase substantially with the level of detail and sophistication of the cost accounting system.

Actually, the cost-of-instruction method of establishing tuition blends different methods. The share of instructional costs that students pay almost always differs betwen resident and nonresident students. As a general rule, it also differs by type of institution (e.g., four-year versus two-year) and often for students at different levels (e.g., undergraduate versus graduate). When Florida first instituted its cost-of-instruction system, for example, it computed general instructional costs for five different student levels: lower-division undergraduate, upper-division undergraduate, graduate level prior to dissertation, dissertation stage, and professional. Initially, Florida proposed, for resident students in its four-year public institutions, to set tuition charges at 30 percent of the cost of instruction at each student level the first year, but the cost and complexity of maintaining and updating this multilevel system were so great it was never fully implemented or updated, and Florida is now examining alternate methods.

Most other states using the cost-of-instruction method establish fewer student levels in their computations and set tuition or fees in their four-year institutions at 20-30 percent of cost, at least for resident undergraduate students, although in 1985 some legislators discussed extending the upper limit to 35 percent. In some states, the percentage fluctuates as frequently as every two years, while in others it is linked to the rate of inflation. Illinois, a former cost-of-instruction state, has switched to a fee adjustment indexed to inflationary changes in higher education prices.

Until the mid-1980s, separate tuition charges for each student-by-student major had rarely been seriously considered on grounds that making such computations would be both expensive and impractical. Although such an approach is currently being studied in a few states, basing the cost of instruction on the student's major field of study has several deficiencies beyond its presumed impracticality. First, no clear-cut relationship exists between costs of instruction in a discipline and the future earnings of its graduates. As a result, the adoption of a cost-of-instruction method based on each student's major would discriminate against those students who choose careers offering relatively low financial rewards, such as teaching, the ministry, journalism, or homemaking. In addition, such a system would tend to discourage students from enrolling in high-cost fields of instruction without guarantee of a high salary in the future. (Nursing is often cited as a good example of a high-cost instructional program whose graduates do not receive high wages.) Thus, this particular approach, implemented at any level, would separate the determination of student charges from decisions about society's needs and state goals and objectives for public higher education.

While the cost-of-instruction method of determining student charges can be fairly objective, determining the percentage of those costs that students pay is inherently arbitrary. Theoretically, the method presupposed that the cost of providing postsecondary education should be shared equitably by all students through tuition and by the state through direct institutional subsidies and financial aid. However, when states set fees by employing different proportions of the cost of instruction in different segments (i.e., community colleges, four-year colleges, and universities), as Washington does, they alter the basic concept behind the cost-of-instruction method, often in response to historic or traditional segmental differentials bearing little relationship to instructional costs. In states with large numbers of public institutions, such as New York or California, developing suitable accounting procedures and securing intersegmental agreements on the assignment of costs is a formidable task. Hence, although the cost-of-instruction method of calculating tuition and fees is being used by more and more states, it seems to work most effectively in those states with a small or moderate number of public postsecondary institutions.

A few states employ a variation of the cost-of-instruction method by basing student charges on a student's academic level—the assumption being that because the cost of educating students varies considerably according to academic level (lower division, upper division, graduate), the amount they pay in tuition should reflect this difference. This approach does not mean that the students' share of instructional costs—that is, the percentage of costs they are expected to pay—should increase with each level, but rather that the amount advanced-level students pay should increase. Proponents of this method argue that keeping charges lower during the first two years of college facilitates access to postsecondary education because it minimizes some of the financial risks until students can more accurately assess their prospects of successfully completing a degree.

The Carnegie Commission recommended that tuition and fees be determined separately for four different academic levels: (1) associate degrees, (2) bachelor's and master's degrees, (3) doctoral degrees, and (4) other advanced professional degrees. Whether this or some other breakdown is used, the approach has some advantages over a budget-based, cost-of-instruction approach; most notably, it more strongly reflects conscious policy decisions about a state's goals and educational priorities.

A highly popular, if often politically abused, method for establishing tuition and fee charges at public institutions can be found in states where governing boards have the legal responsibility to determine student charges—that is, by basing tuition levels in the various segments of institutions on the difference between the amount the governor, legislature, and boards believe is required and the level of support the state can provide. Although this approach allows maximum flexibility for the state and governing boards, it offers no rational or predictable basis for the actual levels of student charges and no substantive basis for the establishment of those levels. In effect, it constitutes an open invitation to the state to alter the balance between state appropriations and student fees whenever it is pressed for funds and a continuous temptation to the boards to pass on higher charges to students whenever there is a state budgetary shortfall. In recent years, whenever this fee- and tuition-setting procedure has been followed, it has merely widened the gap in student charges among segments of public higher education and further eroded the fundamental principle of low tuition: to preserve a suitable balance beteween the individual's proper share in financing a college education and that borne by society via governmental appropriations.

Proponents of treating tuition as simply another revenue-generating mechanism in the state's budgetary process, to be used in meeting shortfalls in annual or biennial appropriations, say that tuition constitutes a "user tax," and, like a sales tax, can and should be raised along with other consumption taxes to help the state balance its budget.

According to Carol Frances, consulting economist to the firm of Coopers and Lybrand, "This rationale for setting tuition is ill conceived. To treat spending for education as a consumption expenditure, like the purchase of food or tobacco, is an error. Spending for education is an investment. Knowledge creates private benefits that continue over the individual's lifetime and social benefits that last even longer. The user tax analogue is simply not appropriate to the requirements for financing a long-term investment. A more workable analogue can be found in bond or mortgage finance.... For most families sending their children to college, education is the second largest investment they will ever make, the first being for housing."

Whether tuition is established as a predetermined percentage of the cost of instruction, or according to the academic level of students, or as a "user tax" designed to help keep a state's budget balanced, a continuing—and unfortunate—by-product of debates on appropriate tuition levels at public institutions is that students and faculty members invariably find themselves on opposite sides of the issue. Students don't want tuitions to keep spiraling upward and make the cost of attending college prohibitive. Faculty members, on the other hand, are often told bluntly by state government officials that, for budgetary reasons, there has to be a ceiling on state appropriations to public colleges and that the only other possible source of funds for salary increases is revenue generated through tuition increases.

From the standpoint of an institution's academic strength, the tactic of pitting students against faculty members every time the tuition issue arises is debilitating. Yet increasingly in the 1980s legislatures and/or governing boards have mandated that requests for faculty salary increases be met from higher tuition scales, rather than increased state appropriations, on the grounds that what students pay should be more closely tied to instructional costs. States where tuition levels were once pegged to 20 percent of instructional costs have raised that percentage to 25 or 30, and, as of mid-1985, members of the Wisconsin state legislature and its university system board of regents were considering plans to raise the figure to 35 to 40 percent at the system's two largest campuses and to place it at 32 percent at the others. While student groups bristled at the threatened increase, it received strong support from faculty representatives seeking to bring the University of Wisconsin's salary schedules more in line with counterpart institutions elsewhere.

Another policy issue that, in recent years, has come to divide both the academic and the political communities is the idea that tuition and fee scales at public colleges should be tied to family income—the concept of a sliding scale or graduated tuition formula based on a student's ability to pay. The most fully developed proposal incorporating the "sliding-scale approach was designed for the State University of New York (SUNY) and the City University of New York (CUNY) in early 1983 by the Citizens Public Expenditure Survey and announced at the annual meeting of New York's Commission of Independent Colleges and Universities (CPES).

Said Richard V. Horan, president of CPES:

> *I am aware that no state university in the country has heretofore attempted a graduated tuition system. I am convinced that if New York were to adopt such a policy for SUNY, it would set the pace for other states. Wherever required state tax resources are failing to meet higher education budget needs, we would see similar policies adopted. Graduated tuition pricing may not have been attempted in any other state, but it is an idea whose time has come. The old philosophical objection of subjecting students to a needs test has been effectively mooted by the overwhelming participation in federal grant and loan programs which gear eligibility to individual need. Also, we are in a protracted period of scarce state resources, where it borders on the obscene to soak taxpayers for the purpose of subsidizing students from rich families while states are scraping the bottom of the barrel to meet health, welfare, housing, law enforcement, environmental and other critical needs.*

Under the CPES plan, tuition at SUNY would range from the 1983 level of $1,075 for the poorest students (those from families with incomes of $14,000 or under) to $4,335 for students whose families had a net taxable income of more than $40,000.

SUNY officials countered the proposal with the following arguments:

- Sliding-scale tuition denies the philosophy that public higher education is a public investment in the nation's social and economic future in which all those academically eligible should have the opportunity to share.

- The proposal violates the basic concept that public services are equally available to all, regardless of income; citizens are not and should not be charged more for public services because they have greater incomes than someone else's.

- The proposal, simply put, would levy a new "tax" on middle-income New Yorkers who want their children to have a good college education while doing nothing to improve or even to preserve the quality of education.

Donald M. Blinken, chairman of the SUNY board of trustees, stated the case against the CPES proposal most eloquently:

> We need to distinguish between the system by which revenues are generated and the efficacy of their use. They are different subjects. SUNY's objective in respect to the use of its revenues, from whatever source, has always been and always will be to provide maximum access and highest quality within the dollars available.
>
> In all American governmental settings—local, state, and national—public services are priced at a uniform fee for all citizens. Since we have graduated tax structures, we ordinarily do not tax a person a second time on a graduated scale when that person makes use of a generally-available public service. . . . For example, access to the judicial system, fire protection, and police services are not linked to income. Similarly, public roads, museums, and libraries are available to all at equal cost. . . .
>
> Any public service or institution is owned by members of the public on an equal basis; that is, all of us to a degree are equal shareowners in roads, public forests, park lands, as well as state public colleges and universities. The proposal for a sliding scale would suggest that we are not equal owners, that those people who have fewer means own a larger part of the service, while those with more means own the lesser part of it.

Developments in New York State will be watched most carefully during the 1980s and 1990s as governors, state legislators, and boards of trustees formulate public policies affecting tuition levels at public colleges and universities. Those so engaged would do well to consider the following guidelines for shaping policies:

- Each state and system of public higher education is unique. Although national studies of tuition recommendations can be useful, a state must test such recommendations against its own demographic and economic needs and realities.

- The total cost of a college education is affected not only by tuition charages but also by living costs and the distance students must travel to school. These other costs are also affected, in turn, by state policies governing the location and type of higher education institutions.

- Every study of issues pertaining to the estabishment of student charges in public colleges and universities has shown that tuition costs affect college-going decisions.

- The issues of equity and opportunity raised in discussing tuition and student aid policies relate to broad social policies, not just to higher education finance.

- Although budgetary stringencies render fruitless the public-service arguments sometimes advanced in favor of "zero tuition," the parallels between free elementary and secondary education, fire, police, and other public services and public postsecondary education institutions are nonetheless valid. Society has a critical stake in its public colleges and universities.

- A more solid foundation for tuition policy can be constructed by relating tuition to education costs and by establishing the individual's share, not as a "user tax" treating education inappropriately as a consumption expenditure but rather as a payment on a long-term investment. Tuition at public institutions often covers approximately one-quarter of the educational cost. "Setting future tuition charges using these principles," Carol Frances concludes, "would probably not move tuition toward one-third to one-half of cost, but toward one-fifth to one-sixth of cost."

13. The Management of Universities of Constant or Decreasing Size
Richard M. Cyert

One of the important factors in university planning today is the possible decrease in enrollments during the 1980s. A recent publication states, "Higher education in the United States has grown throughout most of its 340 years. Now it faces a quarter of a century of little growth or no growth in enrollments for the first time in history. In two decades, 1870 to 1880 and again in 1960 to 1970, enrollments have doubled and also the greatest advances have been made."[1] Since the students of the 1980s were born in the 1960s, there is little uncertainty connected with such predictions. The percentage of high school graduates going on to higher education might increase enough to compensate for the smaller number of graduates, but there is no reason to expect that kind of change. Looking just at private institutions, we must conclude that the problem is even more severe. The private sector continues to lose students to the public sector. The phenomenon occurs because of enrollment ceilings in prestigious private institutions and the influence of lower tuitions in public universities.

These kinds of considerations lead to questions about the techniques for effectively managing a university that is of constant or contracting size. In most of the literature on organization theory and management practice an implicit assumption is made that the organization is expanding or is interested in expanding. This bias comes from the concentration on the business firm where the motivation is always for increasing sales, increasing production, and increasing profits. Many questions arise about how universities that are contracting can maintain excellence, stimulate high motivation in the participants, develop innovative programs, achieve fiscal equilibrium, and continue the viability of the organization.

Organizational Characteristics

Universities by their nature are difficult to manage under the best of conditions. They are decentralized organizations in which colleges, departments, and faculty members are the organizational units. The product is a service that is delivered by a faculty member

---

Richard M. Cyert has served as president of Carnegie-Mellon University since 1972. He was dean of the Graduate School of Administration prior to becoming president.

under conditions that make it wrong for a manager to observe the delivery of the service. The traditions of academic freedom guarantee the inviolability of the classroom. Thus the academic manager—department head, dean, provost, president—will discover problems with the delivery of the product only through the complaints of the student, who pays to receive the service.

The faculty member not only has independence in the classroom but also gains additional independence because he or she is a source of revenue to the organization through research efforts. By getting outside grants he pays for part of his salary and part of the overhead expense of the university. If indefinite tenure is added to the other elements of independence, it can be seen that the concept of "managing a faculty member" can be difficult.

Deans and department heads, being faculty members, can have the same independence. In addition, by building good relations with the faculty members in their department or college, the deans and department heads can acquire a political base that gives them some independence for their administrative jobs.

In short, the university lacks, to a great extent, the elements of authority inherent in the business organization. The hierarchical structure exists but does not carry the same meaning with respect to the reward system or to the roles of subordinates.

When the organization functions effectively, as measured along educational, research and fiscal dimensions, the structure may present little difficulty because only limited central action is necessary. The situation is quite different when a contraction in size is forced on the organization, and it becomes clear that the central administration must take action. The contracting process brings with it conflicts of all kinds in contrast with an expanding organization.

Organizational Participants

Everyone concerned with organizations in our society needs to readjust his or her thinking with respect to the criterion of success. The nature of a market economy makes growth a measure of success. Any organization producing products that are satisfying the market will tend to grow; those organizations that are not will tend to shrink. Thus, we are inculcated by the market system with the idea that growth is good and comes to those organizations that are doing the right things. Further, growth is a creative force in this society. It produces new opportunities for participants in the organization, as well as for other members of the society. Some of the beauties of an expanding organization can be understood from the following description:

> Even a moderate rate of growth in an organization may produce as many (or more) promotional opportunities as are provided by normal replacement—at least in the short run. Even a five percent annual growth may double the annual number of promotions that can be made at each level. This will probably have the effect of (a) increasing each employee's chances of reaching the higher positions, and (b) reducing the average age at which promotions are made. As a result of the growth, larger numbers of employees will also have to be brought in at the lower levels, hence increasing the competition for promotion after the initial impetus has been spent—but still retaining promotional opportunities at a higher level than in a static organization.[2]

For any given organization, the opportunity for promotion for participants decreases as the rate of growth decreases. This reduction in the opportunities for promotion is perhaps the most difficult element to manage in a contracting organization. The low probabilities of progressing in the organization considerably decrease the organization's ability to attract first-rate participants into the organization. This difficulty is compounded when there are organizations in society that are expanding. When an organization is unable to attract outstanding new participants then it suffers a reduction in the input of new ideas and in the supply of future leaders. As a result, the cadre of experienced people available for promotion to the top positions in the organization may not contain the number of high-quality individuals desired. The university may be forced to look outside for individuals for top professorships, for example. Thus, the probability of attaining a top post for those within the organization is reduced further, and the job of attracting bright young people into the organization is made even more difficult.

In fact, the vicious circle in which one action leads to a second and to a third, all of which are detrimental to the organization, is a characteristic of a contracting organization that the university community must try to avoid. The trick of managing the contracting organization is to break the vicious circle that tends to lead to disintegration of the organization. Management must develop counter forces that allow the organization to maintain viability.

Financial Deterioration

A good example of the vicious circle exists in the financial problems inherent in the private university. The university begins to suffer financial reverses because of a decrease in the student body and its only recourse is to increase tuition. An increase in tuition itself will eventually lead to a further deterioration in the number of students coming, and so a vicious circle begins. Other examples can easily be adduced. In order to justify a higher tuition the private university must achieve a level of greater excellence than the public university. To reduce costs, university managers reduce the salary increases paid to faculty and reduce the number of outstanding new faculty members hired. Then, gradually the university's excellence will deteriorate and it will no longer be in a position to justify the higher tuition cost.

In all of the cycles involving financial deterioration one obvious solution to breaking the negative loop is to find more resources. Generally these resources are difficult to find in the environment or the university would not be in a contracting state. The best source of increased resources is improved internal management. The technique is to find ways of achieving approximately the same quality level of education and research that has been achieved but to achieve it with fewer resources. Achieving that result means that management, someplace within the system, has increased productivity.

Management

More generally, it is imperative that the university be well managed when the organization is contracting. This goal is difficult to attain because the greater rewards offered to superior managers in expanding organizations reduce the supply of good managers for universities. The achievement of this end is made even more difficult because academics resist being managed by expert managers and seek to have an academic in the top management position. Only rarely will this approach lead to an excellent manager. This aspect is characteristic of hospitals as well as universities. In universities, the faculty is the dominant participant group and tends to abhor the concept of administration in general and looks toward a scholar to succeed to the top management position. In hospitals where the physicians are the dominant participant group, they wish to be responsible for the important decisions and tend to make the hospital administrator a less important figure. In both of these organizations, however, as the stress from the environment becomes greater and as the deterioration of the organization becomes more obvious through financial decay, it becomes possible to put greater emphasis on managerial ability.

Inflation

The problem of the survival of a university that is not growing is exacerbated when one postulates an inflation rate of 5-7 percent within the environment. The inflation factor means that the organization must continue to get an increase in its total revenues, matching the rate of inflation, if it is to achieve a constant dollar equilibrium. It is clear that economies due to management cannot achieve continued savings. Inflation means that certain expenses continue to increase and that the organization can meet them only by acquiring additional revenue. If the revenue is not acquired, the university eventually becomes bankrupt. If the revenue is acquired by continued tuition increases, it is likely that the organization will be forced into a vicious circle of the kind described. This analysis assumes that higher tuitions will have some impact on student demand for the university's services.

There are other aspects of remaining a constant size in an economy that is experiencing inflation that plague the university. One of these is the role of outside activities of the faculty. It is common, and most universities encourage it, for faculty members to have outside consulting arrangements that will increase the faculty member's professional skills and lead to research and publication. Most universities have some limitation on the amount of time a faculty member may spend on such assignments but the faculty member is given the responsibility as a professional to police himself on both the amount of time spent and the quality of the assignments. In the best of times, there are faculty members who behave unprofessionally. In a period of no growth and falling real income, the temptation to increase the amount of time spent on outside work will tend to become overwhelming. Faculty members who have the opportunity, will focus on the income involved rather then the intellectual quality of the assignment and will, in effect, become part-time faculty. There is an obvious source of potential conflict here if the university management attempts to correct the situation.

Strategic Planning

I have painted this dismal picture because there is another alternative that is important to examine: the development of a new strategic plan for the organization. A university that cannot operate successfully in the conventional way may need to reexamine the areas in which it is offering educational service. It may be possible to develop a plan for operation that would eliminate some of the educational areas where the university is losing money and move into other areas in which the organization has expertise, such as research. Stated more succinctly, it may be possible for some private universities to operate more as a mixture of a research institute and an educational institution than is currently done. Since such universities now offer both educational and research services as part of their product package, the strategy seems feasible. The examination of a new strategic plan would reduce the emphasis on producing educational services and increase the production on research services. Thus students would become less important and outside research contracts and grants more important. This example illustrates only one strategic alternative. More generally there is a need when an organization is contracting to find a new mix of services that can allow it to attain an equilibrium position. Some universities will disappear because there are no services or mix of services that can win support. A good strategic analysis should uncover such a situation and allow the organization to close its doors in an orderly and dignified manner.

In essence, we are suggesting an approach similar to diversification in the business firm. It should be clear that this type of strategy is only one of many possible strategies for a university. Nevertheless, it is worth discussing because it does carry with it potential danger. That danger stems from too much emphasis on survival—almost survival at any cost. It is probably always possible for a university (or any organization) to survive if it is not committed to a set of guiding principles that prevent it from being infinitely flexible. The university seeking alternative strategies must be wary of being seduced into becoming an applied research institute with no standards for the type of research it does. The path to such a position is characterized by an increasing emphasis on contracts and a decreasing emphasis on grants. The contracts tend to prescribe the type of research that must be done and faculty members soon find themselves, in essence, doing research that is not of basic interest to them. Its only virtue is that it pays part of the salary of the researcher. Such a strategic path must be avoided. The university must not only survive, but it must survive fruitfully.

Strategic planning is generally difficult to do within universities, but it becomes more difficult during a period of contraction because certain functions may have to be eliminated. Planners must change their orientation to think in terms of attaining an equilibrium by contraction rather than growth. In addition, financial criteria must be given a heavy weight in developing criteria for eliminating activities, and such an emphasis is contrary to academic thinking. In short, the type of planning that is necessary for survivial requires a significant change in thinking. Clearly, strong leadership is necessary to produce meaningful strategic plans under the circumstances.

It is, of course, far better to begin the strategic planning process before organizational slack is completely dissipated.[3] It is always possible to use some of the slack to ease the transition of the organization to new paths or as side payments to gain the cooperation of certain units.[4] As the pressure builds, the slack will be used to help balance the budget. The early and quick reduction of expenses of a unit generally reflects the elimination of slack that had been built into the organization when times were better financially.

When the organization fails to achieve some well-defined goal (balanced budget, entering class enrollment), the organization will be motivated to search for explanations. Only when it is convinced that a real problem exists, that the structure of the environment has somehow changed, will it be prepared to engage in serious search. The university, like the firm, exhibits problemistic search.[5]

In particular, the university follows simple-minded search procedures and generally searches in the neighborhood of the problem symptom. If the enrollment is down, the admissions department must be doing something wrong. If there is a shortage of funds, get a new president because it is his or her job to raise an adequate amount of money. It is only when the organization has lived with the problem for a time and has begun to develop a more sophisticated model of causation that the organization can begin to make real progress on its problem.

Where solutions are hard to find, and they are harder the greater the contraction, the danger is that aspirations for the organization and for the individual will be reduce in the minds of faculty members. The real danger in contraction is that individuals who by nature desire excellence will begin to settle for mediocrity out of frustration.

Motivation for Excellence

In a contracting organization it is frequently difficult for the participants to maintain the desire to achieve excellence. Some of the difficulty stems from the fear that if the organization is not expanding and in fact is contracting, that it is going to become defunct. The alternative concept of an organization reaching an equilibrium size at a smaller level must be made clear to the participants.

The concept of an equilibrium at a smaller scale of operation is one that is difficult, psychologically, to accept. Under conditions of contraction, however, it is necessary to reexamine the scale of operation of the university. When inflation is present also, the problem of finding the proper scale of operation becomes even more difficult. The usual way of finding a new equilibrium for a university when students were plentiful was to increase the student-teacher ratio by adding more students. This move forced greater productivity on the faculty but risked adversely affecting the quality of education.[6] With contracting size, stimulated by fewer students, everything must be brought into the proper proportion—faculty, space, research, administration, and staff. At the new equilibrium, there will unboubtedly be rooms and even buildings that are closed and taken completely out of use. Administrators must become less specialized—the admissions director may also have to be the financial aid director, the vice president for business operations may also have to be the controller, the president may have to do without a provost, colleges may be merged, and so on. The new equilibrium at the smaller size will, in many respects, be a new university.

Once the concept of an equilibrium position at a smaller size is understood and the fear that the organization is on the road to disintegration is eliminated, it is necessary to develop positive programs oriented toward attaining an increased level of excellence for the organization. These programs may be designed to strengthen the subunits of an organization, such as the departments within a college, or to improve the quality of an important activity, such as the delivery of educational services.

A positive program will, of course, require funds that can be utilized for its implementation. These funds may be obtained from foundations, the utilization of reserves, if they exist, or from a reduction in expenditure in another part of the organization—for example, the administration. A positive program designed to change the attention focus of the faculty from survival to excellence will be most effective when it provides money for faculty members to develop an idea. One effective approach is to make funds available for some objective or set of objectives such as improving teaching or seed money for new research through a faculty-dominated internal foundation. Faculty are stimulated to submit proposals and another set of faculty determine which proposals are financed. The point is that a concerted effort involving the faculty directly will help make the organizational goal of continued excellence real to the participants. Further, the program focuses the attention of the administration as well as the other participants on goals that are professional in nature as opposed to the constraints, which are generally financial or physical (e.g., buildings, facilities, etc.). In fact, the major leadership tasks under conditions of contracting or constant size are to maintain the attention focus of the faculty on the professional goals of the organization and at the same time to follow managerial policies designed to produce the efficient utilization of resources.

The university administration must be careful to maintain standards of excellence in the face of financial pressure. Promotion and salary decisions, for example, should not be made on the basis of a faculty member's capacity to raise money from outside contracts to support his or her salary and research. Further, the university administration must recognize a limit on the proporation of a faculty member's salary that can be financed from outside. The educational goals of the university cannot be compromised.

Conflict Resolution

Within any organization conflicts tend to arise between the goals of subunits and the overall goals of the total organization.

In an expanding organization these conflicts can generally be solved by the simple expedient of finding more resources and applying them appropriately to enable the subunit goals to be achieved without violating organizational goals or constraints. This approach is used in profit-making organizations also. Organizational slack makes the managerial life an easy one because the manager does not have to resist the pressures of the subunits as vigorously as when resources are scarce, as they are in a contracting organization.

In an expanding organization a subunit strives to get more of the organizational resources, frequently by using the argument that strengthening its ability to achieve its professional goals is in conformity with the organization's goals. Knowing that this type of argument has a good chance of being successful provides an incentive for a subunit to be innovative. In a contracting organization the danger is that the subunits will become concerned only with survival, with maintaining a constant rather than an increasing flow of resources, and will no longer strive to improve their capacity to achieve their professional goals. Rather than become "squeaky wheels" the subunits attempt to become "unobstrusive wheels" so that the administration will not use the excuse of the squeaking to eliminate them.

These subunits attempt to behave in such a way that they will go unnoticed and, therefore, untouched. They exhibit little desire for reform but want only the status quo. Such units make it difficult for the organization to improve itself. An organization filled with such units cannot reform itself and a university in such a position cannot achieve the excellence it needs to survive.

Conflict resolution will be more difficult in a contracting organization because the easy method of utilizing more resources for resolution is not available. At the same time it is likely that more conflicts will arise than in an expanding organization because of the emphasis that subunits and participants place on survival. The added dimension of participants competing within a subunit for a limited number of positions and subunits competing with each other for a limited number of organizational slots within the total organization clearly increases the tension level in the organization. The concentration on survival will, therefore, tend to increase the number of conflicts within the contracting or constant size organization since survival of individual subunits or participants will not generally be an over-all organizational goal. Conflicts will tend to be oriented to resource distribution. More specifically, conflicts will tend to focus on inducements and contributions where equity and justice will be evoked as criteria.[7] The conflicts are also exacerbated by the fact that the contracting organization is usually in an industry or region that is also contracting so that the mobility of the participants is reduced.

In a business organization the causes of a contraction can be more easily determined than in a nonprofit organization. A recession in the economy or an increase in competition may be diagnosed as the reason for a fall in profits. Further, the business organization can more easily deal with the conflicts resulting from contraction.[8] Profit is a well-defined criterion of performance and simplifies the measurement of the performance of subunits. Having a quantitative method of evaluating subunits gives management an objective method of settling conflicts. This insight can be a useful heuristic for analyzing conflict resolution methods within the contracting organization.

After all efforts have been made to increase resources within the organization by improved management, more gifts, or higher prices, it will be clear that the internal conflicts remain and these will be forced to the attention of top management.[9] The tendency is to deal with these conflicts through a series of ad hoc decisions made by the head of the organization. These decisions are referred to as ad hoc because there is no generally accepted and publicly known set of goals and priorities for the organization. In universities this condition means that knowledge does not exist within the organization on the relative priorities for resource allocation of the individual colleges. The program for attaining a goal is critical as a first step in the solution of such conflicts. The goal structure provides a framework with an objective basis for the resolution of conflict. Second, it is necessary to develop measures of performance, particularly for academic units. The main technique for resolving conflicts arising within contracting organizations is to find objective criteria on which agreement among the contesting participants can be achieved. Without a broad framework and specific measurements the resolution of conflicts will tend to be based on political considerations—how many decisions have gone against a particular group, what is the effect on the status of the department head or dean of a negative decision, or what will happen to the morale of a department if another decision goes against it. The aim must be to improve the availability of the quantity and quality of information available for rational decision making.

Conclusions

The study of contracting or constant size organizations has received relatively little attention in the management or organizational literature. Growth and expansion have tended to be the objectives of most organizations and the criteria by which success has been judged. It is clear, however, that in education we must be concerned with the management of organizations that are not growing. The problems that must be handled are clear. An equilibrium size must be established as a target. Provisions must be made to keep a constant flow of new participants and ideas into the organization. In order to attain a stable equilibrium it may be necessary to develop an early retirement program. Attention must be given to the programs that will keep participants striving for excellence even though there is no growth. Conflicts must be settled objectively. Efforts must be made to keep an adequate flow of information to the participants so that excessive demands for compensation and fringe benefits are not made. At the same time management must prevent the development of an attitude among the participants that their interests are not being given adequate attention. This attitude can lead to the development of subunits with goals divergent from organizational goals.

The major problem for the organization reaching a static equilibrium is gaining adequate revenue in the face of inflation. Constant size may mean that revenue is also fixed. There must be attention given to increasing the endowment and the gifts to get a higher income. At the same time a continuing effort must be made to find new managerial efficiencies that result in cost savings. There is no simple solution to the problem of managing universities of constant or contracting size. It will be a crucial one since the outlook for the United States and probably for the Western World is for contraction with inflation.

University presidents must take an analytical approach in the hope of developing policies that will counteract the debilitating tendencies of contraction. New ways of thinking about management of universities must be developed if universities are going to play the critical role for our society in the future as they have in the past.

Notes

[1] *The States and Higher Education,* A commentary of the Carnegie Foundation for the Advancement of Teaching (San Francisco: Jossey-Bass, 1976), p. 5.

[2] H. A. Simon, D. W. Smithburg, and V. A. Thompson, *Public Administration* (New York: Alfred Knopf, 1950), p. 345.

[3] Richard M. Cyert and James G. March, *A Behavioral Theory of the Firm* (Englewood Cliffs, N.J.: Prentice Hall, 1963), pp. 36-38.

[4] Ibid., p. 29.

[5] Ibid., pp. 120-122.

[6] There is conflicting evidence about the effect of class size on educational quality. Cf. Dubin.

[7] Simon et al., pp. 498-99.

[8] Cf. H. F. Rainey, R.W. Backoff and C. H. Levine, "Comparing Public and Private Organizations," *Public Administration Review,* March/April 1976, pp. 223-44. This paper contains a relatively exhaustive list of propositions about the differences that exist between the two types of organizations. See R. M. Cyert, *Management of Non-Profit Organizations* (Lexington, Mass.: D.C. Health and Co., 1975), pp. 7-14 for discussion of some similarities between the university and the business firm.

[9] Some of these conflicts may be resolvable by zero-based budgeting. Cf. Peter A. Pyhrr, "The Zero-Base Approach to Government Budgeting," *Public Administration Review,* January/February 1977, pp. 1-8.

14. Should States Support Private Colleges? Yes!
Steven Muller

Arguments between the independent and state-owned sectors of American higher education are all too frequent. But they are inevitable and can sometimes be enlightening. Certainly the issue of state aid to independent universities and colleges is important, and divisive.

Somehow Chancellor Priest* fails to mention why-as he quite correctly states-forty-three of the fifty states (which means almost all the states in which there are independent institutions of higher education) already have programs to assist independent colleges and universities. The reason is simple: it saves money for the taxpayers. It is cheaper by far for states to provide a margin of help to independent institutions than it would be to take them over, or to pay to have their students educated at state-owned institutions. State legislators want to save money, too, and they can recognize a bargain when they see one.

Look at the numbers from Texas that Chancellor Priest provides. If the state of Texas can help to keep a number of independent universities and colleges alive and well for only $7.5 million a year among them, that makes an interesting comparison with the cost to the taxpayers of operating the Dallas County Community College District, which costs $50 million a year in public funds, of which $25 million a year already comes from the state. One can calculate how much it would cost a state to take over the costs of the thousands of students and faculty now in the independent sector, and then demonstrate that only a tiny portion of that cost each year, given to assist that sector, is a wise investment.

That, however, involves two assumptions: first, that it is all right for an independent sector of higher education to exist; and second, that a margin of state assistance is really needed to preserve it. On the first proposition, Chancellor Priest states that he agrees—he says we need "outstanding private institutions." Yet he proceeds to take issue with a statement that only tries to set forth that independent universities and colleges have a unique and important role to play.

Whatever the explanation, it happens to be a statement of

---

*Chancellor Priest's chapter follows this one.

mine to which he makes reference. Unfortunately he does not quote me directly, but only summarizes me, inaccurately. But let me let most of that go by and pick up only one significant distortion, plus one passing comment of his.

The distortion involves Chancellor Priest's claim that I have spoken of private higher education being free of government controls. Neither private persons nor private corporations live outside the law, so in that sense all of us experience government control. Besides, privately financed universities and colleges serve a public purpose. Like other institutions in the private sector that meet public needs—such as hospitals, for instance—they are exempt from taxes in recognition of their public service: in fact, to call them private is less useful than to call them independent. "Private" conveys that their primary support comes from private rather than public funds, which is true enough. But "independent" conveys something more significant: that they are independently governed.

Independent governance means boards of trustees selected by the institution itself, not by public election or appointment. And it is truly important, both historically and currently. Higher education in the United States began primarily with private collegiate foundations, which were incorporated under public or private charter and evolved the American pattern of trustee governance.

The trustees could and did delegate internal administration to presidents, faculties, and students, but they retain responsibility for the corporation. They stand as a buffer between the college or university and the public, and that is crucial when the public wishes to interfere with academic integrity. Academic integrity means that unpopular views may be held and expressed on campus; trustees generally have understood this, and have defended the academic integrity of their institutions.

As public institutions of higher education were founded, their governance was modeled on the pattern that had already evolved in the private sector. Boards of regents were created for state universities, which thus were not placed under the direct control either of the legislature or a state department of education. Independent trustees and public regents alike are responsible, among other things, for the academic integrity of their universities and colleges.

Three aspects of their situation merit special mention. First, had there been no independent sector of higher education in the past, public colleges and universities might easily have become heavily politicized campuses, extensively controlled by the political party in power in a state at any one time—which is exactly what all too often happens abroad where state boards of regents generally do not exist.

Second, were the independent sector of higher education now to disappear, the existing restraint on state legislatures and agencies that prevents their direct control of state universities and colleges would largely disappear, and the academic integrity of these campuses might then be as vulnerable as that of universities abroad has been.

Third, independent governance is not threatened per se by the receipt of public funds. Of course, public accountability is a consequence of public funding, but the difference between accountability for public money on the one hand, and public control on the other, is vast. The receipt of some public funds by independent universities and colleges does not contaminate their independent governance or institutional autonomy any more than the receipt of some private funds by state-owned colleges and universities makes these any less public.

Chancellor Priest also states his concern that his tax dollars are helping someone's son or daughter attend the most expensive school in the state. What he means by most expensive, of course, is only that the institution charges the highest tuition. That does not mean that it spends more per student on education than do other institutions. In fact, the actual expenditures per student for independent and public colleges and universities are very comparable. The difference is that state legislatures heavily subsidize these expenses at public institutions, while independent colleges and universities depend heavily on student tuition payments.

And that, in turn, does not mean that only the well-to-do can attend independent colleges and universities. In fact, the proportion of students from low-income families, and who represent racial minorities, is almost exactly the same in the independent as in the public sector of higher education which does, of course, put a considerable strain on independent institutions who spend a great amount of their own resources on student aid programs to assist students who cannot afford the high tuitions that are now being charged.

When these facts are understood, Chancellor Priest's analogy of a choice between a Chevrolet and Cadillac is misleading. The actual choice is not at all like that. The real difference is between a state-owned institution that charges a low tuition because its operating expenses are paid by the taxpayers to the extent of millions of dollars a year, and an independent institution that receives a few hundred thousand dollars a year from the state to help maintain its quality. The choice is whether those few hundred thousand dollars are a good investment for the taxpayer, as opposed to spending millions more on public higher education should that independent campus fail.

Let us go back to the earlier question of whether independent colleges and universities really need a margin of state assistance. The answer is yes. While financial health varies greatly from one particular campus to another, independent not-for-profit institutions, including universities and colleges, are obviously having a very hard time during a period of higher inflation. Their expenditures are forced to rise at a rate of more than 6 percent a year, and it is nearly impossible to increase their revenues that much each year for an extended period of time.

Why do I say "forced" to rise? Because the degree to which they control the increase in their expenditures is so limited. They cannot function without using utilities, paper, and the buying of books—items whose cost is rising faster than the consumer price index. They must pay wages and salaries, and if they lag far behind the consumer price index each year they will lose their best people. They are employer and are compelled as employers to pay ever-increasing social security taxes. So substantial annual expenditure increases cannot be avoided. To match these steep increases each year from private sources alone is terribly difficult at best, and to do so at a time when the investment market has been depressed for years is virtually impossible.

A margin of state assistance is, therefore, crucial. What the states are spending on aid to independent universities and colleges is only a margin—a tiny fraction of what they spend on public higher education, and as a rule less than one percent of the budget of any single independent college or university that benefits from state assistance. Such minimal aid is not enough to keep a poorly managed independent campus going, and indeed no one has argued that every single independent university or college must be preserved, regardless of quality or management. But for the vast majority of independent universities and colleges the problem is to maintain quality of service in the face of steeply rising costs. For them, a margin of state assistance makes a crucial difference. For the taxpayers of the state, helping them to continue to render undiminished service is a wise and cost-effective investment.

At the end of his discussion, Chancellor Priest plays the familiar zero-sum game: there is only one piece, and if you get a piece, my piece is smaller. I hope he is wrong. Any sensible state legislature will surely recognize the pressure inflation puts on the state's public colleges and universities and will not take the dollars for assistance to independent institutions out of the budgets of state-owned campuses.

I believe that most states will continue and probably increase their assistance to independent colleges and universities; on the other hand, public universities and colleges will seek and receive more and more private dollars. Private fund raising by public institutions is already intense—for years the state universities of California and Michigan have ranked among the top ten universities receiving the most in private gifts each year. I for one do not object to such efforts by public institutions to improve their programs with the assistance of private funds.

And I suggest to Chancellor Priest and my other colleagues in the public sector that they should respect the decision by their state legislatures to give marginal support to independent colleges and universities. That would be the best evidence they can give that they really mean it when they say that they believe, as I do, in the dualism and diversity of American higher education.

15. Should States Support Private Colleges? No!
Bill J. Priest

At the outset, I want to make it clear that while I have grave misgivings about providing state aid to private institutions, I am a proponent of dualism in American higher education. In addition to excellent public colleges and universities, we need outstanding private institutions which are free of the ebb and flow of political support and approval—free to serve the intellectual needs of society without the shackles of government constraint.

The issue is: should the state provide financial assistance to private institutions? Some forty-three states do so to some degree at this time and some basic questions are being asked by both proponents and opponents of allocating public dollars to independent colleges.

In reviewing this question, I find myself viewing the issues from two separate vantage points. One is that of chancellor of a public, multicampus community college district which operates with a $50-million budget, approximately half funded by state tax moneys. Obviously, in a competitive market with money in short supply, I have a professional interest in what and whom legislators choose to support.

The other vista from which I operate is that of a taxpayer: overburdened and, at times, miffed by government spending.

I see three fundamental, relating questions which are applicable across the board and to which answers must be provided before the dilemma is resolved. They are:

1. Are private colleges and universities in such dire financial straits that they need state tax money in order to survive?
2. If such financial needs do exist, is it appropriate for the state to respond through appropriation of tax dollars?
3. If the state does support the private sector, what kind of impact will this have on not only the public schools but on private institutions as well?

The evidence offered by the private sector to justify the emergency nature of its financial predicament is suspect if we accept what statisticians and researchers tell us.

Bill J. Priest was president of Dallas County Community College when this article was written. He also served as a member of the board of directors of the American Association of Community and Junior Colleges.

The Association of American Colleges published a study on private higher education in which researchers Howard Bowen and John Minter show that, contrary to expectations, there was little evidence of retrenchment activities in their sample of one hundred private colleges.

I must conclude that the private sector is not in as bad a shape as some would lead us to believe. Granted, we all could use more money, but my second question is even more fundamental. This involves the appropriateness of allocating public funds for private higher education.

For the sake of argument, let us assume that the private sector is desperate for additional monies. Should the government respond? That is, is it appropriate for public dollars to go to the aid of private institutions—in fact, to preserve private higher education? If so, does it not cease to be "private"?

In attempting to provide answers to these questions, I examined some statements by the president of a prestigious private university on why private higher education is essential in America. Dr. Steven Muller, president of Johns Hopkins University, cited indispensable functions:

1. Help maintain academic quality.
2. Help preserve student choice.
3. Act as a counterbalance to institutions which are publicly controlled and, therefore, subject to government regulation.
4. Help ensure freedom of religion.

The legitimacy of these reasons is subject to debate, particularly on the grounds that these functions are unique to private higher education. I hope, for example, that even in the remote eventuality that private institutions disappear, there still would be academic quality at Berkeley, Ann Arbor, Austin and Chapel Hill, to name only a few. I am not at all convinced that any valid generalization can be made rating private higher education as superior to public higher education. That the Dukes, Harvards, and Stanfords contribute richly to the quality of American higher education is unassailable, but I don't see this as a vital factor in evaluating the controversy.

The question of student choice is perhaps the strongest argument which proponents of the state aid questions have advanced. But it, too, has its failings. We know, for example, that considerable financial aid from federal and private sources is available. Private educators betray themselves in their recruiting pitches when they assure prospective students that if they need aid, it is available.

The "student choice" angle is the primary thrust of the tuition equalization program in Texas. In fact, the T.E.G. program serves as only a tool to be used in competing with public institutions for increased enrollments.

As a taxpayer, I am troubled when I observe that my tax dollars are helping someone's son or daughter attend the most expensive school in the state, when I have already provided quality public higher education. Freedom of choice, yes—but I'd like it to be the same kind I have when I choose a Chevrolet instead of a Cadillac, and that's my personal money I'm spending! Is attending high tuition private college an American birthright?

The third reason offered by President Muller for preserving private higher education is that it is free of government controls. This position is becoming less tenable as each public tax dollar goes into private sector treasuries: it is a myth that government money comes with no strings attached. It is my contention that the very nature of what private educators are trying to preserve—that feature which makes them "private," invulnerable when these institutions become dependent upon state aid. I quote from the statute which created the T.E.G. program in Texas. I believe its message is clear and unmistakable:

Any college or university receiving any benefit under this subchapter, either directly or indirectly, shall be subject to all present and future laws enacted by the legislature.

President Muller's fourth function, which deals with the religious mission, is not an appropriate purpose for tax dollars, and I am unaware of any private educator who espouses state aid for preservation of religious freedom. However, it bears mentioning, simply because there are institutions whose primary mission is directly related to the advancement of religious doctrine. In my opinion, such institutions which receive state aid violate the principle of separation of church and state.

The final question in my analysis focuses on the impact of public funds for private schools, not only on the private sectoor but on public institutions as well. What does it mean when state aid is given to the private sector? How much does a private college lose when it starts feeding out of the public trough? I believe the following implications must be considered.

1. Public and private institutions will extend their competitiveness from the recruiting of students to the recruiting of legislators for increased appropriations. If a private college is dependent on public funds, is it not imperative that provisions be made for

lobbying and pleasing public officials who decide who gets what and how much? In the Lone Star State, the private schools have formed their lobbying group to obtain as much as they can from already scarce public resources. This is viewed by many in publicly supported colleges as the Fort Sumter of the coming shootout.

2. As I indicated in responding to President Muller's statements, I fear that with increased government aid, private higher education will no longer be private. There is a basic inconsistency in private educators seeking public funds. This is, without a doubt, an invitation to state control. If you have state control, particularly when it comes to prescribing educational standards, dictating hiring procedures, and restricting expenditures, you do not have private institutions.

Baylor University in Waco, Texas, is a good example of an institution which refuses to accept public funds. Dr. Abner McCall, Baylor's president, through good, sound management principles, has led Baylor to unprecedented prosperity. Baylor is turning students away—its academic standing rises with each entering freshman class. And it is second in the nation in low tuition rates of major, private universities. Dr. McCall is consistent. He believes in the "special education" of the private sector and does not compromise his belief by accepting government aid. The President of Brigham Young in Utah has made similar pronouncements.

3. Related to the "control" issue is the question, "How much invasion of privacy is the private college willing to accept to keep the flow of public funds coming in?" This would likely include (1) required reports done at institutional expense, (2) audits by government agencies, (3) visitation to determine if standards are being maintained, and (4) imposition of policies which influence or control personnel decisions, institutional philosophy, and internal operations.

4. Another implication which concerns me, primarily as a taxpayer, is the extension of state funds to private elementary and secondary schools. If it can be argued that this is appropriate in higher education, is not the same reasoning just as applicable to the other levels of education?

As I reflect on this matter, a few additional thoughts run through my mind. Some are variations of points I've made, but they seem worthy of restatement in a summary.

One interesting and significant trend among states is the tendency for representatives of private education to seek positions on public higher education planning agencies. One of the purposes of this is to influence planning decisions so that the status of private colleges will not be harmed. Perhaps there is merit in such surveillance and participation.

If so, is it not equally meritorious to have representatives from the public sector sit on private college planning groups to simultaneously monitor and assist them in reaching sound decisions and to voice opposition to plans which may be harmful to public institutions?

A closely related matter is the tendency for states to subsidize private institutions to deliver needed educational services which otherwise would be assigned to a public institution. An example might be the creation of a long-term contract between the state and a private graduate school (i.e., medicine or law) to train a given number of students rather then duplicate the facilities needed if these functions were to be added to a state school. I question the legitimacy of such an arrangement for the same reasons I question any public aid to the private sector.

Private colleges are almost always created by a group of people who wish to develop a particular environment and curricula compatible with their priorities and value patterns. They have historically banded together and pooled resources to found this educational operation on the premise that it will then be theirs to do what they want done. If there is no longer sufficient interest to support this concept, what is the rationale for perpetuating it at taxpayers' expense?

If one believes that past is prologue, how can you assume that private education is not committing suicide when it moves in a direction that will make it dependent upon public funds with which inevitably come public controls? I am for quality in education. This kind of subsidy only dilutes the quality of education in our society. Will the public stand for the across-the-board dilution of quality which is the almost certain outcome of dividing a shrinking public education budget into more and smaller pieces? Will they support two competing systems of higher education with tax dollars in a setting where education has already slipped from first to fourth or fifth place in our national priorities?

In closing, I'd like to share with you a limerick which speaks to the question I've been examining:

> *There was a young lady from Trent*
> *Who said that she knew what it meant*
> *When men bought her wine*
> *And took her to dine—She knew what it meant, but she went.*

16. The Public-Private Debate
Frank H. T. Rhodes

At Association of Governing Boards (AGB) meetings, in the associations, and within the individual states—wherever talented, dedicated, and conscientious education leaders have gathered to discuss the issue—there have been both widespread concern and widespread agreement on some general principles.

Yes, we agree, America's system of higher education is infinitely richer because of the mixture of institutions—public, private, two-year, four-year, graduate/professional, urban and rural, vocational and liberal arts—which compose the whole.

Yes, it is important to preserve access *and* choice, so that students may select institutions most suited to their needs and aspirations rather than to the size of their bank accounts.

Yes, we must share resources, for everything from journal subscriptions to electron microscopes has become incredibly expensive, and few of us can hope to provide all things to all our people.

Yes, we must work to reduce bureaucratic requirements that dilute our educational efforts, for most of us have had direct experience with those voluminous reports that require documentation of virtually everything except our faculty's shoe sizes.

Yes, we must strive for statesmanship and collegiality across sectors, for few of us feel entirely comfortable with the self-serving lobbying tactics that have become a part of our annual budget negotiations.

Yes, we must stand for quality, and we've said so, eloquently and repeatedly, in our recruitment and fund-raising brochures and virtually every other document that leaves our university publications offices.

And yes, both of us, independent and public, fulfill a public trust. If that is so, we've got to put a stop to the snide remark that suggests one sector has a monopoly on quality, selectivity, morality, and independence and the other on democracy, accountability, public service, and educational opportunity. We all know better

---

Frank H. T. Rhodes has served in both public and private universities. He is currently president of Cornell University, an institution unique in that it has both publicly and privately supported segments. He was formerly academic vice president of the University of Michigan.

than that. But agreement in principle too often preempts discussions, in practice, of the hard policy questions that form the basis of any cooperative action.

In the end, it matters less what we say than what each of us is willing to do. Without a proactive strategy that moves beyond generalized platitudes and woolly exhortations, I see little hope that we can resolve the issues dividing us, as indeed we must if we are to achieve a maximum return on this country's $95.5-billion investment in higher education.

The sources of our discord are familiar to most of us, but they are also urgent. A shrinking pool of traditional college-age students; student interests shifting into high-cost instructional areas such as engineering and computer science; new programs for less well-prepared and part-time students; urgent needs for maintenance of our physical plants and improvement of our laboratories—all have strained our resources and prompted us to compete, both within our own sectors and across sectors, for state, private and corporate support.

The problems

Unfortunately, we become so fluent in discussing the merits of our own institutions with legislators and donors that we too often fail to acknowledge that neither sector has a monopoly on excellence or is alone sufficient for a truly healthy and responsive system of higher education.

The strengths of the public institutions are many, but two in particular stand out: broad access and low price. In the years following World War II, public institutions filled a need for which the resources of the independent sector were clearly inadequate and so made higher education available to thousands of individuals, including many from disadvantaged backgrounds, who might otherwise have been excluded.

Between 1950 and 1980, enrollment in public institutions grew from 1.1 million to 9.4 million, largely because of the success of public community colleges where 80 percent of these students enrolled. As our economy shifts away from blue-collar jobs and into service and information industries, this highly educated work force, trained largely in the public sector, may be our greatest natural resource.

Because it is sustained by the taxpayers, the appeal of public higher education must be broad and its programs solid, orthodox, noncontroversial, and as risk-free as possible. Public higher education is not the "generic brand" that some have claimed, nor is it colored in the "committee beige" that some have painted, but it does have a general consistency, if not a uniformity, that is both a characteristic and a strength.

The appeal of independent higher education is not nearly so universal, and, not surprisingly, its growth has been more modest. Beginning in 1950 with approximately 1.1 million students, it claimed some 2.6 million students in 1980.

Despite a smaller "market share," the contributions of the independent sector to higher education have been substantial. It has been estimated, for example, that if independent institutions did not exist, taxpayers would have to spend some $2 billion to build comparable facilities at today's rates and would have to provide additional operating funds in excess of $2 billion annually.

The value of independent institutions is not confined to their cost effectiveness, however. Perhaps their greatest strength is their ability to undertake courageous experiments in style, substance, and context with the support of those citizens who share the institutions' visions.

Because they can often respond quickly to changing conditions, independent institutions have helped chart new directions for all of higher education. One area in which this has been particularly true over the past few years has been corporate support for university research.

Independent institutions, which entered into some of the most substantial early ventures with industry, have helped define the form of agreements that balance academic freedom against industry's proprietary interest in the results of the research.

By and large, it is the nation's selective independent institutions that have been particularly devoted to the liberal arts, particularly concerned with the gifted student, particularly strong in graduate and professional education, and that have set the standards of excellence to which all—public and private—can aspire.

And it is because those aspirations have been transformed into reality in both sectors that higher education has become such an important force in American life.

Actions Required

If we are to maximize the opportunities and minimize the difficulties of the years ahead, if we are to move from exhortation to action, we must be willing to acknowledge the strengths of our dual system and also to support initiatives which, while sometimes difficult for individual institutions, can greatly improve the effectiveness and responsiveness of the larger enterprise. I suggest that there are six major questions of policy that must be addressed by education leaders from all sectors and that must form the basis for any cooperative action.

First, we must be willing to support shrinking, redirecting, combining, or even closing weak institutions in both sectors, so that limited resources may be allocated more productively. Most of us can agree to that in principle. In practice, however, we have seen, on the one hand, the extinction of a number of small independent liberal arts colleges amid rancor, bitter recriminations, and lawsuits, and on the other, unprecedented political wrangling over the fate of some marginally effective public colleges.

Is it simply to be the law of the jungle in the independent sector, as with such obstructive lobbying and political free-for-alls in the public, as to prevent any effective and reasonable action?

Only by agreement on specific criteria, applicable to institutions in both sectors, and by establishing mechanisms for applying those criteria, can we make the reasonable and rational decisions required of us, for without that the problem, already serious, is likely to become critical.

How do we tackle this problem? How can we best develop guidelines, protocols, and models? What about statewide or regional consortia? Dare we take this first step?

My second proposition is that we must build on our strengths rather than developing new weaknesses. We must agree to establish new programs in either sector only with clear evidence of demand, only if the resources for new programs are adequate, and only if the same students could not be served by expanding strong existing programs.

The difficulty here is not with the proposition, but with the political reality. In the public sectors, for example, we have recently seen the establishment of a major new campus dedicated to engineering, despite the critical shortage of engineering faculty members and the unused teaching capacity in existing programs in the region, both public and private. It simply makes no sense to award new educational programs and develop new institutions as regional political prizes, but who will adjudicate?

Third, we must insist on certain essential standards of quality across the institutional spectrum, and we must strive for the highest quality on our own campuses, not simply as an empty slogan in college catalogs, but as an everyday expectation.

The national spotlight is shifting from the schools to our colleges and universities, and it has begun to reveal much that is shoddy and second rate in our undergraduate programs. If we are unwilling to correct our deficiencies, others less well disposed to the welfare of higher education and with less love for learning will undertake the task. But who will address the fact that in some of our institutions, both public and private, there are programs of which we cannot be proud and whose value to students is marginal? Are we ready to act together, across the sectors, on this?

Fourth, we must work together to preserve equality of access and choice across sectors, preserving and enhancing the institutional diversity so essential to meeting the varied educational needs of our citizens. We must especially encourage the flow of talented minority students into graduate and professional programs that will supply the future generation of faculty members.

We have made substantial gains in recent years in attracting minority students to our undergraduate programs, but our record at the graduate level, especially in fields such as engineering and computer seicence, has been disappointing at best.

In 1982-83, for example, only twenty-nine black students completed Ph.D.'s in engineering and only thirty-two in the physical sciences. That, briefly stated, is the problem. But how can we address it? What together can we do to improve it? What can associations do to help us improve this situation?

Fifth, we must come to terms with the tuition gap between the public and independent institutions so that price more closely approximates costs, which are roughly the same in both sectors.

This fall, tuition and fees at four-year institutions will average $1,126, while at four-year independent colleges they will average $5,016. That price differential of almost five to one is a daunting prospect for many students and their families.

A recent poll of parents conducted by the National Institute of Independent Colleges and Universities indicated that although 37 percent of the parents would prefer to send their children to four-year private colleges, only 14 percent expected to do so. Most said they simply could not afford the cost of independent higher education.

We need a realistic tuition policy at our public institutions, coupled with state and federal aid that will permit student choice on bases other than price. It would be unfortunate for both sectors if only affluent and lower-income students were able to enroll in independent institutions while middle-income students could never select anything but public education.

This is not an issue that will go away, nor is it one about which there is candid discussion, either wihin the two sectors or between them. What principles should determine the price of a college education? What criteria should be used to establish tuition levels at public institutions? How do we begin to address the problems?

Sixth, both sectors must work together to find an acceptable pattern of public accountability that respects institutional autonomy. We all face this problem at the state and federal levels, in everything from state support for instruction to federal research funding and student financial aid. All of us have learned that public moneys bring with them public responsibilities, yet institutions in both sectors have a clear interest in ensuring that accountability has as its ultimate goal the enhancement of higher education through the preservation of its dual and distinctive sectors.

But how can we best achieve accountability? I believe that it must be based on academic results and on scholarly and professional standards rather than on financial expenditures. Institutions of higher education cannot long survive if they are regarded by either university administrators or public officials as utilities or state agencies, wherein standard accounting procedures and bottom-line results are regarded as the criteria of institutional effectiveness.

Of course, financial accountability is important, but it is not an end in itself. It is rather a means to an end, and the end is the effective education of the nation's college students and the effective discharge of our research and extension functions. Can we not jointly address this urgent question in a combined approach at both the state and federal level? What can associations do to provide models? One-day symposia won't help here. Careful analysis, rigorous research and thoughtful proposals are what we need.

All this implies we have work to do. Unless we address these questions, I see little hope of moving beyond well-meant platitudes and airy generalities into some pattern of effective partnership that will strengthen all of higher education.

I do not pretend that the task will be easy, for on our own campuses, each of us must deal with asbestos fibers and faculty petitions, microcomputers and union contracts, alumni groups and concerned parents, and the many concerns of students themselves. And we must do our jobs with budgets that too often seem to require some facility in manipulating loaves and fishes.

The danger is that, faced with these pressures, as Richard Cyert has observed, individuals who by nature desire excellence will begin to settle for mediocrity out of frustration. If we are candid, we are compelled to admit that we can begin to see danger signals in the larger enterprise, and we are compelled to acknowledge that self-protection, stagnant uniformity, and safe mediocrity are no substitutes for the bold experiment and constant striving that have long characterized the best of our dual system.

Despite our pressing campus concerns, we must make time in our schedules to serve as ambassadors for higher education generally, and we must enlist the support of others—our trustees, prominent alumni, and local legislators among them—in making the benefits of a strong and diverse system of higher education known in our statehouses and in Washington. And if we are to do that, we must first face and answer the hard questions I have posed.

I sometimes hear presidents, chancellors, and other high-level administrators say that they regret they no longer teach. I believe they are mistaken: all of us in positions of leadership teach every day in the way we undertake our administrative tasks. For, in the end, our primary responsibility is not to deal with admissions goals and program review, with fiscal stability and long-range projections, with persuasive approaches to legislators and convincing appeals to donors. Important as these are, they, too, are means, not ends.

The end is something infinitely more: it is, as Alfred North Whitehead once remarked, the creation of the future, so far as rational discourse and civilized means of appreciation can affect the issue. That is our institutional business. That is our leadership task. And it is a task so immense that it is worthy of the most openhearted and far-seeing partnership of all members—public, private, proprietary—of our educational enterprise.

The Politics of University Planning and Coordination

What role is a public college or university to play in its state's system of higher education? Which campuses will give doctoral degrees? Who will make these decisions? The answers to these critical questions relate directly to the organization, structure, and politics of a state's higher education system.

Since at least the 1950s these issues have been closely related to the growth of statewide systems of higher education coordination. The characteristics of coordinating mechanisms vary among the states, but they generally involve a state board charged with general planning responsibilities and sometimes program review and budget powers. In most states individual universities (or groups of universities) have their own governing boards in addition to the state coordinating board.

Universities have viewed the development of state coordinating systems with mixed emotions. University officials generally recognize the desirability for some type of rational planning mechanism. They are also aware of the advantage of having a structure that can respond to public concern about apparent duplication or inefficiency in higher education. On the other hand, each institution is likely to see the state structure as a potential barrier to certain of its own goals and plans. A university planning a new graduate program in a specific field may find the state board opposing it on the grounds that enough programs of that type already exist in the state. In order to respond to state financial problems, the state board may recommend enrollment limits or the elimination of graduate programs for specific campuses, actions not likely to win the approval of campus-based faculty members or administrators.

Callan and Johnson present a board view of trends in state planning for higher education. Norton's article is a straightforward statement of why these trends are likely to continue. Chambers, long a skeptic about state coordination, discusses the importance of maintaining the maximum amount of institutional autonomy.

In addition to questions about how the state coordinating process will operate are the related issues of what the role and mission of specific institution will be. Will coordination lead to a leveling and homogenization of higher education, or will it help institutions maintain individuality and preserve a unique role? The last three chapters address these kinds of issues. Munitz discusses the problem of the multicampus university in attempting to establish and develop a special mission for each campus. Moos, in a study prepared primarily for the University of Maryland, provides a look at the historical development and future role of land-grant universities. Finally, Birnbaum speculates about the future of the nation's many state colleges and universities, those which were once teachers' colleges in many cases and which Alden Dunham called the "colleges of the forgotten Americans."

17. Trends in Statewide Planning and Coordination

Patrick M. Callan/Richard W. Jonsen

Historically, the pattern of development of higher education in the United States has been highly decentralized; crucial decisions have, in the past, been more often made by individual institutions than by system, state, or federal authorities. In the past twenty years statewide planning and coordination have become increasingly important. The coordinating boards were established by legislatures and governors to assist states in determining state policy in postsecondary education while maintaining the traditional decentralized approach to governance and management. Both the authority and the effectiveness of these agencies have varied widely from state to state. But during this period the primary function of these agencies has been to coordinate growth.

In the 1980s, for most states, the main agency task will be coordinating responses to decline, either in the size of higher education or the fiscal resources available to do it. The tools available for fulfilling this function will be the same tools available during the past decade, but they will have to be used differently. Of course, the phenomenon of decline in enrollment and resources is by no means certain; the decline in the size of the traditional college-age cohort will affect college enrollments in various states in very different ways, and will be modified by factors within and outside of institutional control. Still, demographic changes, the fiscal health of states, and other important factors such as the emergence of noncollegiate institutions and agencies providing educational services, and the increasing competition among institutions for students and resources, are likely to increase reliance on and expectations of statewide planning and coordination. The interdependence of institutions and the complexity of the postsecondary systems that have developed in response to growth suggests greater emphasis on coordination in periods of decline. Examples of that interdependence and complexity are the effects of changes in ad-

---

Patrick M. Callan is director of the California Post Secondary Education Commission. Richard W. Jonsen is deputy director of the Western Interstate Commission on Higher Education (WICHE).

mission or tuition policies in one institution (or sector) on enrollments in another; the effects of off-campus programs at one institution on programs at other institutions; the unequal and potentially destructive competition that can arise between public and independent institutions as a consequence of market pressures.

Because of the magnitude of the typical state investment in higher education, governors and legislatures will expect coordinating agencies and governing boards to develop rational solutions to these difficult problems. The success of these statewide structures has always depended on a volatile mixture of confidence and authority granted them by the legislative and executive branches of state government; on the ability, creativity, and courage of their executives and staffs; on the cooperation and trust they share with the institutions; on recognition by institutions of their long-term self-interest in fair and procedurally proper coordination. Boards and institutions must work harder to establish the common ground of their interest in strengthening higher education.

Most of the problems related to enrollment declines and demographic changes will be solved by the resourceful and courageous actions of institutional leaders. But some problems—even for the ablest of institutional leaders—will need resolution at the state level by the decisions and recommendations of the statewide planning agencies if they are strong and effective or, if they are not, in arenas where partisan politics or the most narrow fiscal perspectives may predominate.

The responsibilities of coordinating boards vary by the functions assigned to them and by the strength and authority with which those functions are performed. The common duties can be characterized as planning, budget review, and program review.

Planning

During growth periods, planning included identifying future needs and institutional and system responses, such as finding sites for new campuses. Now, the critical planning decisions involve reallocation of resources: systematic and programmatic changes necessary to respond to new student needs and interests, new clientele, new delivery systems, and new institutional "providers." An elaboration of some specific planning issues follows. Much greater coordination of effort among institutions, through close examination of institutional roles and missions, will be imperative to planning in the 1980s. Planners will be challenged to preserve the richness and responsiveness to the market that continues to be one of the strengths of American higher education. Planning has been a chronically weak function. In the future, planning may be increasingly linked to authority through the budget and program review.

Budget Review

The question of how state dollars are to be spent is a crucial element in the reallocation of resources. The degree of state agency responsibility for the budget varies a good deal. Governing boards typically submit a consolidated budget to the legislature. Coordinating boards may also do that, or may recommend or simply review and comment on the budgets prepared by institutions or systems. This activity lies at the heart of the agency's operational authority or influence.

Program Review

Despite the centrality of budget review, program review in state agencies has been more controversial and better publicized. The review of proposed programs gives state agencies the ability to prevent duplication among public institutions, and, to a lesser extent, between public and private institutions. But where such reviews have resulted in the closing of programs, as in Washington, New York, and Louisiana, institutions can be expected to challenge the fairness, appropriateness, and legitimacy of the action. More than any other function of statewide boards, program review has the potential to create accountability approved by the legislature and planning that can be used by campus leaders to deflect some of the "heat" for difficult, though warranted, decisions.

Within the three broad functions of statewide agencies, a number of specific issues will, in most states, need serious attention in the 1980s.

Governance

The trend toward consolidated statewide governing boards in the public sector has slowed. As interinstitutional and intersegmental competition for scarce resources and student becomes more intense, perhaps even hostile, governors and legislators may insist on reconsidering governance structures to limit such competition. Consolidating groups of institutions into systems under single statewide boards does not necessarily solve this problem. Many statewide multicampus systems, and institutional boards have been reluctant to define sharply the mission of their institutions if that definition curtails their aspirations. Boards should strengthen their resolve to define institutional missions and to allocate both responsibility and functions to make the most efficient use of total resources.

Social Justice

A major part of the unfinished agenda of the 1960s and 1970s is the equalizing of educational opportunity. Many minority and low-income groups were left behind in the expansion of access to postsecondary education during the last two decades. The state coordinating agencies should lead the efforts to improve opportunity for traditionally underrepresented groups by improving academic preparation, support services, counseling, etc. Opportunities at the graduate and professional levels, as well as in baccalaureate and associate programs, shoud be stressed. Agencies must ensure that programs designed to enhance opportunity are carefully designed and rigorously evaluated. These programs should expand eligibility and opportunity rather than help individual colleges and universities compete with one another for the underrepresented students most likely to matriculate.

Student Aid

In the past, student aid programs were of more concern to the private than the public sector. The pressure to implement or increase tuitions at public institutions will engender a serious review of student aid policies in many states. Such pressure may come from legislatures and from institutions searching for dollars to compensate for constrained general revenue funds and changes in the federal student aid programs, illustrated by the battle over BEOG support levels and the efforts to control costs of the Guaranteed Student Loan Program. Issues that should be addressed include the relationship of state and federal aid program; equity issues involving the appropriate combination of grants and various categories of students; and treatment of nontraditonal students (adults, part-time), independent students, middle-income students, students in private vocational programs, and students attending "high-cost" institutions. The growth of federal and state student assistance programs, both in total dollars and in numbers of students served, and the growing proportion of total postsecondary education expenditures represented by aid have made financial assistance an important aspect of postsecondary education finance. Significant shifts in funding policy could take place because of the student aid issue.

State Policies Pertaining to the Independent Sector

In many states, student aid programs have been the foundation of policies pertaining to the independent sector. As costs rise and student pools decline, the adequancy of student aid programs will be questioned. Decision makers will be pressed to consider institutional types of aid, general "tuition-offset" grants, and policies regarding failing private institutions. On the other hand, the cost saving to the states, once a powerful argument for state support to the private colleges (access could be achieved at a lower cost per student to the state), is less compelling when declining enrollments may produce empty seats in public institutions. Few statewide coordinating agencies have achieved a systematic planning perspective that considers institutions in both public and private sectors, acting together to meet the total higher education needs of the state. Increasingly, they will be obligated to do so. Off-campus programs involving the private sector will surely be an item on many state agendas. Private and public institutions will be competing for the same adults, often at similar tuition rates; because such programs support themselves, some coordination of this activity may be necessary to prevent waste and duplication.

Relationships with Secondary Education

The concern and jurisdictions of secondary and postsecondary institutions overlap in an increasing number of cases, including adult and vocational education. From the perspective of the student or consumer the distinctions between the two sectors may be fairly arbitrary. Eliminating overlap and duplication should be a priority of the respective state agencies responsible for secondary and postsecondary education. Better working relationships between these two agencies is needed in most states.

Secondary and postsecondary institutions and agencies have a mutual interest in the improved academic preparation of students. Secondary and postsecondary educators and public officials share the concern over declining test scores and growing costs of remediation at the postsecondary level. All too often, public criticism and recrimination (Who produced the poorly prepared students? Who trained the teachers that didn't teach?) have been more common than joint efforts to identify and alleviate problems. Statewide coordinating agencies, as well as chief state school officers, should be leaders in developing cooperative approaches.

Educational Opportunities for Adults

Statewide agencies have been ill-equipped to deal with this issue because it increases the range and number of educational "providers" in their planning. Nevertheless, demand (more adults seeking access to learning opportunities), supply (efforts of colleges and universities to expand clientele by appealing to adults), and some other factors (such as new learning technology, changed manpower needs, equity considerations) may force serious review of financing, coordinating, and evaluating lifelong learning.

Funding Patterns

Allocation to instruction, research, and public service. The classic functions of higher education are instruction, research, and public service. Of these, instruction has been the most heavily subsidized by state funds in the public sector. Research has been heavily subsidized by federal funds, and public service by private funds (payments for service in the case of continuing education, foundation and other philanthropic support in the case of innovative community service programs). Financial pressures, societal demands, changes in the internal structure of institutions, and realignments in the relationships among education, the corporate sector, and government may necessitate a rethinking of the present policies that determine the proportions of state support going to these activities.

In some states, establishing new policy means reconsidering the way state funding formulas allocate resources among these activities, as well as reviewing the equity and efficiency of the formulas themselves. Declining enrollments expose the weaknesses of the formulas in "downside" budgeting, where reductions based on averages may be greater than marginal dollar savings. Formulas should be sensitive to fixed as well as variable costs as enrollments decline, should avoid excessive incentives for expansion or punitive losses for decline, and should reduce incentives for cutthroat competition for students.

Quality

As traditional institutions embrace new clients and as new providers enter the learning arena (and become eligible to receive federal and even state student aid), threats to the quality of education become more widespread. The present arrangement for assessing and ensuring quality have been widely criticized, but new structures and new alignments have not yet been forged. Consumer protection and accountability will create pressure (from the public and legislators, respectively) for statewide agencies to involve themselves, to a much greater extent, with standards of quality, assessing institutions by those standards, and enforcing sanctions. Also at issue is the relationship and distribution of power among the three accrediting "partners": states, the federal government, and accrediting associations. These problems will have to be solved satisfactorily if higher education is not to be harmed greatly by loss of public confidence.

State-Federal Relationships

State officials worry about the new Department of Education and federal intentions to respect the state primacy regarding federal policies and practices. Few federal programs at the postsecondary level are coordinated or even channeled through the states. The bulk of federal support for postsecondary education goes directly to students via student aid and veterans' benefits or to institutions for research. The recent battles in some states over "reappropriation" of federal dollars signal the growing importance of this issue, and the need for thoughtful state solutions.

Interinstitutional Cooperation

For years, voluntary cooperation (such as consortium arrangements) has been touted as an alternative to coordinated and centralized planning. The traditional independence of institutions and the academic reward system have effectively barred the extensive development of voluntary academic coordination. Institutions and their faculties hold the keys to the development of truly imaginative interinstitutional activities. States may need to think of new inducements and sanctions to increase interinstitutinal and interstate cooperation. Such cooperation will save money and increase programmatic and institutional effectiveness.

Mission, Role, and Scope

The independent and frequently uncoordinated growth of institutions of higher education has resulted in duplication of mission among institutions in the same locale, state, or region. This competition often has been beneficial. But some activities may be overdeveloped, some programs may be unnecessarily duplicative, some needs may not be met. Where resources continue to be limited seriously, states may wish to look seriously at institutional missions, emphasizing and augmenting distinctive institutions, cutting back on missions or functions that duplicate each other, and revising some institutional missions wherein more effective attention to underserved needs is needed.

The political position of the statewide agencies is sensitive and unstable, and the environment of the 1980s offers little hope of stabilization. Resource constraints and competition for students are likely to intensify conflict—among institutions as well as between institutions and external agencies. The business of coordination is increasingly the business of conflict—and of the resolution of conflict through negotiation and consultation with state and institutional leaders, based on a broad and independent public-interest perspective. The agency and its board must achieve and maintain credibility with politicians (governors and legislators) and be sensitive to the severe pressures on public resources and to the need for efficiency and cost savings. The agency must also maintain the trust of institutions, which means appreciating the importance of institutional authority, quality, and traditional academic values. If the state agency fails in its task, the result will probably be intensified hostility between higher education and state government which will, in turn, predictably lead to more direct oversight of higher education through the political process.

A fundamental question stimulated by the forgoing discussions is this: Can the traditional value of decentralized governance be maintained while the states, the coordinating bodies, and postsecondary institutions face an increasing number of problems requiring sensitivity to interinstitutional and intersegmental considerations? Also, can these competing and legitimate values continue in a state of productive tension so as to improve the way in which the total system functions? The answers will not be uniform, perhaps not even similar, as these issues and forces play themselves out in each state. Even tentative resolutions and accommodations will be shaped largely by the history, traditions, and politics of each state and by the quality of institutional and coordinating agency leadership.

The negotiated resolution of these problems, especially the quality of the relationship between the institution and the coordinating agencies, cannot be overemphasized. Institutions will need to determine how their self-interest can be served through coordination, and coordinating agencies will need to increase their sensitivity to the "academic culture," and be effective interpreters of that culture to the political branches. The ultimate test is the quality of service—instructional, research, public service—rendered to society by the system of higher education. Institutions will provide that service and determine its quality. Statewide agencies can add a critical and valuable ingredient to the decisions that are needed to make such service possible.

18. Ambiguities in the Administration of Public University Systems
Lawrence K. Pettit

Like political science—or perhaps as an emerging branch of that discipline—the study of higher education governance has one unremitting, unassailable (and quite bothersome) law: "It varies from state to state." Consider the organization of public universities into systems. Over one-third of the states (Wisconsin, North Carolina, Oregon, Montana, Maine, for example) consolidate all state universities into a single system with only one state governing board. In California the various "segments" (doctoral universities, other state universities, community colleges) are organized into separate statewide systems. Illinois supports several public university systems, quite different from one another in most respects. Texas supports thirty-seven public senior universities under fifteen different governing boards, six of which govern systems.

Some systems, called "unitary" by Magrath,[1] are essentially single universities with multiple locations. In these arrangements the positions of CEO at the dominant flagship campus and system CEO may be merged. Other systems may resemble single universities because of nomenclature ["The University of (common name) at (different locations)"], but the campuses may have equal legal status, and all campus CEOs report to the same system CEO. Moreover, commonality of campus names does not in itself signal highly centralized authority within a system. Other systems may be highly centralized despite the absence of commonality in campus names. The dissimilarity of names in such cases, however, may result in the component institutions' not being recognized as parts of a system, even in generally reliable national directories. Some designated systems may be only loosely organized as federations with weak central executive authority, often with campus CEOs reporting directly to the board.

Lawrence K. Pettit is chancellor of the Southern Illinois University System. A political scientist, he received his Ph.D. from the University of Wisconsin, taught at Pennsylvania State University, and was head of the political science department at Montana State University. He has been an administrator for the American Council on Education, CEO of the Montana University System, deputy commissioner of the Texas Coordinating Board, and chancellor of the University System of South Texas.

The variety in system arrangements should not mask the important fact that most public universities do not have their own boards, and a significant number of public university presidents and chancellors do not report directly to boards, but to system chancellors or presidents.[2] This phenomenon is not really new, yet insufficient literary attention has been given to system administration by scholars, practitioners, and management experts, and there are few operational guidelines for the appropriate interaction between the system CEO's office and the campus CEO in such matters as implementation of board policy, effective management of the campuses, and ultimate administrative resolution of grievances and other personnel matters.

The rationale for a university system is that it is less cumbersome and more cost effective than it would be were each public university to have its own board. In addition, the system arrangement should enhance interinstitutional cooperation to disperse program availability and enrich campus curricula without costly duplication. Finally, complementary missions and program development under system direction should help achieve state or regional objectives most effectively and efficiently. Joseph Kauffman argues that the "justification for a system is planned, purposeful diversity to serve all of the population better, improved planning and coordination, and keeping the state government officials from deciding academic program and educational priorities by making those tough priority decisions *within the system.*"[3]

If this rationale is to be valid, effective administrative direction of campus activities is required from the system office. Lee and Bowen have written that appropriate system governance, in addition to guaranteeing a high level of campus autonomy, has "direct operational responsibility and is accountable to the state for the sum activity across campuses."[4]

Is it possible for a lay board of trustees, whose members convene only periodically throughout the year, to provide sustained direction of a system in the absence of a strong and effective system executive? Campus CEOs may prefer a weak system CEO to whom they do not report directly, thus allowing them easier access to the board. But such an arrangement might also invite board meddling in campus administrative matters, something that might more easily be prevented if a strong system CEO stands between the board and the campus CEOs. A strong system CEO is not always something to be feared by the campuses. In a ground-breaking study of multicampus sytems, Lee and Bowen concluded that "in the face of pressures to centralize, multicampus systems have been unusually sensitive to the values of individual campuses. As often as not, increased systemwide activity has focused on improving the quality of campus decision making, not on preempting judgments at the systemwide lvel."[5] Moreover, board cohesion under the leadership of the chairman should be enhanced with a more streamlined, centralized reporting pattern, avoiding the formation of a series of campus CEO-board member alliances in the pursuit of parochial goals.

If accountability to the state "for the sum activity across campuses" is to be met, what kinds of authority must repose in the system office?[6] This is not the kind of question typically asked by individuals paralyzed by the prospect of dissension. As Clark Kerr puts it, "The governance of systems is one of the really sore points in American higher education; a few systems seem to exist on the verge of explosion."[7]

In most systems there is probably some discordance between the official allocation of authority through the policy manual on the one hand, and the evolution of administrative practices and procedures on the other. Practices, even if they vary with policy, achieve a legitimacy simply through their repetition, and changing them strains relationships. In that regard, a timid or laissez-faire system CEO may create an untenable circumstance for a successor if he or she allows or encourages practices that undermine his or her formal authority. As Kauffman writes, "The role of the system president . . . will most often be shaped by the early incumbents, rather than by written definitions."[8] In addition, board members may have a proper sense of authority patterns in the abstract but be unable to understand the appropriate translation into practice. In one case involving the creation of a new system, the board routinely affirmed the system CEO's authority over the campus CEOs but unwittingly took actions that undermined that authority.

This all reflects a basic, positive characteristic of academe: persons associated with higher education, whether trustees, administrators, or faculty members, would rather focus attention on the achievement of educational goals than on the organization and implementation of authority. There is something selfless and acceptable about the former, something self-serving and unseemly about the latter. Yet the two are closely related, and in order for university systems to function smoothly in the pursuit of their goals it is essential that policy-making boards occasionally give organized attention to the allocation and exercise of formal authority. As Barry

Munitz observes, "It is amazing how many regents and trustees of multicampus boards have never had a meaningful discussion about the structure itself with their colleagues and their administrators."[9]

Within multicampus systems the relationship that defines the system's character is between the system CEO and the campus CEOs. Even in those cases wherein the two kinds of executives emerge from essentially the same recruitment pool and could easily be interchangeable, the different requirements of their positions result in a clash of perspectives, so that a smooth accommodation between them does not come naturally but must be achieved through effort and strategy. The responsibility of higher education executives may be depicted in a continuum from those most responsible for implementing external controls to those most relied upon to protect institutional autonomy, as shown in Figure 1.

Figure 1

*Chief Decision Makers
in Public Higher Education Systems*

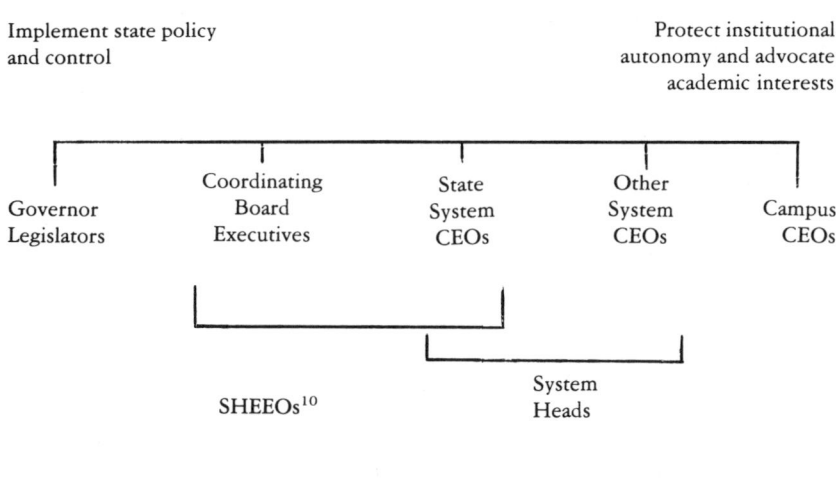

Although both the system executive and the campus executive occupy the "autonomy" side of the continuum, the system executive still has more of a "public" and less a "campus" identity and set of responsibilities than does the campus CEO.[11] It is this seemingly small degree of difference in role that impedes the system executive's shaping and sustaining a visible, legitimate presence conducive to meeting administrative responsibilities. Lee and Bowen conclude, for example, that "midway between state and campuses, system administrators are often the focus of the discontents of both," and that "in attempting to satisfy campuses and state, the multicampus system runs the very real risk of losing the backing of each."[12]

The first of these impediments is the problem of visibility and identity. In contrast to systems, universities are concrete entities, and their names bring to mind vivid images of the collegiate environment and its host of enterprises. People can relate to a *university* in a variety of ways; they understand what it does. Similarly, the public knows essentially what a university president or chancellor is—his or her identity derives from the institution's. A university *system,* on the other hand, is more of an abstraction, particularly when there is no commonality of names among its component institutions or between them and the system itself. All of the events in higher education of which the public is aware happen at particular universities, not at "systems." Unless the system president or chancellor is closely identified with the flagship institution (to the point that he or she virtually eclipses the flagship CEO), that individual will have the same identity and visibility problems as the system itself does: a job that is an abstraction in the public mind. Since the system CEO works with small, attentive publics anyway, this may not cripple his or her performance, but it is one example of a disadvantage in comparison with the campus CEOs who report to him or her, and several such incidences could significantly weaken the authority of the system CEO.

Second is the problem of constituency. Students, faculty members, alumni, athletic boosters, financial contributors, townspeople, the local news media, local legislators, and other political figures may support and identify with a university, but seldom with a university system. The campus CEO is the leader and orchestrator of this potentially powerful constituency, which belongs to the institution he or she heads. The campus CEO enjoys the luxury of acting as an unrestrained advocate of a single campus, regardless of what system or public-interest considerations may dictate. The system CEO does not have such an automatic constituency and must continually balance the interest of one such alliance against others within the system. He or she may command formal authority and a great deal of responsibility, but virtually no loyalty.[13] The system CEO has no constituency per se. He or she depends solely on the unremitting support of trustees, many of whom may be alumni or, in some other sense, partisans of institutions he or she supervises.

Next is the problem of ceremonial prerogative. As stated above, public events take place on campuses, not at system headquarters. Unless there is an explicit board policy or strong custom to the contrary, the campus CEO commands what takes place on home turf, and only personal decency, courtesy, or political acumen may motivate him or her to accord to the system CEO a visible role at commencements, football games, social events, and other campus ceremonies. The view of the campus CEO is valid: he or she needs to remain visibly in control in order to be effective; the individual campus, not the system, is usually what attracts or generates most social and ceremonial events; and the support work involved is performed by campus, not system, personnel. In addition, some campus CEOs believe their effectiveness with both campus and external groups is impaired if they are forced to demonstrate publicly that they report to a system executive rather than directly to the board. The system CEO has another perspective on all of this, especially if he or she resides in one of the campus communities. To include the system CEO at such events as only another face in the crowd, albeit in the VIP section, is symbolically to disassociate that person from the institution's administration (and from his or her profession) and place him or her in the category of its public supporters.

Finally, a residual problem that results from the combined effects of the first three is that of legitimacy. Most system CEOs have probably encountered the blank stare that says, "Who are you and why should you be concerned?" Although campus CEOs may understand perfectly the reporting requirements within their particular systems, their administrative subordinates may not; the faculty is even less likely to understand (and might be horrified if it did), and students seldom know that the system office exists. The prevailing view among those on campus below the rank of vice president is probably that the system CEO is a chief of staff to the board who directs clerical tasks and coordinates agenda, but for whom it is wholly inappropriate to attempt to exert executive authority over the campus. This is an accurate portrayal of some systems and is likely to constitute the campus perspective at others. The reason is twofold: (1) the strongly held, venerated norms and values of the academic tradition create a perceptual screen that makes it easy for an academic to view the system office as a nest of clerks, and (2) the problems expressed earlier—identity and visibility, constituency and ceremonial prerogative—obfuscate the legitimate claim the system CEO has to the exercise of executive authority. Formal authority may be enshrined in the policy manual, but if its exercise is not accepted as appropriate, it lacks legitimacy.[14]

The Kerr Commission on Presidential Leadership recommended that systemwide boards accept special responsibility "to see that a proper balance of authority and responsibility exists between the system and campus heads."[15] In confronting that charge, boards need to understand that the problem of legitimacy requires that in addition to allocating power through the policy manual, they must also support those customs and practices that facilitate the appropriate exercise of authority, and they should award those perquisites that symbolize authority in a manner consonant with the formal allocation of authority itself.

Twelve Salient Authority Relationships[16]

In the twelve dimensions and symbols of system CEO authority discussed below, the first option under each heading represents the highest degree of system authority, the second represents an accommodation between system and campus prerogative, and the third characterizes the most decentralized model, with weak system authority and maximum campus autonomy.

1. Appointment and dismissal of campus presidents
(a) System CEO appoints and board ratifies; system CEO dismisses or recommends dismissal and board ratifies.
(b) System CEO plays a significant role in the appointment, is on the search committee or designates its members, and/or recommends to the board with the board formally appointing the campus CEOs; system CEO recommends dismissal, but the board reaches an independent decision.
(c) System CEO plays essentially a clerical role in the search/selection process; system CEO does not recommend dismissal of campus CEOs.

2. Reporting pattern and access to the board
(a) Campus CEOs report to the system CEO; system CEO reports to the board.

(b) Campus CEOs submit to system coordination or authority on some matters but have direct access to the board; system CEO's authority is derivative, as spokesperson for the board, rather than inherent in executive role. In this arrangement, system CEO and campus CEOs are usually of equal *official* status, but campus CEOs enjoy more prestige.

(c) Campus CEOs report directly to the board; system CEO also reports to the board and performs services for campus CEOs as well; central office is viewed essentially as a clerical/service operation and does not exercise supervisory or administrative authority over the campuses.

3. Setting the board agenda

(a) The agenda going to the board are the system CEO's agenda, who approves all campus agenda in advance and makes the recommendations.

(b) Agenda are mixed: the campus CEOs propose their own agenda, on which system CEO may make independent recommendations, and the system CEO formulates hir or her own agenda. Campus agenda go to the board even if system CEO's independent recommendation is negative.

(c) System CEO simply transmits campus agenda to the board; his or her own agenda are essentially "housekeeping" items.

4. Presentations at board meetings

(a) All action items presented by system CEO. Campus CEOs have minimal role at board meetings and, within a very large system, may not even attend except at invitation of system CEO.

(b) System CEO calls campus CEOs to present campus-related agenda; system CEO presents other agenda and coordinates all presentations.

(c) Board chairman calls on campus CEOs directly to present items related to their respective campuses; system CEO performs essentially clerical duties at board meetings.

5. Personnel decisions

(a) System CEO signs off on all hirings, promotions, and awards of tenure before recommending to the board; system office is locus of final administrative decisions on personnel appeals. Where there is bargaining, system CEO is the official management spokesperson.

(b) System CEO routinely accepts personnel recommendations of campus CEOs and incorporates them into recommendations to the board. Only rarely are personnel disputes appealed to system

CEO. Where there is bargaining, system CEO and campus CEOs have shared, "team" authority on behalf of management.
(c) Campus personnel recommendations go directly to the board without a recommendation from the system CEO. Personnel appeals go directly from the campus CEO to the board. In bargaining, campus CEOs have authority delegated directly to them by the board. System CEO's role is essentially clerical and supportive.

6. Operating budgets and appropriations requests
(a) System CEO approves all campus operating budgets and submits consolidated appropriations requests to the board.
(b) System CEO transmits campus operating budgets and appropriations requests to the board with independent recommendations.
(c) System CEO transmits operating budgets and appropriations requests to the board without formal recommendations.

7. Academic program review
(a) System office initiates and conducts or supervises academic program reviews.
(b) System CEO may initiate or propose program reviews, but they are conducted at the campus level and usually initiate there.
(c) Campuses initiate and conduct academic program reviews without direction from the system office.

8. Contracts for goods and services
(a) System CEO acts on all major campus construction, service, and purchasing contracts, either giving final approval or making the final administrative recommendation to the board.
(b) System CEO does not give final approval but transmits to the board, with recommendations, most significant contracts.
(c) All contracts are approved and signed locally on the campuses or are transmitted directly to the board without system office approval or recommendation.

9. Legislative relations
(a) All legislative relations are conducted by the system CEO, who gives consolidated testimony on appropriations; campus CEOs do not go to legislature without clearance from system CEO.
(b) System CEO coordinates legislative relations and involves campus CEOs who may participate actively.
(c) Campus CEOs conduct their own legislative relations without supervision by the system CEO, or the board itself conducts and controls legislative relations and system CEO has no particular role, or no greater role than the campus CEO's.

10. Recruitment pathways
(a) System CEO is expected to have credentials and background similar to campus CEOs' and may have been a campus CEO earlier.
(b) System CEO is more likely to have spent part of his or her career in government or politics, and the time invested thereby may have resulted in fewer academic accomplishments than those of the typical campus CEO, whose career is more likely to have been entirely academic.
(c) System CEO is not likely to have been either a political executive or a campus CEO but is more likely to have been recruited from the same bureaucratic pool as state agency heads.

11. Compensation package
(a) System CEO is paid more than campus CEOs and has similar or better provisions for housing, automobile, entertaining, and other executive perquisites.
(b) System CEO has equal or higher official salary than campus CEOs' but does not have as effective access to perquisites and lifestyle maintenance, and total compensation may be less than major campus CEOs.
(c) System CEO is paid less than major campus CEOs within the system.

12. Fund raising
(a) There is one consolidated foundation for the system, with centralized fund raising, and the system CEO is the primary linkage to the foundation board.
(b) There is a single foundation but with separate accounts for each campus and mostly decentralized fund raising; campus CEOs are likely to have more extensive development staffs than does system CEO.
(c) Each campus has its own affiliated foundation, independent of the governing board and the system CEO. System CEO and staff do not have access to private funds.

Because of the several limitations on a system CEO's exercise of authority, not the least of which is authoritative ambiguity, one could argue that the only significant leverage the system CEO has in working with campus CEOs is the power to hire and fire them.[17] In the absence of that prerogative, the system CEO may be left in a posture of constantly negotiating authority while responsibility and accountability remain constant. Moreover, if the sytem CEO does not have the authority to appoint and dismiss administrative subordinates, the only avenue of appeal in cases where his or her authority is questioned is to the board, and the very process of invoking the board's adjudication places the two contestants on an equal footing and suggests that there is no administrative hierarchy through which such disputes can be settled.

Whatever the pattern of authority relationships, board members must adjust their expectations of accountability to the realities of power dispersion. Obviously, if a system CEO's role is typified by option "c" in each of the twelve examples presented, one does not have an effective system in the sense that while the member institutions may be governed by a common board, they are not administered as a system by an effective CEO. In such a case the board can hardly hold the system CEO accountable for much beyond getting the agenda materials to them on time. If any system is accurately described in option three for any one of the twelve dimensions, the system CEO is seriously weakened. At a minimum, system authority patterns should follow option one in dimensions two, three, and eleven; in addition, if the system CEO is held accountable for what happens on the campuses, he or she should have the power of appointment as represented in option one in the first locus of authority listed. The political and academic cultures (meaning the history, traditions, customs, and patterns of attitudes associated with both politics and higher education in a particular state or region) will dictate these authority relationships to some extent, but in any setting there should be some latitude for governing boards to make deliberate decisions about how they will allocate authority between system CEOs and campus CEOs. Many of the campus and system CEOs involved would probably be as interested in the elimination of ambiguity as in the allocation of authority itself.

Power and Purpose

The only justification of power is the purpose it is to serve, and all higher education administrators would do well to remind themselves of that daily. If we cannot justify effective power in the hands of system CEOs, then we should not have systems. We must remember our calling to serve *students*. Creating optimum opportunity for high-quality education is certainly our central purpose, but we have public service and research responsibilities as well and, deriving from those, the obligations of interpreting and transmitting a cultural heritage and enhancing the present cultural environment.

How does a university best create, transmit, and use knowledge?

Between the extremes of the anarchist who believes that society will automatically support a faculty and that students will miraculously appear in the absence of any administration at all, and the cost accountant or systems engineer who believes that all functions in higher education should be uniform and justified by quantitative measurement, there must be a middle ground. Surely each campus must be accorded sufficient autonomy to pursue its unique mission in its particular location, and the educational process should be as unfettered as possible. High quality usually is associated with the maintenance of traditional faculty prerogatives in academic matters, and where the actual work of instruction, research, and public service takes place, there should be little administrative interference. We all subscribe to that catechism, but we sometimes differ on what it means. Often both campus and system administrations are simultaneously accused by the state of being overly protective of faculty autonomy and accused by the faculty of ignoring scripture from the AAUP Redbook.

Public universities exist in a political environment of strong countervailing claims on the public purse and, especially in recent years, the growth, legitimation, and acceptance into the political mainstream of anti-intellectual cults. Standing at the nexus of politics and academe are those CEOs who report directly to boards; in order to protect and promote public higher education, these executives have leadership responsibilities that extend far beyond the day-to-day stewardship of campus affairs. Stanley Ikenberry has lucidly formulated the leadership requirements of higher education. In his scheme, the responsibilities are (1) the articulation of a system of values and beliefs, (2) the integration of higher education within the larger environment, and (3) the creative use of power, including the capacity to create power and the willingness to disperse it.[18]

The broad purpose guiding system CEOs is to create the best possible external and internal environments for the campuses to achieve their missions and goals. In dealing with external decision makers—for example, legislators and governors—the system CEO is held accountable for what happens on the campuses, and insofar as that CEO lacks authority to affect what happens on the campuses, his or her effectiveness in representing them is undercut. This is not to say that the sytem CEO should be involved in day-to-day operations, but that he or she should have effective line authority over campus CEOs and should be kept informed by them regularly.

It may be helpful to think of the system CEO's responsibilities as comprising three sets of functions: nurturing, leading, and managing. The first requires that the system CEO
1. promote academic values in general and the particular norms and values of the individual campuses,
2. provide the support and autonomy necessary for the campuses to achieve their missions effectively,
3. promote diversity within the system and the uniqueness of each institution, and
4. remain attentive to the needs of the campuses and serve as the conduit for the expression of their views to the board and other important groups and individuals.

The second set involves leading, wherein the system CEO should
1. provide for the campuses a unified and coherent presence in the region, state, and nation,
2. shape the development of a culture for the system that enables it to establish priorities, articulate a purpose, and plan for the future,[19]
4. coordinate the external relations of the system, maintaining communications that clarify for others the missions and aspirations of the campuses and that create shared meanings within the system,
5. provide adequate vision for the charting of new directions for the system and its campuses, and
6. coordinate and direct strategic planning for the complementary, rather than competitive, development of the campuses.

Finally, there is an administrative or managerial set of functions appropriate to the system CEO: managing, involving the responsibility to
1. discharge administratively the legal responsibilities of the board, and meet the collective and individual accountability of the campuses to the state,
2. interpret and implement board policy, and
3. oversee (but not be directly involved in) the general management of the campuses.

The preceding discussion should clear away some of the ego-threatening brambles that inhibit the open discussion of system

CEO-campus CEO authority relationships. One could hope that as long as the system CEO and campus CEO are reasonable persons with shared values and a common organizational purpose, they would resolve any differences that emerge. But good will and shared values are probably not enough, in the face of cultural and structural frustrations, to ensure the exercise of legitimate authority by either kind of executive. The governing board alone has the prerogative of defining power relationships, and it has enormous influence in establishing customs and promoting practices consonant with the officially defined pattern of authority. Systems are here to stay, and the objectives of higher education would be best served by reducing ambiguity where it now exists in the system CEO's authority, and by granting to system administrators the authority to do their jobs.

Notes

[1] C. Peter Magrath, "Mini-System, Maxi-System, Land-Grant System: One Participant's Perceptions," in *The Monday Morning Imagination: Report from the Boyer Workshop on State University Systems* (New York: Aspen Institute, 1976).

[2] Clark Kerr reports that "more than one-half of all students in the United States are on campuses that are parts of systems, and approximately one-half of all public campuses . . . are combined within systems." Clark Kerr, *Presidents Make a Difference: Strengthening Leadership in Colleges and Universities* (Washington: Association of Governing Boards of Universities and Colleges, 1984).

Creswell, Roskens, and Henry illustrate the variety in developing a typology of multicampus systems. Their typology includes four factors: control (public or private), jurisdiction of board (statewide or less), comparability of campuses within the system (homogeneous or heterogeneous), and administrative structure (separate central office of flagship administration). The infancy of efforts at understanding and classifying systems is reflected in the fact that their "complete list of U.S. systems" omits several. John W. Creswell et al., "A Typology of Multicampus Systems," *Journal of Higher Education,* 56:1.

[3] Joseph F. Kauffman, *At the Pleasure of the Board: The Service of the College or University President* (Washington, D.C.: American Council on Education, 1980), p. 72.

[4] Eugene C. Lee and Frank M. Bowen, *Managing Multicampus Systems: Effective Administration in an Unsteady State* (San Francisco: Jossey-Bass, 1975), p. 148.

[5] Lee and Bowen, p. 147.

[6] Magrath argues that a "small university system must operate on a unitary basis, even though the fiction is preserved that there is [only] a coordinating [system CEO] . . . the ultimate chief executive, whatever the title, must be perceived as the central directing officer. . . . . This much is expected of these chief executives, both by their boards and by the state governments." He adds that in large systems it is possible for the system CEO to be simply a planning, coordinating, and political chief executive, but that even here the system CEO "must have discretion to call the shots on issues that become salient statewide educational concerns" (Magrath, pp. 19-20.).

[7]Kerr, p. 71.

[8]Kauffman, p. 66.

[9]Barry Munitz, "Memo to a Multicampus Trustee From a Flagship CEO," *AGB Reports,* September/October 1981, p. 23.

[10]In an earlier work Kirkpatrick and I focused on all statewide higher education executive officers (SHEEOs), both those who work for coordinating boards and those who are CEOs of consolidated statewide systems. Lawrence K. Pettit and Samuel A. Kirkpatrick, "Combat Leaders Without Troops: State Higher Education Executives," *Educational Record,* Summer 1984.

[11]Millett formulates the difference as follows: "The system chief executive officer should be perceived as having fundamentally an administrative/political role, while the campus chief executive officer should be perceived as having fundamentally an administrative/scholarly role." John Millett, Report to University of Texas Board of Regents (1978).

[12]Lee and Bowen, p. 147. Compare with the following observation about SHEEOs: "This constant imperative to maintain both academic legitimacy and political credibility, in the absence of either an academic or a political constituency, is what we believe distinguishes the state higher education executive officer from other administrators or executives in either academia or government" (Pettit and Kirkpatrick, p. 7).

[13]This phenomenon from the perspective of constituencies pulling on the campus CEO in a manner that impedes his or her relationship with the system CEO is described by Munitz: "If the system administration is strongly in support of the campus executive, often the campus constituencies feel he or she has compromised their interests. Therefore, the campus officer often only gains credibility with constituencies by confronting the very system administration which must ultimately determine his or her working conditions" (Munitz, pp. 20-21).

[14]Leon Epstein knowledgeably discusses problems of administrative legitimacy generally within the academic community, and acknowledges the special problems of administrators who are removed from the campus. Leon Epstein, *Governing the University* (San Francisco: Jossey-Bass, 1974), pp. 110-114,214.

Durward Long makes a similar point: "In the academic ideology, the image of a university system and its administration carries negative freight, only a half-step above that of government agencies and coordinating boards." Durward Long, "Notes Toward a Theoretical Perspective," in *The Monday Morning Imagination: Report from the Boyer Workshop on State University Systems,* Ed. Martin Kaplan (New York: Aspen Institute, 1976), p. 60.

[15]Kerr, p. 73.

[16]The first three categories discussed here have been used recently in a somewhat different format by the staff of the Ilinois Board of Governors in an effort to classify public university systems throughout the United States. Pamela P. Meyer, "Survey of the Relationships between the System CEO and the Campus CEO at Selected Multi-Institutional Systems with Multi-Campuses," unpublished ms., Board of Governors of State Colleges and Universities, 1985.

[17]Kerr, for example, argues, "There should be a clear understanding that all matters requiring action by the board must be reviewed by and (with only agreed-upon exceptions) presented to the board by the system executive, and that all campus heads should be appointed *on the recommendation of the system head"* (emphasis added). Kerr, p. 74.

[18] Stanley O. Ikenberry, "Dimension of Leadership in Higher Education," in *State Government,* Summer 1985.

[19] Note the leadership prescriptions of Peters and Waterman for successful corporations: "to harness the social forces in the organization, to "shape and guide values," to "make meanings," and to shape the appropriate metaphors and myths. Thomas J. Peters and Robert H. Waterman, Jr., *In Search of Excellence: Lessons from America's Best Run Companies* (New York: Harper and Row, 1982), pp. 6,75,105,282.

19. Who's Afraid of the Statewide Board?
James A. Norton

Back in 1973 a task force of the Education Commission of the States published a report entitled, "Coordination or Chaos?" It was the perception of the task force that the growth of higher education—more students, more cost, newer technologies—and the changes in attitudes—broader recruitment, equality of access, more student financial aid—were part of a changing complex of priorities within society and within education itself. With the stresses to come from a decline in the number of high school graduates and challenges from new methods of delivering the services of higher education, centralization seemed more plausible than laissez faire, and it was clear to the task force that better coordination was an alternative to a wasteful, chaotic situation.

A great many persons have observed that by 1973 it was already too late to choose between coordination or chaos. It was already our fate to have both. Certainly anyone who ever tried to explain the system of higher education that serves our country had to account for a primal disorder involving institutional types, specialties, and experiences, with an almost infinite variety of governance, offering services, nostrums, hopes, and opportunities in every conceivable package.

Despite the organizing threads in federal policy, historical precedent and public expectation, the fifty states with their individualities required any out-of-stater to relearn the basics if he or she wished to comment on a situation. A given state might challenge being characterized as chaotic, but to claim a chaotic situation nationally required only mild hyperbole. And within most states the process of determining public policy often seems threatened by near unimpeded diversity.

Coordination was certain. The public investment, both governmental and private, was too great for it to be otherwise.

The idea was not new. New York had created an agency to coordinate all education in 1784. The first operative higher education coordinating board was authorized by constitutional amend-

---

James A. Norton is a professor of political science at the University of Virginia. He formerly served as chancellor of the Ohio Board of Regents and executive director of the Greater Cleveland Foundation.

ment in Oklahoma in 1941. Even before that, sixteen states had put all their public, senior-level institutions under statewide governing boards. Since then, primarily in the 1960s, when we were expanding public higher education as fast as possible, every state that hadn't some form of coordinating structure moved to create at least the semblance of an agency. In the amendments to the Higher Education act in 1972 Congress added its enticement for coordinated planning with grants to implement commissions designated under Section 1202.

Nor is coordination a phenomenon peculiar to the United States. It is worldwide. According to Dr. Nell Eurich, who with Jim Perkins and some colleagues has made a comprehensive study of contemporary higher education around the world, every country seems to have moved toward centralization or coordination.

Assuming the evident fact of centralized governance or coordination, we may best move ahead and talk about it. I propose that we talk first about the agenda of state coordination, then about alternative mechanisms, and then about the challenges involved.

First, let's review the agenda. Right at the top, it seems to me, is the decline in the student-age numbers. We've heard about this so much that we probably have begun to discount it, but the students who will be graduating from high school in the 1990s have already been born, and we can count them. In Ohio the decline between now and 1992 will be 30 percent. Cuyahoga—the central county of the Cleveland metropolitan area—will have a drop of about 50 percent.

If you do not have the figures for the market area served by your school, you should demand them. Different schools are going to be affected differently, but every school that has served the traditional age group is going to be affected.

That leads to a second part of this agenda item on enrollment change. The leaders of many institutions have felt that they could develop new clientele groups. They have seen that many more persons beyond traditional college age are turning to colleges and universities for things they missed, or to expand or update the education they received. These leaders know that the recent population bulge in the 10-24-year age range will soon be thirty to forty-four years old. If we could just capture more of them, there still would be a strong demand for our services.

As many of you have said, services to the older student will continue to increase in importance, especially for the schools that are in the right location and are sensitive to market demands and able to package their wares appropriately. But as it said in the song we used to sing around the campfire, "Everybody talk about heaven ain't going there," and those charged with the guidance of institutions must be careful.

First, we are talking primarily about part-time students, students who don't fill dormitories and are not uniformly distributed across the nation. Second, these persons are already on our campuses in large numbers. In some places the increased enrollments of the past few years were made up of these persons as the institutions drew a smaller percentage of the still growing high school graduating classes. The average age on many campuses—especially two-year campuses—is twenty-seven or twenty-eight years. Schools already may be mining what we thought of as reserves.

There is also the third consideration that should bother us—about the older enrollee. Society—speaking through our state legislatures—may not be as eager to subsidize those students as much as it subsidized the younger adults.

That brings us to a second item on our agenda: this business of finance. Today the catchwords in many conversations seem to be "Proposition 13," or "Tax revolt." To me the term *tax revolt* does not seem as appropriate as "general disenchantment." We have lost any euphoria about solving society's ills and come to focus on our own. The reality of inflation in what we buy is more evident to most of us than the inflation in our income. We discount the latter and complicate evaluation of the former with our higher expectations. We ask government to do more for us at every level because so much of what we want to improve in the quality of life requires the broad reach and participation of government. Then we fail to count its costs—and its successes.

All this boils down to a very pervasive disenchantment. It includes higher educaton and our private and governmental financing of it. Operationally in the public sector it has begun to show up most clearly with new budgeting, PPBS, cost-benefit evaluation, zero-based budgeting, and so on. They are wrapped up in the concept "accountability." Each of the techniques has value. And each of us believes in "accountability." More and more of it for government in general. But each of us worries about it in the activity for which we are being held accountable.

This issue of accountability differs for the tax-assisted and the independent sectors of higher education. But it applies in each case. What do you purport to do? Is it worth doing? Why are your goals changing? How do you do what you claim to do? Can't you be more efficient? These questions are being asked—in a more sophisticated way in some places than in others, but the weaker questioners are learning. On how well we answer these questions will depend whether we get continued financial support, and how much.

A third item on the agenda for coordination is the development of new systems responding to new demands. As is the case with the changing clientele and demands for accountability for fiscal support, this item is not merely on our future agenda, it is present right now.

Some of our institutions may be able to repackage their offerings for the new market, but many of our potential clients are already producing and packaging their own programs. There is a tremendous demand for higher education services in the professions and in the private corporate sector. Under state laws, or the mandates of insurance companies, physicians are required to study the latest information in their field or lose the privilege of practicing. Ohio requires this of optometrists. Soon there will be similar requirements for nurses, dentists, engineers, attorneys, public accountants, and consultants. Professional societies and corporations already are retraining and educating their employees.

A market this rich attracts entrepreneurs of every description. Packagers of learning technologies go beyond their collegiate customers to compete for the colleges' clientele. Consulting firms turn trainers. New schools spring up. Established universities strike out for new profit centers. There are great opportunities here, as well as the spectre of chaos unlimited.

If you take the market our higher education institutions traditionally serve, diminish it with the shrinking numbers of high school graduates, enhance it to an unknown degree with an improbable clientele that demands new services, throw its traditional pricing and funding mechanisms into disarray, question its validity, effectiveness and efficiency, and bring new players and undefined rules into the maelstrom—if you do all this, you outline much of the agenda for higher education for the next decade. You also explain why one of the responses is coordination of one type or another.

Turning to the mechanisms for coordination.

Assuming that coordination is likely to be a state-level activity, one can distinguish gubernatorial coordination through an executive budget office or department; legislative coordination through a committee staff or legislative budget office; and coordination under an independent board. Theoretically there could be voluntary coordination under an informal or nongovernmental agency. It has been tried often in the past, but voluntary coordination requires two things that are impossible in the next decade—a universal willingness to abide by decisions that limit resources or programs or clientele, and the participation of all the actors in the game.

Someone would have to say who all the legitimate parties were, and even then they would not agree to abide by the results. The politics of institutional self-preservation makes it impossible for trustees, presidents, or faculties voluntarily to accept recommendations that their constituents perceive as being to their disadvantage. Voluntary coordination rarely works in splitting increasing resources; it is not a reasonable alternative when resources are shrinking.

Some governors feel strongly about the autonomy of universities. Many governors like to build great new facilities and to bask in the company of college presidents. If there is no alternative coordinating process in a state, the governor's task of recommending allocation of funds in the budget becomes a minimum level of coordination. If the agenda I outlined is at all reasonable, however, there are many specific issues to be addressed that are not likely to make friends. Governors have a history of finding their calendars crowded so that even their friends soon seem to be demanding too much time and attention. Staffs look for ways to protect their boss from his or her friends. However competent, the staff members inject considerations that "balance" all the forces they perceive.

Everyone wants the governor as a friend; no one of sound mind wants the governor as an enemy. But to want every issue finally decided in the few minutes a governor can give to it, you must be exceptionally confident that he or she is and will be your partisan. If the chief executive coordinates higher education through the budget agency, the work probably will be done by persons whose rewards do not relate to the success of higher education. If he or she operates through a cabinet department, higher education may suffer by department-level competition with the other functions included in the department.

Equally, some state legislatures have served as coordinating agencies with good results. They may operate through education committees, or, more probably, through subcommittees of finance or appropriation committees, or through legislative budget offices. Regardless of whether a legislature takes total charge, as some have in recent years, they surely are becoming more important. Across the country legislators are increasing their staffs both in numbers and in competence. In many states they are having longer sessions or devoting more time in inter-session research, hearings, and oversight, as the members move, in effect, toward becoming full-time legislators. With the weakening of party structure the legislature becomes more independent of the executive. It is not difficult to imagine a period of legislative dominance for the last part of this century.

One example, however, will clarify some of the problems that reliance on this branch of government for coordination will encounter. Because of the length of their terms, legislators are likely to plan in two-year cycles. Most of the problems we face on our campuses require a longer time span for effective action that does not do violence to our traditions and our contracts. Consensus-conscious organizations with the weight of tenured faculty do not move easily.

Legislatures are complicated in their processes. Power is not distributed equally among their members. The institutions in the districts of powerful patrons should appreciate the special favors they receive, and they should carefully check the teeth of gift horses. The more negotiating that goes on, the greater the chance for some new programs to be mandated or new actions to be required.

Legislative staff, like those of governors' offices, are improving greatly these days. But like those in governors' office, they have wide ranging interests that may lead to strange compromises, and rarely do they plan lifetime careers in their posts.

It is both because of problems inherent in executive and legislative coordination and because of its own characteristics that the independent coordinating boards have been established. Governors have recommended them, legislatures have provided for them, on occasion the voters have given them constitutional status. Experience as well as theory suggests that those with institutional representation are less able to take initiatives than those required to be free of institutional ties. The requirements of Section 1202 of the federal higher education act for participation of many groups that had been ignored for some years (such as proprietary schools, and, in some states, independent schools) was a corrective for the exclusion, but where the requirement were met literally there have often been the problems of planning by consensus.

The greatest advantage of an independent coordinating board for a state is its single-purpose visibility. By no means does it eliminate gubernatorial or legislative politics, but it does offer the governor, the legislature, and participants in higher education an excuse for doing right. Without suggesting any inherent wisdom in a board, we can note that it is likely to recruit a staff whose judgments are colored by career ambitions in higher education. As we noted, a gubernatorial or legislative staff must prove its political sagacity. Boards can take a view longer than that which must focus on the next campaign. They can adopt consultative procedures not unlike those on campuses.

Boards also can take abuse. At least all of them do. Criticism comes from the institutions, where it is more or less expected, for the same reasons that college boards and presidents expect criticism from collegiate departments and faculty members. It also comes from governors and legislature. They threaten to strip away a boards' powers and sometimes do.

Before you relax into thinking that coordinating boards will all be abolished, however, note that the most frequent criticisms arise from board weaknesses—their lack of power or their belief in decentralization. Ohio is not atypical as a case study. The present governor attacked the board of regents as "too powerful" and "useless" in his campaign and in his inaugural address. Then in the next four years on every occasion when he had the option to assign functions or powers, as with federal programs, he assigned them to the boards of regents. Not once did he threaten to veto new legislative assignments. Also he appointed some very strong perons to the board who quickly asserted their intention to be stronger. Nasty words cause headaches, but they have to be read in context of actions.

This leads us directly to some of the challenges we ought to discuss. Without deprecating the success of centralized governing boards where they exist, most of us in states without them worry about coordination being just a way station to centralization. If you dislike centralization, it is a reasonable concern. There probably never has been a policy maker or administrator who at one time or another did not wish he or she had more authority to affect that for which he or she was responsible. My observations suggest that it is not this feeling about which we need worry. There are many state administrators so imbued with belief in institutional autonomy that their momentary frustrations are unimportant.

The greatest potential force for centralization seems to be the propensity for an occasional institution to foul up its own situation and then claim special privilege for relief. Large states can take this if the number of problem schools is small enough and if they move rapidly enough to correct their problems. But when several schools fall down on their job, those that don't fall down see "their" resources eroding. Legislators cannot tolerate gross unfairness for a long time and their response may well be greater centralization.

The fact of the matter is, all our higher institutions are more in the same boat than anyone wants to admit. In the public sector there is too much backbiting between long established schools and those more recently created, two-year colleges and four-year, research universities and others. Add the public-independent-proprietary fights and we seem ridiculous.

The big challenge for the next decade is to work through a problem-filled agenda together. The teaching, research, and other services that are the stock in trade of higher education are more important in many ways than ever before. To give the public—students, government, corporate and association sectors—full value is going to require substantial readjustments. We are going to need intensive participation of faculty members, administrators, presidents, trustees at many insitutions, and broad concern by society in general.

One of the mechanisms we have invented to help with this process is the coordinating board. College presidents have come to recognize the legitimacy of participation of their trustees in many schools; it should not be too difficult for presidents and trustees to recognize a role for coordinating boards. To be effective coordinating boards must represent appropriately the concerns of state government. But they are part of the process of higher education. They can help provoke, promote, and ameliorate change. Achieving coordination is a challenge with promise.

20. The Point of the Discourse
M. M. Chambers

The aim here is to discover something of the nature of higher education as a function of society, and inklings of an optimum *modus vivendi* for the partnership of public higher education and the state.

Elsewhere the author has written that a key to productivity in higher eduation is good morale among those immediately engaged: students, faculty members, administrative officers, and members of governing boards. This indispensable *esprit de corps* is derived in part from the judicious trust and confidence of parents, donors, taxpayers, legislators, and governors. "Morale cannot be forced; it can only be fostered."[1]

This sentiment is not original. It is and has been understood and held by many. Observe, for example, the words of Arthur G. Coons, late revered educational statesman of California:

> *In the midst of controversies over finances, or structures, or functions, or programs. . . . It is important to remember that what takes place in fact rests on the attitudes and intentions of the persons who are involved. Dependence primarily on power, whether by directives or by demonstrations, will fail.*[2]

On the matter of public confidence, consider what was written in 1967 by Terry Sanford, a recent governor of North Carolina, known for his breadth of wisdom concerning educational issues:

> *In at least one activity, it is undisputed that over the years the money from the states has achieved excellence. That is public higher education. The nation has become strong through the support the states have given public higher education. . . . Much of our preeminence as a social and governmental system {and} the university capacity of America couldn't have been put together in a crash program. It has grown over many years by state nurture.*[3]

M. M. Chambers, professor of higher education at Illinois State University, perhaps best known for his annual reports on state support for higher education, is also an ardent spokesman for the independence and autonomy of higher education.

In many states this clear view has been clouded somewhat by distrust, some real and some feigned, by some legislators and state administrative officers who grumblingly question the efficiency of the management of state universities and colleges and the efficiency of statewide development of public education. Only rarely are such innuendos reducible to a specific complaint. Rarely is any factual evidence adduced in their support.

It is well to be candid and recognize that some of this alleged lack of confidence is sincere, even if mistaken; and that some of it stems solely from a power struggle by overambitious office holders and would-be office holders for control of the expenditure of large sums of state tax money.

Early in the present century the effort to remove some of the confusions and abuses of nineteenth-century state governments took hold. One of the thrusts was to reduce the large numbers of miscellaneous state agencies, departments, bureaus, and commissions, and compress them into a much smaller number of major departments whose heads would be appointed by the governor and directly responsible to him.

Another thrust was to introduce detailed administrative and fiscal controls emanating from a state department of finance, a state personnel board or civil service commission, a state department of public works, and often central agencies such as a state printer, a state architect, a state engineer, and others.

Granting that the motive was good (but not without noting that a state adminstrative reorganization almost invariably means opportunity for an incoming governor to "throw the rascals out" on a large scale, and install his or her own followers), and conceding that state governments are now generally better than they were half a century ago, it is nonetheless important to notice that push toward centralization has led to vast increases in unnecessary paperwork, delayed decisions, and harmful rigidity in administration.

These are especially damaging in public higher education, where half of the total of annual operating expenditures is on contracts for salaries of persons at high levels of professional training and general education. Inflexibility and undue delays in the management of recruiting and of changes in salary and rank can cause failures in obtaining or retaining prized talents—to say nothing of depressed morale—with resultant imponderable losses in productivity and quality.

These matters are managed generally with skill and dispatch, and in admirable style, by the leading private universities, and by the great constitutionally independent state universities, all of which are free of any vast overlay of smothering officiousness from the statehouse. A study team for the Southern Association of Colleges and Schools, reporting in 1968, was eloquent on this point:

> *Effective higher education absolutely requires a maximum of freedom for the exploration of ideas and concepts. This makes wholesome relationships between higher education and state government even more necessary than may be true with other functional areas of state service and makes direct political involvement in the control of institutional personnel and operations intolerable. The uniqueness of higher education should be recognized in organizational patterns and relationships with other agencies of the state.*

More specifically, the report concludes, "An educational institution can neither conduct a sound educational program if its operational procedures are set by legislative act, nor can it be properly administered if an agency outside the institution exercises undue and restrictive financial control." Once funds have been appropriated for an institution (either for building construction or operations), budget making, establishing priorities, and control of expenditures should be entirely within the institution under the jurisdiction of the governing board subject to general policy provisions enacted by the legislature and to the commitments represented through budgetary requests by the institution.

> *State financial and administrative officials adversely affect the educational and academic process when they exercise specific and detailed control over matters which can and should be handled within the institution. Recognition by educational representatives of the responsibility of state officials for the post-audit function and the general enforcement of reasonable budgetary law is imperative; however, the educational function of an institution must not be controlled through the use of budgetary techniques or controls by financial officials outside the institution.*

This statement, a studious revision of an earlier one after the completion of the study, was recommended for inclusion among the association's *Standards for Colleges*.[4]

The other and related thrust toward bundling the governance of all or many of a state's public universities and colleges into the hands of one statewide governing board, or the alternative of superimposing a power-laden "coordinating board," deserves equally careful examination and monitoring. To the extent that this movement diminishes or destroys the autonomy of the university or college by removing decision making from the campus to the statehouse or some other remote point, creating a species of "absentee landlordism," it tends to shortchange and insult the constituency, and to debase the institutions.

To be sure, the interests of all the people of the state are superior to those of any institutional constituency; but statewide public interest can be well served without the power play involved in the abolition of governing boards or their reduction to impotency. The solution is in the limiting of the statewide central agency to the work of facilitating interinstitutional liaison, performing data gathering, research reporting, making planning studies, disseminating of public information, and aiding in the representations of statewide public higher education to the governor, the legislature, the institutional governing boards, and the general public—all in an advisory capacity and by means of permissive and persuasive methods free of the exercise of raw power.

A state university is not properly conceived as an inanimate mechanism that can be operated by remote control, with Big Brother pushing the buttons on the control panel on the twentieth floor of the state office building. Instead it is a living organism with its own complex skeletal and muscular structure, its own circulatory and nervous systems, its own capacities for encouraging initiative and inventiveness and maintaining the atmosphere of expectancy most conducive toward discoveries in various fields of learning. Its morale, and its productivity, can be greatly diminished or destroyed by rude chopping off of fingers and toes: by a power-laden "superboard."

> *The disadvantages of a "super-board" setup, in extra overhead cost, in added but unproductive work at all levels, in impairment or even loss of flexibility in an era of rapid and often major change, in interference with faculty control of courses and curricula, in lost time of administrators, in standardization of important things, some of which can only become and others of which are likely to become mediocre if standardized, in the frequent and almost inevitable "substitution of rules for brains," in the erosion of responsibility right along with authority, to my mind far outweigh any presumed benefits from supposed avoidance of unnecessary duplication of programs within a state system.[5]*

Fear of "duplication" of general undergraduate programs is a relic of Depression days and earlier, when public higher education was a very thinly spread enterprise. Virtually all undergraduate curricula and courses, whatever their labels, contain large infusions of liberal arts or general education, which indeed needs to be "duplicated" (or better, diffused, diversified, and dispersed) until it is accessible to all citizens. Wariness of alleged "duplication" would have some point with respect to costly advanced graduate studies and research, were it not for the fact that the scholars and scientists who lead these enterprises are always aware of what their counterparts in other institutions in the same state, if any, are doing and planning. Within the fraternity of top-level scholars and scientists there is intercommunication often unknown to administrators and others, and on a level that would be uninteresting and unintelligible to lay citizens and even to professional persons not immediately concerned in the special fields involved. This is insurance of a sufficient degree of "coordination" without the intervention of uniformed fiscal clerks. Wise governing boards and administrators know their best service is to encourage it, not impede it or clumsily meddle with it. The story of Iowa, infra, provides an illustrative example.

Twin menaces to optimum reasonable autonomy of state universities and colleges for more than half a century have been (1) unduly detailed and oppressive central fiscal and administrative controls from a dozen statehouse offices, and (2) the push toward overcentralized statewide structure for the governance of higher education. These are persistent forms of "overreaction" to the shortcomings of state governments in the nineteenth and early twentieth centuries. In many states, though by no means all, they have been applied in varying degrees to state colleges and universities in ignorant or willful disregard of the fact that they tend to cause lengthy, needless delays, confusions, and frictions; to depress the all-important morale of governing boards and faculties, administrators and students. This can only result in ultimate wasteful losses—diminished educational productivity per tax dollar invested.

Some states have enacted "autonomy bills" which have relieved their state universities or colleges of some of the worst features complained of; for example, Rhode Island (1939), Massachusetts (1956 and 1962), Ohio (1965 and piecemeal in several earlier years, with respect to custody of student fees and other institutional receipts), and New Jersey (1969). But in most instances the gains were only partial and sometimes were eroded in subsequent years. The analogy between the bureaucracy and an octopus is vivid: cut off one or two tentacles and you are constricted by half a dozen others.

Through the Fifties and most of the Sixties the press for the abolition of institutional governing boards was dormant; instead many states set up a statewide "coordinating council" or similar board by whatever name, whose prescribed duties were largely or wholly confined to making studies and recommendations and acting in advisory capacity. Such statewide councils or boards wholly advisory and without any powers of mandate were established in California (1960), Michigan (1963),[6] Louisiana (1968), Washington (1969), and Alabama (1969). The statutes creating such boards in some twenty other states between 1950 and 1970 were usually cautious and often ambivalent about conferring coercive powers. Almost always the function with regard to institutional budget askings was no more than the duty to examine and make recommendations.

Often in these statutes there is wording about "approving or disapproving" the addition or deletion of major departments or schools within a university, but it is usually unclear whether this authority is intended to be final. This is in fact a rather unworkable idea, because departments and schools are not ordinarily created by fiat, but only labeled and recognized after the essential nucleus of professors, students, books, and apparati has been painstakingly assembled over a period of several years. Clumsy attempts at such regulation by remote control can also produce very embarrassing problems when it may result in loss of substantial philanthropic grants or governmental subsidies, and consequent departure of one or more distinguished professors and many advanced students.

If the main point of this discourse were to be stated in a single sentence, it would be that state universities and colleges should be extricated (in reasonable degree and with moderate dispatch) from the unnecessary and burdensome mandatory ministrations of statehouse fiscal and administrative offices, and from the rigidities of overcentralized statewide structures of governance or coercive "coordination."

The myth of "wasteful duplication"—a ceaseless incantation for half a century—has lost its force among knowledgeable persons with the coming of universal education beyond the high school in economy of abundance, and with the development of interinstitutional and interstate cooperation in many forms. Coordination by consensus is the productive policy, and this is increasingly recognized and practiced everywhere, even by legally power-laden statutory authorities.

Notes

[1] *Higher Education: Who Pays? Who Gains?* (Danville, Illinois: The Interstate Printers & Publishers, 1969), p. 210.

[2] Arthur G. Coons, *Crises in California Higher Education* (Los Angeles: Ward Ritchie Press, 1968).

[3] Terry Sanford, *Storm Over the States* (New York: McGraw-Hill Book Company, 1967), pp. 63-64.

[4] The quotations are from *Higher Education and Financial Control by State Govenments in Southern Association States* (Atlanta: Southern Association of Colleges an Schools, March 1968). Edward J. Boling and J. Jefferson Bennett were joint chairmen of the committee making this report. Robert Cornett and Joe Johnson were staff members.

[5] Elvis J. Stahr, president of Indiana University 1962-1968, in his State of the University Address to the Faculty, 1966, unpublished.

[6] The Michigan Constitution of 1963 created a State Board of Education and designated it a "coordinating body" for education at all levels, including higher education; but the same constitution makes each state institution of higher education explicitly autonomous.

21. Memo to a Multicampus Trustee from a Flagship CEO
Barry Munitz

The first major analysis of multicampus systems was undertaken by Eugene Lee and Frank Bowen under the auspices of the Carnegie Commission on Higher Education. I was a member of Clark Kerr's staff when their work began, and the classic text which they produced continues to serve as the standard reference. They described a relatively new organizational phenomenon, which sought better information for planning, and finer educational diversity to serve the general population. Most critically, the system concept attempted to establish academic priorities in an environment which reduced external political intrusions.

Several years later, as Dr. Kerr recognized the rapid spread of multicampus structures, he invited Lee and Bowen to undertake a follow-up study. In his foreword to *Managing Multicampus Systems,* Kerr concluded that

> *The central lesson of the analysis provided by Lee and Bowen seems to be, therefore, that if multicampus systems are going to make the most of their unique advantages for survival and effectiveness, their flexibility must be considerable and needs to be protected. Such flexibility may be endangered by undue intrusions of state governments, by their own highly bureaucratized central administration, by authority that is too widely dispersed and too absolute at the campus and department levels, or by the introduction of new coordinating centers with control over institutional procedures.*[1]

Thus a number of difficult challenges have arisen for the system administration. The momentum which continues toward more comprehensive multicampus systems can be traced to pressures for realigned political influences and for more cost-effective resource allocations. Yet, even though the political buffers, the better coordinated development of academic programs, and the more efficient allocation of educational resources have been often achieved,

---

Barry Munitz served with two multicampus universities: University of Illinois and University of Houston. At the time this was written, he was chancellor of the latter's central campus. He is now president of Federated Development, Inc.

those results have been accompanied by serious organizational and interpersonal problems.

The structure has created particular challenges to the relationship between system and campus administration. Multicampus system heads protect the component chief executives and educate the board on the one hand, as they protect the board and educate component executives on the other. Joseph Kauffman commented on this exquisite balance:

> *Although it is difficult to generalize about any leadership role in the diverse systems of higher education, it seems clear that the system presidency is the least stable and often the least personally satisfying. . . . System presidents get caught between the ambiguous expectations of single boards and the tendency of the respective campuses to blame all ills on the system administration.*[2]

The system president's role is to interpret and to strengthen academic and administrative values. Failure in this function from the board's perspective is a failure that cannot be overcome by success in any other aspect of that position.

Trustees are well aware that the vitality and responsiveness of our universities depend upon the granting of considerable autonomy. Trustees should expect administrators who request such flexibility to be accountable for their decisions and they fully expect to be held accountable. However, many board members feel uncertain about how colleges and universities actually work, and as a result many regents and trustees stubbornly freeze flexibility for judgment, discretion, or innovation. Kauffman urges that board members virtually force chief executives to educate them (even when their own security is jeopardized), for the trustees,' the presidents', and the institutions' sake. That is a difficult enough concept to implement in a single campus system. Within a multicampus environment the task is excruciatingly complicated yet it remains essential.

Viewing the Campus Executive

My own work on the evaluation of chief executives and boards has brought me repeated awareness of this delicate balance. Most campus administrators have a considerable range of legitimate worries about the responsibility and style of the system office and its staff. Furthermore, the division of functions between campus and system administration is not consistent between any two multicampus systems in this country. "Most people, including the central governing board members, may be oblivious to the dynamics that flow from these concerns. The campus chancellor, however, feels the impact of the system more than anyone else in higher education."[3]

How is the chief executive of the campus to be judged? If the system administration is strongly in support of the campus executive, often the campus constituencies feel he or she has compromised their interests. Therefore, the campus officer often only gains credibility with constituencies by confronting the very system administration which must ultimately determine his or her working conditions.

Facing such problems, several years ago the University of Texas asked John Millet to clarify the distinction between the campus and system chief executive officers. Millett began his report by emphasizing that "there was substantial difference in a multicampus system between the system as an organizational construct and the campus as an educational enterprise. There is some question as to whether or not the substantial difference has been clearly understood by the Board of Regents as the governing board for a considerable number of separate educational entities."[4]

Millett assumed that the basic organizational issues relate to how the system administration provides educational leadership for all campuses, and how it is involved in the management of campus support programs. His guiding principle was:

> *The multicampus system is an organizational construct for leadership and management. The campus is a learning environment bringing together faculty members, students. . . . The system chief executive officer should be perceived as having fundamentally an administrative/political role, while the campus chief executive officer should be perceived as having fundamentally an administrative/scholarly role. Campus chief executive officers need the confidence, the assistance, and the encouragement of the system, but above all else, the campus chief executive officer needs the support and the cooperation of campus constituencies.*[5]

The three-way interaction among board, system administration, and the campus chief executive is likely to heighten the potential for conflict between levels. Most multicampus governing boards delegate to the system executive responsibility for finding and reviewing leadership on each campus, only taking direct board initiative on rare occasions. The irony is that large systems require above all that trustees understand the basic needs of their campus components. Such understanding often is best acquired during search and/or assessment activities, but people in your position must gather such insight without undermining the authority of the system executive.

In turn, system presidents must understand the importance of having credible and imaginative leaders as the heads of their campus components, rather than middle management bureaucrats caught between irreconcilable organization pressures. Without this understanding fewer excellent people will accept or stay in campus executive positions, and our growing number of multicampus systems will move further in the treacherous direction of stifled and then frozen passivity. Kauffman insists that "if strong and imaginative leadership at the campus level is still desirable, and I consider that indispensable, we must be mindful of ways in which the campus chancellor's role may be crippled and trivialized in systems.[6]

If board members comprehend this warning they will ask about the improvement of educational services and the strengthening of educational opportunity, rather than emphasize the political distribution of power and the bureaucratic enhancement of efficiency. Harold Enarson addressed this concern:

First as a guiding principle, remember that decisions should be made at the appropriate level within any organization. In higher education I believe these appropriate levels are as close as possible to the point of impact. Campus officials should be delegated authority to administer their campuses effectively and held quickly accountable after the fact. If on occasion an administration abuses this discretion, it makes more sense to replace the administrator than to remove discretion.... Second, realize that there ia a certain amount of error inherent in large systems. Even the most stringent regulation will not eliminate it. But over regulation will cost far more in diminished creativity and vitality than could even be saved through tight control of every action.[7]

Specific Problems to Examine

After all the polite employer-employee phrases are uttered, and all the appropriately deferential gestures of mutual respect are observed, the fact remains that chief executive officers at major components are in a particularly awkward position. While they attempt to enhance the status of subordinates, they must pay careful attention to relationships those same subordinates establish with their functional counterparts at the centralized system level (this is particularly true for the interaction between campus and system fiscal officers). While they struggle to convince their internal constituencies that the best interests of their campus are being duly protected, they must also satisfy the chief executive at the system level in whose hands their own professional fate rests.

Now, as a multicampus system trustee, how can one help? Look beyond the cliche to the substance. Many members of multicampus governing boards, chosen for their experience and expertise with governmental or corporate agencies, tend to press for more efficient use of resources. Such pressure is politically, professionally, and personally tempting. It often leads to a centralization of functions, and elimination of alleged duplications, and a proposed streamlining of decision-making processes. There is nothing intrinsically wrong with these values—unless the absence of adequate translation from a holding company to a university setting sacrifices educational principles.

Trustees assign the system chief executive primary responsibility for balancing campus autonomy and system accountability. I emphasize that he or she has the burden of educating and protecting constituencies both below and above if the system is to function with integrity and with quality. Therefore, trustees must learn the difference between alleged duplication and the necessary distribution of functions to a variety of component campuses. They must learn to distinguish between services which truly can be provided more effectively at a centralized level, and those where close proximity to the user is more important. They must know why campus chief executives are chosen, after a complex search process, and what issues they will confront during their likely tenure in office. Indeed, one critical measurement of success will be sustaining the inevitable constructive tension created by bright and aggressive administators at both campus and system levels, without falling into the destructive conflict which results if board members and the system chief executive do not provide courageous and sympathetic leadership.

The likelihood of staying on the constructive side of that tension is increased substantially if board members and system administrators comprehend the unusual ironies facing flagship campus administrators. Quite often, the main campus existed before a multicampus structure was created. Many board members, and most senior alumni, remember only the flagship campus. They identify their emotional and financial commitments with entity. This situation is particularly poignant as it relates to the athletic program, since in many multicampus systems the most visible and perhaps the only athletic program exists at the flagship.

Complications in fund raising inevitably emerge when more than one campus exists within the same geographical region. Major resources which were given to an institution when only the main campus existed are seen by many faculty and staff members at that campus to be wasted, or politically distributed, or even unethically seized if they are administered by the system administration or by the board. The legislature, which often welcomes a multicampus structure because it reduces political battling between campuses in the state capital, can become confused about system-campus priorites. In turn, constituencies on the main campus naively see any major appropriations to other components as taking away from what would have been theirs. Since in many states the main campus is not in the largest city (having been placed during the land-grant movement), political battles often emerge between the more established but rural legislative group, and the larger urban legislative caucus.

Conflict can also arise on another level. In many states the system officers are located on or close to the flagship campus. Questions about the chancellor's residence contrasted with the president's, relationships between the chancellor's and the president's senior staff, the role of each executive spouse, and a multitude of image and social issues can create symbolic but nonetheless painful confusions and misunderstandings.

For all of these issues the most logical response is a candid and early conversation among system administration, campus administration, and board about their governance expectations. A periodic review of those expectations is equally important, since campus executives must learn and live up to system and board requirements. It is amazing how many regents and trustees of multicampus boards have never had a meaningful discussion about the structure itself with their colleagues and their administrators.

I hope trustees understand why they have felt the danger was particularly strong at the "flagship campus." The traditional, comprehensive, high-quality institution is threatened with lower common-denominator decisions that spread programs and resources across a number of different campuses without distinctions in mission or priority. Each component must strive to be excellent in its own assigned role and scope.

One's role as a board member is to urge the system staff to establish appropriate mission for each component, to allow flexibility for campus operations, to monitor their success in achieving quality, and to ensure that the very best at each function are not sacrificed to some concept of general benefit which undermines the values of all.

> *If the multicampus governing board tends to act as if it were the governing board of a single campus, its agenda may become unwieldy and time-consuming, its actions may be interpreted as undue interference with or favoritism toward a particular campus, and the decisions may appear to be remote from the influence of campus administrators, campus faculty members, and campus students. A multicampus governing board has to learn how to act on broad policy matters and to leave greater areas of discretion to both system administrators and campus administrators than might be the case with the governing board of a single institution.[8]*

Trustees should approach this responsibility with a sensitive understanding of the academic requirements at component campuses. They should maintain an honest commitment to the professional and personal requirements of the campus executive and their system counterparts. Otherwise their colleagues will eventually govern finely tuned administrative structures that preside over second-rate educational institutions.

The respect for campus distinctions, the understanding of programmatic dissimilarities, and the protection of local flexibility are burdens placed squarely by the board on the shoulders of our finest system administrators. In the name of increased efficiency for the deployment of vital educational resources, we may jeopardize the scarcest resource of all—first-rate and deeply committed people.

Notes

[1] Eugene C. Lee and Frank M. Bowen, *Managing Multicampus Systems,* (San Francisco, Jossey-Bass, 1976).

[2] Joseph F. Kauffman, *At the Pleasure of the Board: The Service of the College or University President* (Washington: American Council on Education, 1980).

[3] Ibid., p. 70.

[4] John Millett, *Report to University of Texas Board of Regents,* 1978.

[5] Ibid.

[6] Kauffman, pp. 71, 72.

[7] Harold Enarson, "Quality and Accountability," *Change,* October 1980.

[8] Millett.

22. The Future of the LandGrant University
Malcolm Moos

This report is based on the assumption that just as leading universities shape their society, so powerful social forces shape the university to a considerable extent. I believe profoundly in the life of the mind and the independent role of the university in enriching that life. But I also believe that universities must respond creatively to major shifts in the culture and to the pressing challege to our civilization.

The underlying assumption is that today's research universities are the most precious institutions in our society, the life-giving springs from which flow tomorrow's leaders, tomorrow's ideas, and the new knowledge we need. They are the homes of our intellectual and artistic heritage and the model for our pursuit of truth and meaning. Tomorrow, even more than today, no state or region can claim to have a high quality of life or to possess the basics for economic and social progress without a first-rate public research university in its midst.

As for planning, I think universities have done too little. Mostly, universities have patched, cobbled, and adjusted to spasmodic growth. As a result, universities have often ignored the consequences of changing birth rates, of declining financial health, of creeping regulation and ominous intrusions of new economic, social, and international conditions. When they do plan, it is mainly for enrollments, new buildings, or next year's budget. It may be that universities simply aren't organized to respond to crises in their way of life. They weren't organized for the youthquake of the 1960s and may not be organized for the oilquake of the 1980s. But excessive government regulation has proved to be an often disastrous alternative as a way to change higher education.

The remedy is clearly a renewal from within the universities. The best university faculties and leaders know they face a decade as financially constricted as any since the 1930s. Yet they also know

---

Malcolm Moos, former professor of political science and president of the University of Minnesota, was commissioned by the University of Maryland to undertake a study of land-grant universities. This article, completed shortly before his death, is part of that study.

that the nation needs their teaching and research more than ever. The trick is to cut back and move forward at the same time.

The best method seems to be strategic planning, or the rational selection of courses of action that are most likely to bring success in the future, based on a scrutiny of the changing environment, inner strengths, and assessment of new opportunities.

What does it mean to be a state university in America in the 1980s? What features distinguish a public research university from a private one? What are the obligations of the 1862 land-grant universities 120 years later?

Any state university preparing to redesign its operations for the next decade or two needs to ask itself these questions. And it must propose some answers. The role of a major public research university is quite different from that of a state college or community college, and its emphasis is different from that of a major private research university. But what is the role of a land-grant university in the new society we are entering?

The answers are imbedded in the history of state universities and land-grant colleges and in the new tasks imposed on public universities by contemporary conditions.

Since the birth of the idea of a state university in Georgia in 1975, the purpose of these publicly supported institutions has had a different flavor from that of America's private colleges, most of which were founded by religious sects or devoutly religious laymen. Public institutions were to support the infant republic, help citizens, and promote economic development as well as train minds and improve manners. Thomas Jefferson, who wrote the charter of the University of Virginia in 1818, defined his state's university as "an institution in which every branch of knowledge useful at this day is taught in its highest degree." The word "useful" is significant. Jefferson also listed these as the purposes of a state university:

1. to form the statesmen, legislators, and judges, on whom public prosperity and individual happiness are so much to depend;

2. to expound the principles and structure of government, the laws which regulate the intercourse of nations, those formed municipally for our own government and a sound spirit of legislation, which banishing all unnecessary restraint on individual action, shall leave us free to do whatever does not violate the equal rights of another;

3. to harmonize and promote the interests of agriculture, manufactures, and commerce, and by well informed views of political economy to give a free scope to the public industry;

4. to develop the reasoning faculties of our youth, enlarge their minds, cultivate their morals, and instill into them the precepts of virtue and order;

5. to enlighten them with mathematical and physical sciences, which advance the arts and administer to the health, the subsistence and comforts of human life;

6. and, generally, to form them to habits of reflection and correct action, rendering them examples of virtue to others, and of happiness within themselves.

While objectives 1, 4, and 6 were similar to the purposes of the early private colleges, goals such as those to train people in democratic principles and laws, to "promote the interests of agriculture, manufactures, and commerce," and to educate young people in mathematics, physical and natural sciences, and the health sciences were radically different as was the idea that public universities should contribute to the health, subsistence, and comfort of all the state's people rather than to the prosperity, morality, religious piety, and intellect of the individual, tuition-paying collegegoers. State universities from their earliest years had purposes that were practical, scientific, economic, and protective of democratic government. They were to serve the general public that supported them.

The Morrill act of 1862, establishing land-grant institutions in every state, reinforced Jeffersons's objective. It also revolutionized American higher education.

At the time education at nearly all private colleges, and at some of the state's universities which had veered toward becoming gentlemen's colleges, was devoted to the classics, Greek, Latin, and Hebrew. Subjects like history, literature, and science were ignored, as was training for work. As James Garfield (later U.S. President Garfield) complained in 1867 about Harvard's curriculum,

> *A few weeks of the senior year to Guizot and the history of the Federal constitution, and a lecture on general history once a week during half of that year, furnish all that a graduate of Harvard is required to know of his country and the living nations of the earth. He must apply years of arduous labor to the history, oratory, and poetry of Greece and Rome; but he is not ever required to cull a single flower from the rich fields of our own literature. English literature is not even named in the curriculum.*

College enrollments were declining prior to the Civil War; many sons from leading families did not bother to go to college; women were excluded. As W. J. Kerr, one-time president of Oregon State, observed:

> *Education was still the type imported from Old England . . . traditional and classical. . . . The common attitude toward applied science was expressed in a New England newspaper of 1816, in opposition to a plan for street lighting: "Artificial lighting is an attempt to interfere with the divine place of the world, which called for dark during the night time." It had no relation to the resources of the country or to the occupations and objectives of the great mass of the people. . . .*
>
> *Between 1820 and 1870 industrial conditions in the United States were completely reorganized. The percentage of people engaged in agriculture dropped from 83 to less than 48, while the percentage engaged in manufacturing, trades, and transportation increased from 16 to more than 31. . . . The number of patents per year increased from 200 to 13,000. . . . The old education did not minister to the new wants.*

The rejuvenation and expansion of state universities through the Morrill Act changed all of this forever in at least three ways.

First, the act urged "the liberal and practical education" of students in "the several pursuits and professions of life." The primary objective was to use public higher education as a preparation for work more than for artful leisure or character formation. Specifically, the law required each land-grant college to offer programs in agriculture science, the "mechanic arts" or engineering, and the rudiments of military science (for defense of the republic). Suddenly, previously unheard-of programs appeared at the land-grant institutions: schools of agriculture, engineering, business or commerce, forestry, mining, home economics, education, architecture, journalism, and applied science. And some of the private institutions also began to add more practical programs of study. Prior to 1860 there were only four engineering schools in the country, and one of them was West Point; by 1885 there were 85. Before long Yale added a school of forestry, Harvard a school of business, Columbia a school of mines, and Princeton a school of engineering.

The new preparation for work brought science into the universities. Whereas applied scientists like Thomas Edison and Luther Burbank did their work outside universities, the land-grant institutions unashamedly emphasized experiments, invention, scientific discovery, and technology and brought scientists and engineers into the universities. Within a few decades the entire peach, poultry, and apple industries were transformed. The University of Missouri introduced the soybean to America. The water supply and sanitation of America's cities were modernized. Land-grant research invented the modern carburetor, isolated vitamins, and put the ceramic industry on a scientific basis.

The Morrill Act also brought military science onto college campuses. It prevented the U.S. military from becoming a separate professional caste by establishing ROTC programs at the universities. During World War I, 30,000 army and navy officers were graduates of land-grant institutions. Preparation for defense of the nation became a duty of land-grant colleges. (The University of Maryland required ROTC for all male undergraduates until 1965.)

Second, the Morrill Act changed instruction in higher education. The Latin, Greek, religion, geometry, and logic of the private colleges of the antebellum period relied chiefly on deduction, lectures, countless recitations, and book reading. But as one retired president of Washington State University remembered in the 1930s,

> *The new system to which the charter of 1862 gave life involved the use of the inductive system. When things were to be studied, the student must rely on analysis and synthesis, on observation and comparison. He must see, feel, smell, taste, weigh, measure, record. What a revolution! . . . Memory of verbal forms accents, idioms, and vocabularies had been the chief virtue of the gifted student, and dictionary, grammar, and text his chief instruments. Under the new regime, test tubes, flasks, scales, thermometers, reagents, microscopes, telescopes, plants, minerals, animals, apparatus and machinery, ad infinitum, were the necessary instruments, and inquiry and determination the method.*

Land-grant colleges brought discussion classes, experiments, field trips, and laboratories to higher education. It was their purpose to train students less to quote Thucydides, Virgil, or Tennyson than to use their senses, experience, and the scientific method in their working lives as farmers, engineers, businessmen, educators, and even as politicians.

The objective was succinctly expressed by historian Frederick Jackson Turner in a 1910 commencement address at the University of Indiana. To him, public universities and their research should help produce a contemporary kind of American pioneer:

> *General experience and rule-of-thumb information are inadequate for the solution of the problems of a democracy which no longer owns the safety fund of an unlimited quantity of untouched resources. Scientific farming must increase the yield of the field, scientific forestry must economize the woodlands, and scientific experiment and construction by chemist, physicist, biologist, and engineer must be applied to all nature's forces in our complex modern society. . . . It is the test tube and the microscope that are needed rather than the ax and the rifle in this new ideal of conquest.*

Third, equally as important as changing the content and teaching styles was Congress' determination to open higher education to the children of clerks, artisans, storekeepers, farmers, miners, mechanics, teachers, and laborers as well as to the children of clergymen, lawyers, physicians, and wealthy merchants. As Jonathan Turner of Illinois, one of the godfathers of the land-grant colleges noted in the 1850s, colleges were mainly for what he called "the literary and leisure classes, the 5 percent," whereas if the United States was going to be a real democracy and a land of opportunity it needed higher education for "the industrial classes, the other 95 percent." The new land-grant colleges and refurbished state universities did just that in the last quarter of the nineteenth century.

Women who had been allowed to attend college only at a few places like Oberlin were admitted to the land-grant colleges. Young people came to college from lumber camps, dairy farms, factory villages, and behind grocery store counters in small towns. Except in the South—of which Maryland was part—young blacks ventured out, too. Roy Wilkens attended the University of Minnesota, Whitney Young Kentucky State, and Ralph Bunche the University of California at Los Angeles. Unlike a number of religiously affiliated private institutions, land-grant colleges accepted young persons of any religious commitment.

In his Carnegie Commission study, *American Higher Education,* the Israeli sociologist Joseph Ben-David observed, "For some time now there has been less class discrimination in education in the United States than in other countries, including the socialist countries." State colleges and universities have been the major force that made this possible.

In addition to the three consciously designed new purposes of the Morrill Act, the state universities quickly became different from private colleges and universities in several other ways.

As Allan Nevins pointed out in *The State Universities and Democracy,* the orientation of some universities to their states or community colleges to their counties is an American invention. The Universities at Oxford, Heidelberg, or Oslo are not primarily devoted to uplift of their geographical areas. Nor are Amherst, Princeton, Vanderbilt or Vassar. State universities became allies of their state governments in furthering the economy, health, and cultural life.

Nevins also noted that many state universities and land-grant colleges virtually created their state public school systems by fighting for better schooling in the legislatures, training teachers, helping design curricula and write textbooks, and inspecting schools for quality. He says, "In the year of Lincoln's election the United States possessed only 243 high schools outside Massachusetts." Illinois had 10, Wisconsin 7, Minnesota 1. When the University of Kansas opened its doors in 1866 not a single student was prepared for collegiate-level work. In 1904 Georgia had only 350 high school graduates in the entire state—and only one-third were interested in going to college. During the first several decades, Wisconsin and Michigan had to devote one-fourth of their budgets, time and efforts to their "preparatory departments." In 1908 Harvard had to admit 58 percent of its freshmen class "not fully prepared," Yale 57 percent, Columbia 55 percent, and Princeton admitted 301 of its 360 freshmen "with conditions." It is one of the lesser-known facts of American educational history that the state universities and colleges were the prime movers in developing their state public school systems, not the other way around.

Land-grant universities have always had a special relationship with the people, industries, and government of their regions. After 1914, when funding for Cooperative Extension Services was added by federal law to the land-grant institutions, much of the latest research and knowledge of the state campuses was carried out to working farmers and homemakers, as it is to this day. Many state universities have established working and research relationships with the leading companies and industries in their states. Many have also forged bonds with their county and state government agencies, training county officials in public administration, aiding budget or planning officials with the latest techniques, and serving as the research arm of state agencies of transportation, environmental affairs, or economic development.

Not all state universities and land-grant institutions behaved in the same fashion, but most of them stressed the policies and programs we have described. Nearly one-half of the states, for example, established their land-grant colleges apart from their traditional state universities. In these states, the state universities were preserved as classics and humanities centers, emulating the better private colleges; and the land-grant institutions became a second, more practical kind of state university. This was especially true in the South and parts of the Midwest and Northwest, where social factors often played a part. Male children of leading families went to the "old" state universities, while sons and daughters of many backgrounds went to the new shirtsleeves land-grant colleges. Thus, Virginia built VPI, South Carolina added Clemson, Alabama built Auburn, Texas created Texas A & M, North Carolina built North Carolina State away from Chapel Hill, and Mississippi built Mississippi State downstate. In the Midwest, Indiana built Purdue and Iowa, Michigan, Kansas, Colorado, South Dakota, and North Dakota added separate "state" colleges such as the Montana State College of Agriculture and Mechanical Arts at Bozeman. Utah, Washington, and Oregon did the same.

But the other states folded the new land-grant spirit into their existing public universities: Georgia, Minnesota, New Hampshire, Tennessee, Wisconsin, Illinois, Ohio, Missouri, and Nebraska. Maryland was one of these states. In these state universities, Latin, French, the arts, economics, history, law, and medicine rub shoulders with dairy science, engineering, business, horticulture, fisheries management, and schools of education and journalism.

This distinction is critical to keep in mind in planning the future of state universities. The University of Maryland is not similar to, say, the state universities of Virginia, North Carolina, Oregon, or Michigan, where the state university and land-grant university are separate. It is more similar, however, to the University of Georgia, the University of Tennessee, the University of Wisconsin, and the University of Illinois, where there is no split between the "gentlemen's" institution and the "aggie" college.

But if the land-grant institutions once were radically different from the elite private colleges and universities, those difference have narrowed. Private institutions now also teach engineering and business, sociology and applied science. They have ROTC programs, admit women (or men) and minorities, and they have creased scholarships for talented students from poverty backgrounds. They have jumped into adult education and career programs. They perform applied research for industry and government agencies.

The differences between state colleges and universities and private colleges and universities are increasingly ones of tone and style rather than substance. In numerous states, private campuses now receive appreciable financial subsides from their state governments. In Maryland, the fourteen private institutions were given more than $9 million in 1980-81, up 54 percent from only two years ago. While the percentage of the state's general funds in the University of Maryland's budget has shrunk from 43 percent in 1971 to a proposed 31.5 percent in 1982, several of Maryland's private colleges now receive more than 10 percent of their operating revenues from taxpayer dollars.

Also, to locate objectives of a major public research university in the post-land-grant era one can no longer look at the state university in isolation. The state university must be seen as one special part of a network of state colleges and community colleges, all of which collectively carry out the enlarged land-grant mission. In the post-land-grant era the emphases and connections of the public research university are the main components of its mission.

These emphases should be of three kinds. One emphasis should be on the maintenance of the old land-grant themes, but with an updated approach. A second should be on the revival of a few old land-grant themes that have been allowed to atrophy, but which need renewed attention because of new conditions. The third should concentrate on new themes that seem appropriate for public research universities in the 1980s and 1990s.

Land-grant emphases that should be continued are these:

The study of agriculture should remain a strong concern, especially since private institutions avoid it and since the world's food supply is getting tight. The research work of the Agricultural Experiment Station should be as vigorous as ever, as should the mass education efforts of the Cooperative Extension Service. But food comes from the sea as well as from on land, so marine science, coastal waters research, and Sea-Grant extension activities should increase at state universities on America's seacoasts. The University of Maryland has a special obligation here because of its proximity to Chesapeake Bay. Also, agricultural help for foreign nations should be increased.

Engineering and applied science at state universities should intensify. But traditional engineering should be renovated for the 1990s. The public research universities have an urgent mission here: to help their states and the nation with technological innovations. Closer ties are needed to the basic sciences that affect engineering work and with the burgeoning field of computer science because knowledge and technology now drive each other forward with increasing interplay.

Education for work should also continue as an emphasis, although mere vocationalism must continue to be shunned. Professional schools should be first-rate and receive fully equal treatment in terms of equipment, quality appointments, and research with departments teaching the equally vital liberal arts and sciences. Though theory should never be neglected, state universities have a special obligation to provide what Thomas Jefferson called "knowledge useful at this day."

Instruction should emphasize the acquisition of learning skills. Students should be active learners with experiments, analyses, writing, and discussion so that they can apply scholarly techniques in their many activities after their university studies end. Whenever possible, undergraduate research should be encouraged.

Admission to the state university should stress higher education for all talented and eager people regardless of social difference or economic background. Public universities have a special obligation to students who are poor and to minorities, especially blacks. Tuition should be kept as low as possible. As tuitions rise, scholarships for the least able to pay should increase.

The land-grant emphases that should be revived are these:

1. Service to the state and its key agencies and to the state's leading organizations. Structures should be established to permit smoother consultation and exchange between the state university and the region's leading organizations and corporations. As research universities increasingly become the driving force for improved quality of life and economic development, a closer partnership between government, business, and the public research university is essential.

2. The state university in the 1980s should return to a closer and productive interplay with the schools. In past decades schools and universities have increasingly gone separate ways. Now new links, interpenetration, and exchanges of instructors are needed to improve the quality of preparation of students and to enlighten the

universities about the needs of schools, their teachers, and their students.

3. *Military affairs.* A continuing military draft, even in peacetime, is becoming a possibility. The military portion of the federal budget is now the largest expenditure item, after social security payments. Strategic weaponry means push-button international nuclear warfare is conceivable. Arms expenditures are increasing worldwide. And the state of American university scholarship about the military and its practices is extraordinarily weak. Study of the military's role in American life and a more active role in defense needs should be a new responsibility of public research universities.

There are some new emphases, too, for the post-land-grant university in the 1980s.

No one campus is sufficient any longer to carry out the land-grant mandate. State universities thus need to have a multicampus organization; and states to provide for opportunity for their citizens should have local community colleges and some smaller state colleges, strong in teaching to complement the public research university and its special role.

The state university in the future must pay increasing attention to the quality of life. The quality of health, social services, environment, water, cultural life, recreational facilities, and the physical appearance of communities for all the citizens of the state is becoming more important, and in such cases as toxic wastes or child abuse a matter of life and death.

As higher education becomes more and more a lifelong, continuing matter, adult and continuing education will need greater emphasis. This is important both for continued economic vitality and for personal enrichment and intellectual growth.

International concerns and training should increase at the state universities. Economic development now means international trade and marketing. People live more than before in a pluralistic, many-nationed world which is increasingly interdependent. World peace and America's security depend heavily on better knowledge of the people outside the United States.

23. State Colleges: An Unsettled Quality

Robert Birnbaum

The rapid enrollment growth of many state colleges, their mission development from a single, unifying purpose to multiple and often incompatible purposes, and society's increased expectations of higher education create a significant identity crisis for these institutions. As George Weathersby has pointed out, they are often easier to define by what they are not (not research institutions, not liberal arts colleges, not community colleges), than by what they are, because they have lost whatever distinctiveness they once possessed. "Such vagueness of purpose and mission has in turn led to confusion in the minds of students, employers, potential donors, and legislators about the identity, purpose, and priorities of these institutions."[1]

Given this identity problem as well as the differences among the various institutions in the sector, it is difficult to specify values that uniformly apply to, or uniquely set apart, all state colleges from other institutional types. There are, however, general similarities in outlook probably shared by a majority of the institutions in the sector. Three characteristics help account for whatever general attitudes may be held.

Values

First, all members of the sector are under public control, and while the implications for institutional practice differ state to state, there is no doubt that it creates an environment qualitatively and quantitatively different from that in the private sector. Among other things, state colleges are embedded within a public bureaucracy that controls many administrative processes, they are constantly under public scrutiny and often must discuss sensitive matters under state "sunshine" or open meeting laws, and they are often pressed to respond immediately to new state public-policy initiatives without an opportunity for full campus discussion and consultation. Second, because of their public status, many of these institutions are caught in the middle of an often competitive system in

---

Robert Birnbaum is professor of higher education at Teachers College, Columbia University.

which state college roles, prestige, influence, and resources are defined in relation to those of public research universities or "flagship" campuses on one side, and community colleges on the other. Third, most state colleges belong to the American Association of State Colleges and Universities (AASCU), an organization engaged in research development, publication, and public information in support of its members (as well as nonmembers to whom it refers as "AASCU-like institutions"). AASCU meetings and publications are influential in articulating and sharing values in the sector.

To the extent that a state college *sine qua non* exists, it would probably be the concept of "access." The colleges proudly proclaim their role in serving blue-collar, first-generation, middle-America students, and defend the importance of offering education to those not served by "elite" institutions. The concept of access is seen in perhaps its most elemental form at the historically black institutions, which have traditionally admitted large numbers of underprepared students who were victimized by an inadequate secondary school system. Even at many of the older or multicolleges, however, barriers to admission usually have been and remain low enough to admit students graduating in the top two-thirds or three-quarters of their high school class, with special procedures for students not meeting even this modest criterion.

Although the admission of underprepared students has probably always taken place at state colleges, recent concern about student performance and attrition rates has led, on many campuses, to major programs of developmental or remedial education. Publicity of these programs (many of which were probably initiated to support special admissions programs for minority students but which are now seen as essential for large numbers of other students as well) has helped confirm both on- and off-campus the image of the state colleges as democratic institutions concerned with the provision of equal opportunity.

Access assumes more than just relatively nonselective admissions requirements, however, and the state colleges strongly believe that higher tuition costs are increasingly becoming a barrier to college attendance. AASCU was instrumental in forming, with two other associations, the National Coalition for Lower Tuition in Higher Education, an "organized political effort to work effectively for low tuition, to make possible educational opportunity for all . . . to fight for higher educational appropriations, which are necessary to make low tuition and quality education possible."[2]

Faced with competition from community colleges, which also support access and low tuition, state colleges are likely to point out to potential students the greater academic expertise of their four-year college faculty as evidenced by their higher proportion of doctorate holders, the advantages of remaining in a single institution for an entire program rather than suffering the discontinuities of tranfer, and the higher completion rates and greater probabilitiy of achieving career goals for students in four-year, as compared with two-year colleges.[3] Challenged for students by public universities in the same state, they are likely to call attention to their emphasis on teaching rather than research, to suggest that their smaller size will enable more personal attention, and to remind students that at a state college they will be instructed by experienced faculty members and not by graduate teaching assistants.

Although with few exceptions the state colleges are comprehensive institutions offering both liberal arts and professional programs, emphasis is clearly on preparing students for careers. This thrust is evident in all groups within the sector. For the older institutions and multicolleges it represents a continuation of the teacher education tradition, although new fields such as business now predominate. Historically black colleges have always emphasized the role of education in preparing students to compete for employment in a discriminatory society, and the new colleges, many developed in urban areas during a period in which "relevance" was the watchword, often matched their programs to the expected vocational interest of their clientele.

The liberal arts thus play a secondary role. They may assume greater importance in the future with renewed interest in general education as an essential degree component, although it is questionable whether concerns about improving competency in basic English and computation will eventually manifest themselves in more advanced humanities, science, and social science study. On some campuses, the liberal arts faculty has increasing difficulty recruiting students as majors; on others, the liberal arts faculty sees itself as a beleaguered support department, rather than the college's intellectual core.

Although many of these values derive from the traditions and expectations of the colleges themselves, they are reinforced by the college's function as an agency of the state. Driven by enrollment-related funding formulas, and with few opportunities to buffer themselves financially against short-term reversals, the colleges to survive must offer what students want, regardless of what they may be thought to need. Faced with the unlimited demands for service on one side and the harsh realities of public accountability on the other, the colleges may move away from a rhetoric of education toward a rhetoric of administration and management. "Student credit hours per full-time equivalent faculty" becomes a term heard as often in the faculty lounge as in the president's office; fiscal exigency, layoff, and retrenchment become part of the argot as well as the environment; and discussion of access, quality, and other core values are displaced by contingency planning, new managing systems, and the need to collect data for external accountability even though they may have little campus utility.

The Environment

Because of their mission, public control, and place in the higher education system, state colleges will remain vulnerable to developing social, economic, and political forces. Although many important environmental changes will surely take place, only the known decrease in the college-age cohort during the next fifteen years, and the projected consequent decrease in college enrollments, can now be considered with any certainty.

In examining the potential effects of demographic changes on various sectors of higher education, the Carnegie Council identified the state colleges as occupying a position of average to above-average vulnerability. This means that the sector might expect an undergraduate enrollment decline by 1997 of approximately 10-15 percent. Decreases at any specific college could be significantly larger and would of course depend on many factors such as location, program, and the existence of other institutions competing for the same applicant pool.

Institutional resources are dependent on enrollments, and in the scramble for enrollments created by demographic trends, the state colleges are likely not to fare well against either the community colleges, usually less expensive and more convenient, or the doctoral or system flagship universities, which are more prestigious. The state colleges are also likely not to have the political clout of either of these other institutional types and so are less likely to increase the level of public appropriations on which their budget depends. Local community college boards often have direct access to revenue sources or agencies. They are usually composed of men and women with important local political connections who can forcefully articulate their college's needs in the battle for community fiscal support, and who, both in terms of total numbers and connections, can be an important collective force in battling for additional resources at the state level as well. The trustees of research and flagship universities are fewer in number but in many states occupy positions considered to have great prestige and influence. They interact with legislative and executive bodies that often include as members large numbers of university undergraduates or law school alumni and may also have a statewide constituency developed through their university extension and outreach activities.

State college boards of trustees have neither the numbers and intensive local support of the community college system, nor in most cases the well-placed alumni or statewide interest afforded the public university. In the past, the power of state colleges was often magnified by their close political relationships to statewide teachers' organizations. The state college's reduction of emphasis on education programs has significantly diminished the strength of this traditional coalition and, in many cases, eradicated it.

The lack of a strong political base means not only that the state colleges may have greater difficulty acquiring resources but also that they are easier targets for retrenchment. A recent study indicated that of 4,000 faculty members (1,200 with tenure) laid off or dismissed in the past five years from four-year colleges and universities, virtually all came from either state colleges or less well-known private institutions.[4]

In the search for new clientele, the state colleges are likely to try to strengthen their positions in technical education, lifelong learning, and community service, thus increasing their competition with community colleges. They are also likely to attempt expansion of their range of graduate offerings, particularly in professional areas, thus increasing their competition with the public universities. In both cases the political constraints they will encounter, from other institutions as well as from state coordinating boards, suggest that they are not likely to fare well.

The projected demographic changes, and the competition probably to ensue, will create many critical problems for state colleges. As interest in career-related programs increases, issues such as the nature of general education and the relationship of colleges to business and industry will have to addressed. Enrollment shifts may force consideration of the very survival of certain liberal arts. Greater interest in accepting transfer students from community colleges may create increased difficulty in articulating programs to permit two-year students to transfer their previous work into the upper division and may tend to homogenize the general education components of both institutional types. State colleges will have to continue experimenting with new delivery systems and materials to respond to part-time, older students and other new learner populations, thus placing greater stress on already overloaded administrative structures and further reducing the possibility of developing a sense of campus community.

Resources

The personnel, facilities, and financial resources of individual state colleges relate to a number of variables including their history, location, and size.

State college faculty members increasingly have terminal degrees in the areas in which they teach, although there are still smaller and more isolated campuses at which a faculty member with a doctorate is the exception rather than the rule. Along with other faculty members, their purchasing power has been significantly eroded over the past decade. Average salaries in comprehensive state colleges in 1982-3 were $26,940, and in general baccalaureate state colleges $24,490.[5] Their average salaries, as well as their salaries at each rank except instructor, were lower than those at public universities. The largest difference was at the full professor rank, with universities averaging $38,180, comprehensive state colleges $33,490, and baccalaureate state colleges $30,770. The average teaching load is about twelve contact hours a week, higher than the 6-9-hour loads typically expected of university faculty members. State college faculty members are quick to notice these differences in teaching responsibilities and compensation, particularly in systems in which both types of institution are controlled by a single board, and to recognize that they reflect public perception of the state college's place in the academic pecking order.

Facilities run the gamut from outstanding to inadequate. In many states community college physical plants, more recently constructed and less constrained by the regulations of state building agencies, are both more attractive and more functional than those of the four-year colleges. Libraries, science laboratories, and areas for instruction in technological subjects in particular often were constructed at state colleges for a smaller and more specialized student body and may not have not been improved to support new activities adequately. Capital projects of any magnitude require approval at various levels of state government and often depend on voter approval of bond issues. The state colleges are usually at a political disadvantage when they attempt to compete with public universities for funds.

Over the past decade, because of depressed economies and projections of enrollment downturns, states have been particularly reluctant to approve new college buildings, and in the near future those institutions with significant capital needs are unlikely to find relief. At the same time, renovations and other maintenance needs have been deferred to effect short-term economies. Because it is politically easier to justify the maintenance of buildings than the maintenance of faculty, some colleges may be called on over the next few years to make budget trade-offs and to cut faculty size to support the physical plant.

Equipment budgets have been particularly problematic for many state colleges. The movement into new scientific and technological arenas has not always been accompanied by appropriate equipment support. Expensive machinery or electronic components may be viewed as "frills" and disallowed by state budget offices, even though they are critical to the development of a sound program. Many colleges rely as much on gifts of used equipment from industry as on their own operating budgets, when they can get the equipment at all. Particularly when dealing with rapidly changing biological and physical sciences, and high-technology areas such as computer science, colleges often find themselves instructing students on badly out-of-date equipment no longer in use in the work place.

This equipment problem has been exacerbated in recent years by restricted state budget support and the tendency of colleges facing budgetary constraints to transfer funds from equipment and other accounts to personnel accounts in order to maintain faculty positions. Consequently, support for library books and equipment has become a critical issue for many campuses.

The educational and general revenues for the state colleges in fiscal 1981 came primarily from state and local appropriations (64 percent) and from tuition revenues (19 percent), revenue sources that are highly sensitive to enrollment levels. Approximately 2 percent of their revenues were from gifts and contracts, for a total of 17 percent. In contrast, public university revenues in these latter three categories were 4, 7, and 15 percent respectively, thus affording universities a larger buffer (26 percent) against revenue losses caused by enrollment declines or vagaries of the state.

During the same year, the state colleges expended approximately $2,030 per student for instructional expenses and an additional $410 for academic support. It is virtually impossible to compare this with the expenditures of public universities, since university data do not separate expenditures for undergraduate and graduate students. Comparable figures for all public institutions indicate instructional expenditures of $2,240 and academic support of $410, but this is an average that incorporates a range of $1,421 and $230 at public community colleges on one hand, to public research universities with medical schools at $3,520 and $829 on the other. When compared with private comprehensive and baccalaureate institutions, however, the state college expenditures for instruction are similar. State colleges are likely to spend much more for public service and much less for faculty research than are comparable private institutions.

The Chimera of Excellence

Excellence is easy to support but difficult to define. Over the past forty years it has become common in higher education to refer to a rather narrow range of beliefs, activities, and outcomes, focusing attention primarily on cognitive performance and meritocratic values. These are the characteristics of the "university colleges," which Jencks and Riesman identified as providing the model to which other colleges aspire, but can never really achieve.[6]

Probably nowhere in American higher education is the discrepancy between aspiration and performance more apparent than at state colleges. Dunham clearly identified the irony that the transformation of their values (sometimes internally induced, sometimes externally imposed) had the potential of changing first-class teachers colleges into third-class universities. Probably to some extent this has happened. However, even third-class universities can have some areas of "excellence" if the definition is expanded to include a wider range of desirable values than the traditional one.

The dimensions of excellence. Excellence is commonly tied to the academic performance of students as measured by achievement tests, to faculty qualifications as reflected in scholarly accomplishment, or to institutional reputation. Compared with major universities and selective, independent liberal arts colleges, state colleges must be judged on all these counts before being deemed as deficient. Such judgment, however, tends to overlook at least four important issues. First, colleges have many goals beyond the ostensibly academic. Second, academic goals themselves are often multiple, conflicting, and inconsistent. Third, the organizational and institutional structures and processes that facilitate the effective achievement of one goal often inhibit the achievement of another. No college exists that can optimize achievement of *all* its goals. Fourth, perceptions of excellence depend on the perceivers. Legislators and parents, foundations and community groups, administrators and alumni, cosmopolitan faculty members and locals, Merit Scholars and remedial students, and others are likely to have legitimate definitions that differ markedly.

The notion of excellence also tends to become confused with other ideas that appear equally desirable, if no less difficult to specifiy, such as "standards," "educational effectiveness," and "quality." Of these, *standards* and *quality* appear to connote student requirements or achievements at or above a stated criterion, while *excellence* and *effectiveness* usually relate to the impact an institution has on improving performance. Because institutions have many purposes, it may be presumed that excellence or effectiveness may be of various kinds, and in fact one scholar has developed an instrument to measure nine "dimensions" of effectiveness perceived by various campus constituencies: student educational satisfaction, student academic development, student career development, faculty and administrative employment satisfaction, professional development and quality of the faculty, system openness and community interaction, ability to acquire resources, and organizational health.[7] Of these, only two—student academic development and faculty quality—appear related to commonly held notions of excellence.

The relatively unidimensional views in rhetorical vogue today ironically ignore the pluralistic approach to values that John Gardner identified as a foundation of excellence. This does not mean that all values are of equal worth in a higher education institution, but it does suggest there is no universal definition that can be usefully employed.

The Measurement of Performance. Even if everyone were to accept a narrow definition of excellence involving only student intellectual outcomes, the problem of measurement remains. At least two approaches, "criterion-referenced" or "value-added," can be taken. Using the former, one presumably can evaluate the comparative excellence of two institutions by measuring the knowledge or skills of the students they produce and comparing them to benchmarks. The institution whose students obtain the higher test scores would by definition have the greater degree of excellence.

The value-added concept pertains to the extent to which student performance has changed as a result of the college experience.

Institutions whose students evidence the greatest amount of *improvement* would be judged excellent, regardless of the maximum performance level reached.

Comparisons of the quality of institutional student "outputs" indicate they relate to the quality of student "inputs." Accordingly, relatively nonselective state colleges would be expected to have lower-scoring graduates than those at more selective institutions. However, there is no evidence to indicate that when the academic achievement of entering students is statistically controlled the performance of state college graduates is noticeably higher or lower than that of other graduates.

In general, state colleges have not achieved the same level of "excellence" as have, for example, selective liberal arts colleges or flagship research universities. Given the earlier comments on correlates of student performance, it seems clear that public perceptions of excellence depend not on education process or output but, rather, input. High admissions standards are considered evidence of excellence. To a great extent this creates a no-win situation for state colleges: low admissions requirements and extensive remedial education lead to demands for "standards"; low admission requirements and high attrition call forth attacks on the "revolving door." But raising admissions requirements challenges the essential mission of the colleges to offer access to students of varying background and abilities.

Considering the dimensions of these issues provides new ways of looking at the concept of excellence. At some state colleges excellence will be achieved as a scholarly and proficient faculty provides instruction to well-prepared and sophisticated high school graduates and holds them to universal standards of performance. At others, excellence will mean that a dedicated faculty will introduce provincial students for the first time to profound ideas that will transform some and be ignored by others. Excellence may also be found at a college that accepts disadvantaged students and, in addition to providing basic skills and advanced vocational and technical training, also significantly improves their self-image, feelings of competence, and dedication to community service. A state college can also achieve excellence in serving as a protective half-way house for potentially brilliant students who would be unable to cope immediately with a university environment, as a workshop in which students can experience racial integration for the first time and develop the understanding and tolerance necessary for helping to build a multicultural society, or as a training center from which business and industry can draw competent students to fill technically demanding positions. Through various activities state colleges can also increase the aspirations of potential students, expand the cultural life of a community, assist its economy, and provide opportunities for lifelong learning. In these and many other ways, excellence can be manifested, even if it cannot be precisely measured.

External Constraints on Excellence

Despite the disagreement about what constitutes excellence, there are clearly many factors that limit the effectiveness of some state colleges. Externally these factors include state/system coordination and control, funding provisions, and collective bargaining.

State coordination and control. During the past fifteen years there has been an increasing tendency of decisions of importance to campuses being made by external groups. In some states, individual state colleges have no independent boards of trustees and are controlled instead by a single, consolidated governing board responsible for a system of two or more institutions. These systems sometimes also include institutions that are not state colleges. There are 118 state colleges (31 percent of the total) functioning under such an arrangement. In addition, there are many state colleges that have their own trustees but remain subject to the authority of a state coordinating board with has extensive budgeting and rule-making authority. Both consolidated governing bodies and statewide coordinating agencies can be generically referred to as "superboards." In most cases, institutions in states without superboards are subject to similar control and review by other agencies of state government, particularly in their fiscal and capital operations.

The functioning of superboards tends to remove from direct campus control many critical aspects of institutional functioning, often including new program development, facilities planning, personnel policies, administrative structure, research activities, internal budget allocation, and the like. In the name of accountability such agencies can become exceptionally intrusive into the internal conduct of campus business. Moreover, the need to oversee several disparate institutions leads to the creation of uniform regulations to bring presumed order out of apparent chaos and to offer the appearance of fairness. Many such systems were created both to provide governmental oversight and to protect the campuses from improper governmental intrusion. The ambiguity of this charge is difficult to resolve to the mutual satisfaction of both campuses and governors, and faculty members and administrators at many institutions are convinced that these agencies exist primarily to carry out the will of the state rather than protect important institutional interests. Superboard members are usually political appointees and, like all trustees, fulfill their responsibilities on a volunteer, part-time basis. As these systems have become more complex and difficult for laypersons to understand, effective influence has often shifted from superboards themselves to their staffs, which do the day-to-day business. As the locus of functional authority moves sequentially from campus trustees to superboards and finally to complex state bureaucracies, colleges may begin to operate more as regulated utilities than as institutions with an identifiable character, style, and environment.

It can be debated whether the decisions made by disinterested superboards, acting from a broader perspective and assisted by extensive staff expertise, are "better" than those made by local campuses with more parochial and presumably self-serving interests. Even if data were available to inform such arguments, they would neglect to demonstrate an essential point: increasing limitations on campus autonomy leads to feelings of powerless, anger, and scapegoating on the part of the college faculty and administration alike. Their sense of ownership of the enterprise is eroded, their profession becomes a job, and accountability disappears because authority is too diffused to be grasped. Faculty members may find refuge in their personal interests; administrators may find it in adherence to rules and regulations. The acknowledged reduction in morale and levels of personal commitment is evident to the state and is used to justify further intrusion.

Funding provisions. State colleges share several characteristics related to their funding arrangements: they are enrollment driven or enrollment related, they often have limited flexibility, they usually provide no incentives for prudent management, and they are uncertain. Each of these can severely constrain an institution's concern with excellence.

Enrollment-related formulas as a primary mechanism for determining support levels for state colleges were a major advantage during the growth era of the recent past but are now a significant handicap during the present period of stability or decline. Although some states have moved beyond simple formulas toward more sophisticated models with time-lag provisions and others are attempting to develop nonenrollment-related alternatives, many state colleges lack buffering from environmental shifts. These institutions thus remain extraordinarily sensitive to market conditions. For survival purposes if for no others, issues related to student retention, grading, and transfer, for example, must be decided with an eye to the impact on enrollment as well as on educational quality. Low enrollment programs, regardless of their educational merit, are particularly vulnerable not only to institutional administrators under pressure to reallocate resources but also to superboard staff members anxious to identify (and then to regulate) such "obvious" examples of inefficiency and organizational slack.

Regulations that limit flexibility often constrain the expenditure of funds even after they are allocated to a campus. At many institutions, line items developed when a budget was originally planned eighteen months earlier cannot be allotted to newer purposes a changed environment requires without extensive negotiation with, or approval by, various state agencies.

Other rules (in areas such as purchasing, for example) often prevent colleges from securing supplies and equipment not covered by master state purchase agreements, or require extended sequences of advertising and bidding with absurdly low dollar thresholds. These kinds of limits on flexibility prevent administrators from responding to emerging needs in a timely manner and contribute to feelings of powerlessness. They can also create campus tensions when faculty members, unaware of external constraints, attribute intolerable delays to inefficiency and lack of support for academic priorities on the part of campus administrators.

Incentives for prudent management are provided to colleges if moneys saved by efficiencies in one area can be applied to another and savings generated during one time period can be used in the future. At public institutions, inflexibility in making expenditures inhibits the former; the annual budget and appropriation cycles of the state usually prevent the latter. For most state colleges, funds must be spent in the year appropriated, and unexpended balances revert back to the state treasury. This leads, at many campuses, to the traditional end-of-budget-year spending orgy for equipment and supplies, whether essential or not, to avoid unspent end-of-year balances. This apparent irrationality becomes understandable when it is realized that state budget offices may use the existence of unexpended balances (often created by their own Byzantine regulations) to reduce future budgets on the grounds that they indicate a lack of need.

Uncertainty in budget support is an accepted phenomenon in state college budgeting, but one that has recently acquired new dimensions. In the past, state colleges would typically plan their budgets in cycles beginning eighteen months or more before the fiscal year, even though the actual appropriations would, in some cases, not be decided until the fiscal year was well underway. Under such circumstances, institutions had to be extremely conservative in making expenditure decisions, and positions often remained unfilled because they were approved too late to permit adequate recruitment. Once authorized, however, institutions could generally count on expending their annual budgets, subject only to the annoyances in some states of preaudit controls and regular demands in other states for mandated savings during the current fiscal year.

Within the past few years, however, this has changed. Colleges in some states have faced significantly altered budgets related to state fiscal crises during the course of the current fiscal year itself. In some cases the projected discontinuities have been great enough to lead superboards to propose changes in personnel policies that would permit the colleges to circumvent existing regulations on periods of notice for faculty nonreappointment, or to specify criteria for a declaration of "fiscal exigency" that would presumably permit the layoff of tenured faculty members in response to sudden financial shortfalls. The effects on faculty morale of such proposals, let alone their implementation, can be devastating.

Collective bargaining. Contracts with faculty unions exist on approximately one-third of all state college campuses, making the sector one of the most unionized in American higher education. Although bargaining appears to be related to reduced institutional effectiveness, it is more likely a consequence—rather than a cause—of ineffectiveness. To a great extent, much faculty interest in unionization is a defensive response to the feelings of powerlessness and loss of campus control related to increased intrusion by the state. Once in place, however, bargaining may, ironically, tend to strengthen the centralization that spawned it. It may also accelerate tendencies toward uniformity (particularly in multicampus systems in which one contract is negotiated covering all institutions); toward loss of academic focus (particularly in those situations in which nonfaculty belong to—or are a majority of—the bargaining unit); and toward increased intrusion by the state (particularly in states in which "management" is represented at the bargaining table by a public official unrelated to the college administration or board).

Internal Constraints on Excellence

The status and expectations of the faculty, and the background and preparation of students, are important internal considerations affecting institutional excellence.

The status and expectations of faculty. Probably the single most critical, current, faculty-related influence on organizational functioning is the high tenure density at many of the state colleges. Until recently, it was common practice to award tenure to almost all faculty members completing the probationary period. Although aggregate data indicate that approximately 62 percent of full-time faculty members in public four-year institutions are tenured (higher than the 54 percent seen in all institutional types combined), a large number of the state colleges have a tenure density of between 75 and 90 percent.[8] This builds inflexibility into the system, making it difficult or impossible over the short term to adjust staffing allocations to respond to changing enrollment patterns. Even as enrollment in education, history, or English decreases, for example, no faculty positions are freed to support burgeoning enrollments and large classes in business and computer science. Tenure density poses a particular problem for state colleges because they cannot increase flexibility through the use of graduate assistants, as the universities do, nor do they rely on part-time instruction to the extent reportedly utilized by community colleges.

A related phenomenon is the tension on some campuses between the "old" faculty, often from education or related areas, with doctorates (if they have them) form second-tier graduate institutions, little if any scholarly productivity, and senior rank, and the "new" faculty, often of lower rank, trained in research-oriented doctoral programs of national reputation, and recruited to bring their institution into the academic mainstream. These two groups are likely to have different expectations about the proper processes and criteria for personnel actions such as promotion, differing perceptions about the appropriate role of the faculty in governance, and different expectations concerning the role and mission of the institution. Given the frequent lack of a clear institutional identity, there are often no consistent norms or values that can help to resolve these differences, and the contending parties may fall back on bureaucratic or political mechanisms to arrange temporary working truces. If consensus cannot be developed on the relative emphasis to be given teaching (or the means of assessing it), or the importance of scholarship and publication, then by default seniority reigns. The old guard-versus-young Turk conflict is present in its rawest form when junior faculty members see themselves held to new standards of performance that were not applied to the senior faculty now judging them, and high tenure densities mean a lower probability of achieving tenure, even for the best and brightest of the newcomers.

Students. State college students cover a wide range of abilities and aspirations that in many ways make them "typical" of higher education enrollment in general. Compared with freshmen at all institutions in 1983, for example, state college freshmen closely resembled overall averages in their political orientations, high school grade distribution and rank in class, family income distribution, high school courses taken, and plans for study for a higher degree.[9] As with other freshmen, their major reasons for going to college were (in rank order) to get a better job, to learn more about things, and to make more money.

Approximately 39 percent of state college freshmen report high school averages of "B+" or higher, making them on average academically stronger than students in some institutional categories (for example, public community colleges at 27 percent), but weaker than students in others (for example, public universities at 54 percent). Approximately 21 percent of the state college freshmen report high school grades of "C+" or lower, identical to the national average but twice as high as that in public universities. It is likely that all levels of academic performance, increasingly at lower-grade levels, there are numbers of indifferent students for whom college is a socially acceptable means of marking time. This number may even be increasing. Despite concern about grade inflation over the decade, fewer state college freshmen in 1983 reported high school grades of "B+" or higher, and more reported grades of "C+" or lower than in 1973.[10]

Conclusions About Excellence

An assessment of the present level of excellence in state colleges to a great extent depends on the definitions chosen and reference groups selected. Although there are few hard data to support any clear conclusions, one would be hard pressed to develop a strong case that the alleged "rising tide of mediocrity" has diminished the effectiveness of the state colleges as a group. Indeed, both short-term and long-term evidence suggest the contrary.

Short-term data. An example of short-term data includes a recent survey of higher education institutions in which chief academic officers reported that new faculty members hired in 1981-82 were more competent than those hired a year earlier. These data further indicated that faculty members at state colleges were seen as more concerned about their teaching and student advisement reponsibilities, more willing to innovate, and more productive in research and scholarship than previously. Overall, 58 percent of the respondents identified the quality of state college faculty performance as increasing, while only 3 percent believed it to be decreasing. At the same time, it was reported that secretarial and related support for the faculty was decreasing (although support for research was up). Teaching load had slightly increased, and other workload responsibilites in advising, committee work, and related nonclassroom functions had grown. In general, it appeared that resources to support the enterprise had diminished, but quality, at least in terms of faculty performance, had increased.[11]

A similar earlier survey compared the characteristics of state college faculty members, students, and finances in 1979-80 with those of the previous year. Again, teaching load, advising, and committee responsibilities were all seen as increasing, while secretarial and travel support were seen as decreasing. In addition, the survey asked state college chief academic officers, student personnel officers, senior faculty members, student newspaper editors, and student association presidents to evaluate changes in the quality and content of educational programs during this time period. The general consensus of all groups (with the occasional disagreement of the student newspaper editor) was that there had been improvement in the overall quality of the learning environment, the quality, competence, and performance of the faculty, the rigor of academic standards, the availability of a wide range of student services, and creativity and innovation in teaching. Overall, the chief academic officers and chief student personnel officers of state colleges overwhelmingly reported an increase in the "overall quality of student learning." The presidents of these institutions reported the same patterns of increased effectiveness and decreased resources. Although almost 60 percent of the presidents surveyed said their institution was losing ground financially, 48 percent said the academic condition of the institution was improving (none said it was losing ground), and 52 percent noted an increase in the quality of student services.[12]

Long-term data. The responses of college presidents must be reviewed cautiously. Presidents tend to be optimistic, particularly when reviewing changes in quality that have taken place under their stewardship and presumably as a consequence of their educational and fiscal leadership. Faculty members, on the other hand, may tend to be much more critical about their institutions. For this reason, the results of a recent study of faculty perceptions of changes in institutional functioning over the ten-year period from 1970 to 1980 is instructive. In responses to the Institutional Functioning Inventory (IFI), state college faculty perceived improvements in a number of areas, including development of the intellectual and aesthetic extracurriculum, concern about undergraduate learning, and concern about advancing knowledge on their campuses during this ten-year period. At the same time, they saw their colleges as becoming more diverse in terms of student and faculty background and as being more concerned with meeting local needs. In addition, there appeared to be a slight increase in faculty morale during this ten-year period, even though morale at these institutions continued to be among the lowest of all institutional types included in the study.[13] A review of state college faculty responses to specific IFI items related to concern about undergraduate teaching indicates that, compared with 1970 data, faculty members in 1980 were more concerned about how better to communicate knowledge to students, more willing to spend time talking to students about their personal concerns, more sensitive to the needs and aspirations of students, and more willing to consider teaching effectiveness in faculty recruiting. Complementing this emphasis on teaching, faculty members also saw research and related scholarly activities being given greater emphasis by college administrations and boards, and reflected in an increase in faculty publications. In responding to the item "The college is doing a successful job in achieving its various goals," 65 percent of the faculty agreed in 1980, compared with 59 percent in 1970.[14]

If the quality of faculty and program is seen as improving, there is a general consensus that the quality of state college students, as defined by traditional measures, has been deteriorating. Scores of students on the Scholastic Aptitude Test declined moderately between 1970 and 1980, paralleling the decline seen in all other higher education sectors.[15] Chief academic officers at state colleges reported declines between 1978-79 and 1979-80 in the secondary school preparation of their students in reading, writing, mathematical skills, humanities, social sciences, and sciences.[16] More recent data collected from chief academic officers suggests there has been little if any improvement in student preparation, even though academic standards and grading practices are reported to be more rigorous.[17]

Evaluating the level of excellence. There is a tendency to define a problem in terms of the availability of data. Recent dramatic criticisms of higher education calling attention to test scores and relying on judgmental reports have tended to obscure the fact that there is a dearth of information that might more directly reflect educational quality. The data now available, which by default have become proxy for the concept of excellence, do not indicate whether students are now learning more or less than in the past, whether the increase in remedial education has resulted in more or less social justice, whether graduates are more or less able to function as effective civic and occupational participants, or whether collectively and individually the state college student is more or less likely than in the past to lead a life of increased meaning and reward as a consequence of graduation. These are profound and perhaps unanswerable questions. But a proper consideration of excellence requires that they at least be asked.

To some extent, present concern about the state college reflects the continuing tension in this country between the concepts of mass and elite higher education. Critics of the level of excellence in state colleges point to lower admissions averages and test scores, and increases in the number of remedial courses offered, as indicators of serious problems requiring attention. These criticisms are often leveled without recognition of the political and social context that led these institutions to become more flexible in offering admission to previously underrepresented groups and to take steps to ensure an open door for these underprepared students that would offer reasonable opportunities for success. Other aspects of state colleges can also be identified as mitigating the quality of the undergraduate experience. For example, characteristics thought to be related to quality, such as small institutional size, continuity of program and staff, and a clear and coherent institutional purpose—are not often found in state colleges.[18]

It is useful to examine the conditions of excellence in state colleges and to ask how they might be improved. At the same time, in light of their political and financial constraints, their heterogeneous student bodies, and the many conflicting claims on their resources and energies, an equally intriguing question is how they have managed to be as successful as they have been. Care must be taken lest well-meaning proposals for improving excellence at these institutions inadvertently disrupt those aspects of institutional functioning that have permitted the creditable performance of a most difficult task.

The major thrust of recommendations by national as well as statewide commissions and study groups to improve the quality of state colleges appears to focus on raising admissions standards and on moving toward the elimination of remedial courses at the college level. These are appealing ideas to some, not only because they begin to clarify some of the differentiation between secondary and higher education that may have eroded over the past decade, but also because they are likely to reduce enrollments and save state funds. This position appears to have been adopted by AASCU, as reported with approval in an information bulletin under the headline "Educational Standards Alive and Well in State Colleges and Universities":

> *Tougher college admissions standards are being put into place at state colleges and universities around the country. There are many reasons for these tighter standards. In many states, severe budget cuts have forced colleges and universities to curtail enrollments. Raising standards has proved to be an effective approach to solving this problem. By raising admission standards, higher education institutions also hope to shift some or all of the expensive remedial programs they now administer back to the secondary schools. Employers have become vocal in requesting that colleges and universities produce better quality students.*[19]

The nature of the proposed solutions puts into bold relief the underlying values accompanying the concept of "excellence." The solutions appear to accept a criterion-referenced rather than a value-added approach and to take a unidimensional rather than multidimensional view. They also seem to accept the notion that quality can be improved by inspection rather than "built in" by the application of resources to students, and that excellence can be appropriately addressed by controlling the input rather than by improving the delivery systems and strengthening the educational process.

Two polar views can be taken on the appropriate way of achieving excellence in the state colleges—one remedial, the other developmental. The remedial approach finds great deficiencies in the quality of state colleges, which must be corrected through bold initiatives. These include delineating college mission with greater precision, raising admissions standards, requiring satisfactory student scores on achievement tests as a condition for moving from sophomore to junior status, further centralizing program development and curriculum evaluation processes to ensure uniform application of traditional quality standards, and abolishing tenure or reducing the time required for notice of faculty nonreappointment to make allocation of personnel resources more responsive to student interests and needs. Each of these structural changes might increase excellence as traditionally defined but could also have significant, unintended, unavoidable, negative, and long-term consequences. For example, centralizing program criteria and review processes could stifle innovation, and abolishing tenure would almost certainly lower faculty morale and institutional commitment, and lead to an increase in faculty militancy. And while erecting barriers to access will raise test scores, it is unlikely to increase social equity or to raise the level of national discourse.

The developmental approach recognizes that the condition of state colleges is the result of many societal and educational forces over which the colleges have had relatively little control. To try to delineate the goals of these institutions is in a real sense an attempt to define the goals of the complex, multifaceted society these colleges have been asked to serve; this is seldom possible to do and usually dangerous to try. The developmental alternative is to maintain the present configuration of these colleges and to attempt to improve them at the margins. Fiscal support for programs and activities that enrich and refresh a tired faculty, equipment quality and quantity that demonstrate societal commitment to the education of the young, enough budget slack to make life more pleasant but not luxurious, and sufficient autonomy to encourage people of talent and conviction to consider campus administration as a career—each of these could make a significant contribution to state college excellence, however defined.

Notes

[1] George B. Weathersby, "State Colleges in Transition," in J. Froomkin, Ed., *The Crisis in Higher Education* (New York: Academy of Political Science, 1983), p. 26. Using the new classification system of the National Center for Education Statistics (NCES), *State College* includes 256 public colleges identified as "Comprehensive Institutions" and 121 categorized "General Baccalaureate Institutions." The concept of "comprehensive" as used by NCES refers to the extent to which an institution offers postbaccalaureate, nondoctoral programs. In contrast, in this paper the term "comprehensive" is used to refer to institutions characterized by a mix of liberal arts and professional programs such that no more than 80 percent of its degrees are awarded in either category.

Unless otherwise identified, statistics in this paper have been calculated by the author from data supplied by the National Center for Higher Education Management Systems (NCHEMS) from current data tapes.

[2] *Low Tuition Fact Book* (Washington, D.C.: American Association of State Colleges and Universities, 1983).

[3] Alexander Astin et al., *The American College Freshman: National Norms for Fall 1973* (Los Angeles: cooperative Institutional Research Program, University of California-Los Angeles).

[4] M. G. Scully, "4,000 Faculty Members Laid Off in 5 Years by 4-Year Institutions, Survey Shows," *Chronicle of Higher Education,* 26 October 1983, p. 21.

[5] American Association of University Professors, "The Annual Report on the Economic Status of the Profession, 1982-83," *Academe,* 69:2-75.

[6] C. Jencks and D. Riesman, *The Academic Revolution* (New York: Doubleday, 1968).

[7] K. Cameron, "The Relationship Between Faculty Unionism and Organizational Effectiveness," *Academy of Management Journal,* 25:6-24.

[8] National Center for Education Statistics, *The Condition of Education,* 1980 (Washington, D.C.).

[9] Alexander Astin et al., *The American Freshman: National Norms for Fall 1983* (Los Angeles: Cooperative Institutional Research PRogram, University of California-Los Angeles, 1983).

[10] Astin et al., *The American College Freshman: National Norms 1973.*

[11] B. T. Watkins, "Competence of New Teachers Improving, Faculty Quality Up, Survey Finds," *Chronicle of Higher Education,* 20 July 1983.

[12] W. J. Minter and H. R. Bowen, *Preserving America's Investment in Human Capital* (Washington, D.C.: American Association of State Colleges and Universities, 1980).

[13] R. F. Anderson, Finance and Effectiveness: A Study of College Environments (Princeton, N.J.: Educational Testing Service, 1983).

[14] R. K. Anderson, Unpublished data, Institute for Higher Education, Teachers College, Columbia University, 1983.

[15] Anderson.

[16] Minter and Bowen.

[17] B. T. Watkins, "Basic Skills of College-bound Students Show Little Improvement, Survey Finds," *Chronicle of Higher Education,* 15 June 1983.

[18] G. D. Kuhn, *Indices of Quality in the Undergraduate Experience* (Washington, D.C.: American Association for Higher Education, 1981).

[19] American Association of State Colleges and Universities, "Educational Standards are Alive and Well in State Colleges and Universities," *Background,* July 1983.